8/8/13 .

Happy Birthday !

SIGNS CURES
&WITCHERY

German Appalachian Folklore

SIGNS CURES
& WITCHERY

Gerald Milnes

The University of Tennessee Press • Knoxville

All photographs are by the author unless otherwise noted.

Milnes, Gerald.
  Signs, cures, and witchery: German Appalachian folklore /
Gerald Milnes.—1st ed.
      p. cm.
Includes bibliographical references and index.

ISBN-13: 978-1-57233-878-4
ISBN-10: 1-57233-878-4

1. German Americans—Appalachian Region—Folklore.
2. German Americans—Appalachian Region—History.
3. Occultism—Appalachian Region—Folklore.
4. Persecution—Germany—History.
5. Freedom of religion—Appalachian Region—History.
6. United States—History—Colonial period, ca. 1600–1775.
7. Appalachian Region—Folklore.
I. Title.

GR111.G47M55 2007
398.2'08931074—dc22   2006026740

Contents

Illustrations

Introduction

Much has been written about the Anglo-Celtic, Scots-Irish, and/or English folkways of the Appalachian people, but few studies have addressed their German cultural attributes and sensibilities. Only a handful of early-to mid-twentieth-century writers even mentioned the irrefutable evidence of a strong Germanic presence in the southern Appalachians. John C. Campbell's 1921 work, *The Southern Highlander and His Homeland*, quotes census facts and figures that clearly establish that Germans were, as they continue to be, a considerable presence in the southern Appalachians. Today, a number of good historians base their studies on facts and figures, and they get it right, but some writers continue to promote the old, entrenched view of the ethnicity of Appalachian people.

Regarding cultural influences, Campbell cites the words of ballad collector Cecil Sharp. Sharp, who notes that he is not qualified to speak to the "racial" origins of southern highlanders based on statistics (he leaves that to Campbell), offers these thoughts: "Their predominant culture is overwhelmingly Anglo-Saxon, or perhaps, to be more accurate, *Anglo-Celtic*."[1] Campbell then opines that Sharp's Anglo-Celtic designation is one under which everyone can unite, and he deduces that these Appalachian Anglo-Celts are true Americans.

In the books of the early "color writers," among those who claim first notice of these "forgotten people," our "contemporary ancestors," there is ample misleading information. Maud Karpeles's introduction to *Eighty Appalachian Folk Songs* (1968), for example, notes, "The inhabitants of these mountains are of British descent—English, Scots and Scots-Irish—their ancestors having left their native shores about two hundred years or so ago."

Speaking of his ballad sources, John Jacob Niles says that Appalachians are "the direct descendants of the hardy English settlers who came to the shores of the American continent in the 17th and 18th centuries." Perhaps Niles is building on an earlier statement by fellow Kentuckian and anglophile Jean Thomas, who said, "These sturdy Anglo-Saxons have held safe and unchanged the balladry of Elizabethan days." She also wrote, "The wilderness, the pure air, the rugged outdoor life have made them so: a people in whom the Anglo-Saxon strain has retained its purest line." Similar comments run strong within early studies of southern Appalachian culture.

Cratis William's important work, *Southern Mountain Speech*, examines the possible ethnic origins of mountain dialect and speech, yet neither the word *German* nor any of its variations appears. Are we to assume that German ethnicity surrendered its identity so meekly, contributing no vernacular words or pronunciations to the Appalachian dialect?

In Campbell's 1921 study of "Anglo-Celts" there are some outstanding early-twentieth-century photographs that relate to his text and depict rural Appalachian folklife. Most of these photographs inadvertently reveal aspects of the Appalachian people's German ancestry. There is a mountain rifle (developed by Pennsylvania Germans), a Saxon spinning wheel (named for its German place of origin), a mountain dulcimer (of German folk origin), and a man harvesting rye grain, a traditional German foodstuff. The majority of Campbell's photographs represent the material culture of German people, but this is left out of the text.

By the mid-twentieth century, the idea of Appalachia as a distinct region in America was firmly in place. Color writers made more romantic observations and fanciful determinations about the ethnic background of Appalachian people. Regarding the historic importance of Pennsylvania German culture in the southern mountains, Henry Glassie said, "[It] has been obscured by nonsense."[2] According to both the 1990 and 2000 U.S. Census figures, more people who live in the mountainous areas of southern Appalachian states consider themselves to be of German extraction than of any other ethnic group. This faction of our population has been discounted because of patriotic ideals stemming from twentieth-century world conflicts.

Shapiro's 1978 work, *Appalachia on Our Mind: The Southern Mountains and Mountaineers in the American Consciousness, 1820–1920*, discusses the formation of the idea of Appalachia as a separate and distinct cultural region. In general, his thesis determines that Appalachia, as a region, is a concept invented by outsiders.

Strewn throughout Shapiro's work are references to the "white, Anglo-Saxon, native-born population," "Englishness," "preservers of the folk culture of Merrie Olde England," and so on. Nowhere in his work is the word *German* or *Germany* used to indicate the origin of Appalachian people or culture. The writers critiqued in Shapiro's study not only wrought the concept of a new and distinct American region but also left out a huge portion of the population by getting the demographics wrong.

In the last three decades, much meaningful attention has been given to Scots-Irish culture in the southern Appalachians. This is good. However, all of the roots and aspects of Appalachian culture deserve attention. One good study (long out of print) about German Appalachian folk traditions is *The Pennsylvania Germans of the Shenandoah Valley* (1964), by Elmer L. Smith, John G. Stewart, and M. Ellsworth Kyger. Samuel Kercheval's early *History of the Valley of Virginia* (1833) mentions Germans as a distinct part of the region's social history during early settlement.

Beyond some studies in the "Great Valley," where German oral and material traditions are irrefutable and overwhelming,[3] related works are sparse. However, one can go into the countryside—whether it be in West Virginia, western North Carolina, eastern Tennessee, or eastern Kentucky—observe the cultural landscape, and converse with local people to obtain good ethnographic and cultural information. German culture did not influence, nor was it subsumed by, Appalachian culture; it has been a seminal part of that culture since earliest European settlement.

German culture presents itself in numerous ways in West Virginia's eastern counties, where eighteenth-century Germans found homesteads. Foodways reflect a strong Germanic presence. Local Pendleton County favorites are vinegar pie, sauerkraut, *pon haus*,[4] pickled beans, smoked sausage, and *snitz*. In Pendleton County, people speak of "snitz and knepp"[5] and "turkey spalooch," a stew made with turkey, rice, tomatoes, and onions. A folk song found in central West Virginia mentions *speck* (fat meat).[6] A strong tradition of fried foods (in much of Appalachia) indicates a strong German presence. In contrast, Scots-Irish people traditionally boiled their food.[7] Some German families in Pendleton County still eat specific foods on Shrove Tuesday (the day before Lent), such as crullers with maple syrup. The last person of the family to get up that day was called *Old Foss*. The last person up the next morning (Ash Wednesday) was called *Ash Witch* or *Ash Hutch*.[8] In Pendleton County, this tradition is no longer connected to religious belief; it survives as a folkway.

So who were these early settlers, these German "hillbillies," and just what were their contributions to the make-up of Appalachian culture? I have found they had a spiritual world view that embraced a belief in the occult, including belief-oriented curing methods and an intricate cosmology, a belief that lingers today.

In 1999, I received a West Virginia Humanities Council Fellowship to research folkways in the upper South Branch Valley of Pendleton County in the Potomac Highlands of West Virginia. On most weekends and on many free days over a year's time, I headed to the North Fork of the South Branch of the Potomac, going into Germany Valley through Judy Gap (the name comes from Tschudi, a common Germanic surname here). Then I would cross North Fork Mountain, descend into the South Branch Valley, explore the branches of Thorn Creek, and go over to the upper South Fork. I noted and photographed log buildings, rail fences, German/Swiss or Pennsylvania "bank" barns, and other features of the cultural landscape that present themselves at practically every turn in the road. I also found Germanic ritual celebrations and German folk art motifs and oral traditions, including occult practices, in surprising quantity. These subjects, in context, appealed to my interests, and to my reckoning they pointed to the fact that many oral and material traditions in Appalachian folkways are strongly influenced by Germanic culture.

Naturally, English is the main language of oral traditions in an English-speaking region, but much German folklore, including songs originally sung in German, made the transfer to the New World and then to the English language on the Appalachian frontier. In my field work, I have recorded oral folklore in West Virginia still spoken in the German language, among people whose ancestors immigrated to western Virginia before 1750.[9]

German ethnicity is even more strongly reflected in Appalachian craft and architectural tradition. Material objects found in folk cultures are exactly what they appear to be. They are three dimensional, tangible, undeniable, and relatively easy to explain in terms of provenance. Symbols are symbols, form is form, and style is style, and unless an object is of a revivalist nature, it is hard to refute its stylistic origins. In the early folk cultures in the New World, such objects commonly are of a design, type, shape, and so on found in defined areas of northern and western Europe.[10]

I subscribe to the idea of southern Appalachia being a distinct cultural region. Scots-Irish, German, and English immigrants, with far lesser numbers of Africans and Native Americans (among others), came together at a time, in a somewhat isolated place, in a way that solidified a culture by way of necessity. These people in general were religiously different and culturally apart from the Anglican English in Tidewater Virginia (whom they still call Tuckahoes), the Quaker English of Pennsylvania, and the Puritan English of New England.

As western expansion commenced in Pennsylvania, pioneers soon ran into the Appalachian Mountains, its ridges running parallel in a south-southwestward direction. Substantial numbers of German and Scots-Irish families, in roughly even numbers, headed down the Great Wagon Road to the western frontier in the early to mid-eighteenth century.[11] In some western Virginia counties west of the Blue Ridge, Germans made up as much as 70 percent of the population.[12] Others were home to similar percentages of Scots-Irish immigrants.

Unlike their English neighbors to the east, these pioneers' ties to English colonial government and the state-sponsored church were weak and distant, a major factor in this region's substantial contribution to the upstart army of the American Revolution. However, because Pennsylvania required an oath of allegiance during the war, many Brethren and other Germans of a religious pacifist persuasion headed to the Virginia Appalachian back country to avoid conscription.

Pendleton County has been called the "Dutchiest county in West Virginia" and was ripe for research. I identify traditions there and in other areas of the state that are strongly tied to eighteenth-century German culture and link those traditions to others found in the southern Appalachians as a whole. Since German culture in this area came from the first wave of eighteenth-century immigrants by way of Pennsylvania, the studies of Henry Mercer, Don Yoder, Alfred Shoemaker, Richard Wentz, Louis Winkler, and others regarding German culture were particularly useful. In fact, some of their findings accurately portray folklife activities that persist in the southern Appalachians but have died out in Pennsylvania.[13] To the south, Klaus Wust's keen research and observations about early German pioneers and Elmer Smith's numerous published works were a welcome addition to a rather sparse bibliography on the subject.

In 1947, the late Wayland Hand said that German folklore in this country was being overlooked, and he suggested what could be done about it. He believed that folkways derived from German religious patterns and German agricultural customs would prove worthy of study. Sadly, at least in the Appalachians, other than studies in the Shenandoah Valley, such a study did not come to pass in his time.[14]

The lower part of the Shenandoah Valley and the Potomac watershed of West Virginia became the home, hearth, and launching pad for culture-bearing German and Scots-Irish pioneers into later-settled areas of the upland South.[15] Today, a regional identity has overcome ethnicity in all of the southern uplands.[16]

Make no mistake, Appalachian folklore is full of Anglo-Celtic traditions, mostly attributable to the Scots-Irish, but there is more to Appalachia than that, and the German element deserves its due. Unfortunately, the distaste for two twentieth-century world conflicts involving Germany as a foe has promoted historic revision in this country, a phenomenon now recognized as the "paradox of American identity."[17] I intend to show that German culture, as much as any other ethnic influence, pervades what has come to be widely known as Appalachian culture.

I introduce primary field work into a discussion about the cultural derivations of Appalachian folklore. Much of the folkloric material I present here is in the occult vein. The Germanic origins of this material are strikingly apparent with only cursory references to Old World sources.

Germany is considered the most prodigious country in Europe when it comes to sources of occult traditions, and Appalachian folklore is rife with this material. When people hear the word Appalachian, it should automatically reflect an ethnic origin that includes a Germanic presence.

Several of my best informants were advanced in age and have since passed on. Their collected lore supports an underlying thesis of this book, which is that a portion of the expression of Appalachian folklore, folk art, and cosmology is of German origin. I make no moral or value judgments and take no stand regarding the belief systems and folklore documented here. I am comfortable in being, for the most part, the messenger, but I do open discussion about those beliefs and their origins when appropriate.

Some might find it curious that people in the twenty-first century, such as many of my informants, harbor traditional occult beliefs. It is hard to refute the reasoning of my sources regarding witchery, for, as one informant stated to me, "If you don't believe it, you ain't a-believin' the Bible."

I begin with a brief early European overview of the beliefs of my sources. I then explain how and why those beliefs were brought to America, who brought them, how those beliefs evolved within New World religious contexts, and how they arrived on the frontier with the first pioneers. I describe some specific families and individuals who have contributed the folkways I document, and, finally, I offer a discussion of those beliefs and practices as I have found them and the prospects of those beliefs continuing in the postmodern world.

Use of Terms

In this book, I use the word *spiritual* in the sense that it allows for the belief in the reality of spirits. The word *occult* as used here simply means "hidden" or "hidden meaning." Some aspects of the material and lore might be considered *esoteric*, a term interchangeable with several used by my informants. The words *magic, witchery, witchcraft, witch business, curing, sign cures, omens, tokens,* and *charms* are used to imply hidden or mysterious meaning. *Talismans* are luck charms, and *amulets* guard against evil. Various occult practices allude to *divining*, which simply means "knowing."

The religious *mystics* I mention are relevant historical figures who, through their spiritual practices and aspirations, sought a perfect union with God. Many seek ways to such a union through practices that are in the esoteric realm. *Heretics* hold beliefs that church authorities consider outside of accepted church doctrine. Old World *hermetic figures* were followers of Hermes, the Greek god of mysticism, astrology, and alchemy. Much is written here about *folk spirituality*. This term encompasses all of the intangible beliefs and practices that people use in everyday life to guide their activities in ways that support their cultural values, successful endeavors, and noble aspirations. It also pertains to values expressed in their (tangible) folk art.

The term *German* or *Germanic* refers to sources from the German-speaking areas of Europe, including Austria, Silesia, Alsace, and Germanic cantons of Switzerland. *Anglo* and *Anglo-Saxon* refer to the English and the culture that emanated from England. *Anglo-Celtic* refers to the lowland Scots, border English, and Scots-Irish. *Celtic* and/or *Gaelic* refers to the Catholic Irish, the highland Scots, and the Welsh.

My West Virginia informants refer to the *Valley* when speaking of the Great Central Valley of the southern Appalachian Mountains, and I do the same. In West Virginia, *the mountains* usually refer to the eastern part of the state, although the whole state is mountainous or, at least, hill country.

While medieval scholars, anthropologists, and archaeologists make no distinction between religion and magic, there is a clear separation today in the minds of Appalachian theologians, and I categorize the two accordingly. Both allow for concepts and actions that belie scientific justification. I use a wide definition of the term *religion*, in that it is man's explanation of the universe.

Tree of life gravestone, Old Propst Church cemetery.

Chapter 1

The Old World

The word dies when we seize the pen,
Wax and leather lord it then.
—Goethe

The annals of Bamberg, Germany, chronicle a history of intrigue and vibrant life, a life that may still be experienced in the town's eleventh-century cathedral and thirteenth-century pubs, streets, and plazas. It is where rulers were assassinated, where Hoffmann began his literary career, where Goethe's Dr. Faust had dealings, and, alas, where a dreaded "witch house," or torture chamber, was located.

In 1999, I visited this small cathedral town located on the Main River in northern Bavaria. Walking through the charming streets of Bamberg, I found it hard to imagine that hundreds of accused witches had been tried, tortured, and burnt at the stake here. Indeed, a strong prison, the Drudenhaus, was built especially for sorcerers by the prince bishop of Bamberg.[1]

On June 28, 1628, Johannes Junius, the burgomaster of Bamberg, was implicated, examined, and charged with witchcraft by the authorities. As was typical, Junius's accusers were tortured and executed witches. He ardently denied all accusations. He was again examined and again he fervently denied all of the charges, saying he would not and could not ever deny his God. At this point the dreaded torture began, consisting first of thumbscrews and then of leg screws. He was examined for the "witch mark," and finding a bluish mark on his body, the examiners pricked it "thrice," but it would not bleed (a sure sign).

Junius was relegated to a cell. Many more examinations and torture sessions ensued, including eight encounters with the infamous strappado in which he was drawn up by his arms, which were tied behind his back, and released. At one point, when Junius was being led back to his cell after a torture session, the executioner said, "Sir, I beg you, for God's sake, confess something, whether it be true or not." He went on to say that the torture would only get worse and would not stop until he confessed.

Junius was tortured more and eventually confessed. He implicated many others and, in the end, was burnt alive. But one detail about his case separates it from the tens of thousands of others like it. Just before he died, he smuggled a letter out of prison to be delivered to his daughter. In it, he fervently renounced any belief in witchcraft, saying he was entirely devoted to God and that he confessed only because he could no longer bear the pain. He described the plea of the executioner, who could no longer bear to watch the torture, and confirmed the innocence of those he implicated under duress. He outlined the complete fantasy he made up and gave at his confession, a description that matches the trial records.[2]

Throughout the latter decades of the seventeenth century, stories based on witchcraft accusations and fantastic events found in the confessions of people such as Junius circulated throughout the German countryside. A vicious circle, in which coerced lies were so prevalent that they became truth, however illusionary and imaginary, was set in place. In effect, these fantastic notions became perceived reality through the oral folk process and eventually solidified into an occult world view that existed within a religious sphere.

Christians who promoted the Inquisition found support for their witch hating (and torturing, burning, and hanging) in the book of Exodus: "Thou shalt not suffer a witch to live" (22:18, KJV). Along with fears introduced by the Reformation more than a century earlier, it brought about major religious conversion. Soon after Junius's tribulation, the Rhine and Main Valleys were ablaze with religious ferment. After having endured the infamous Inquisition and a more or less constant state of on again/off again war for over sixteen hundred years, then enduring the punishing Thirty Years' War, which ended in 1648, people were looking for fundamental change. Then, "the Palatinate" experienced still more attempts by European rulers to gain control of this lush garden spot of Europe.

By the end of the century, continuing pressure from both governmental and ecclesiastical powers were forcing entire sects to look westward across the Atlantic for relief. Religious persecution, oppression, and strife became widespread because of Protestant differences with the Catholic Church and the struggle for supremacy among various Protestant factions.[3] When war between France and Germany ended in 1697, the Roman Catholic Church seized the property of Protestant churches, which helped induce an immigration of numerous religious sects to the New World.

Eighteenth-century powder horns with Germanic symbols. Courtesy Darby Collection, Davis and Elkins College.

By the end of the seventeenth century, thousands of Swiss-German Anabaptists, many original followers of Huldreich Zwingli, had escaped persecution in Germanic Switzerland and joined Lutherans and German Reformed[4] in the Rhine Valley. The Pietist movement there, a growing faction, hovered on the outer fringes of mainstream religious thought of the period. It introduced many to a mystical cosmology that included magical and occult aspects of alchemy, astrology, and numerology, and utilized some Christian aspects of the Jewish Cabala. Formal religion in the Palatinate would hardly allow such radical movements. Continued persecution forced many to the New World, where greater religious and personal freedom, as well as prospects of peace, were reported.

William Penn made a visit to the Palatinate in 1671. During later timely visits, he invited the religiously persecuted to join his "holy experiment" in the new English colony of Pennsylvania.[5] In the 1680s, Penn published and distributed pamphlets in English, German, Dutch, and French that promised religious freedom in the New World. For the most part, it was Germans and Germanic Swiss Lutherans, Reformed, Anabaptists, and various other smaller factions who were severely affected by religious intolerance. They responded accordingly by abandoning their homeland and its bleak prospects for their spiritual aspirations.

Chapter 2

The New World

They find impunity
In cosmic unity.
—Goethe

Sizable numbers of Germans fled their homeland as family groups. Pennsylvania, the most common destination of the oppressed religious outcasts, was where the many German factions found religious freedom.

In the late seventeenth century they came in timid numbers, but soon after, they arrived in droves. In 1709, thirteen thousand fled the Palatinate for William Penn's colony.[1] In the mid-Atlantic region, the port of Philadelphia became the funnel through which most immigrants passed. Among these various Christians, it was a connection to mystical thought, religious fervor, and occult beliefs born of study, fear, and the persecution and economic troubles it had begot that provided the great impetus to seek the New World. Soon after settling in Penn's colony, they sought the vast mountainous and forested landscape of the Appalachian back country. This process coincided with a remarkable explosion of Christian pluralism in the middle colonies of America, largely because of the attraction to William Penn's declaration of "liberty of conscience."[2] Penn's religious "experiment" is now deemed a success by historians, and some of the diverse religious factions he attracted have had influence in excess of their numbers in relation to the larger mainstream denominations that surround them.[3]

By 1776, between 110,000 and 150,000 Germans had come to Pennsylvania, many of whom belonged to nonmainstream sects. They were reproducing in staggering numbers, as noted in family genealogies. With Penn's tolerance and help, Pennsylvania became the spawning ground for even more radical religious thought in the New World. Penn's notions of religious freedom were instilled and affirmed in the groups who immigrated to the

Virginia frontier in the eighteenth century. This caused some problems, however, within colonial Virginia, where, with its English church/state rule, there was less tolerance of nonmainstream religious views compared to Pennsylvania. Most of the Anabaptist sects in Pennsylvania were formed within the seventeenth-century Pietist movement of Germany. Many of the more adventurous pioneering Germans among them had radical religious ties.

Once here, the lure and foreseen freedom of westward expansion was irresistible to many. Beginning in the 1730s, serious westward expansion in the New World had begun. These westward-moving pioneers harbored strong occult traditions from their recent European experiences, however deranged. Many who were born in the Old World and had personally known those affected by inquisitions, made it to the western Virginia frontier.

Adventurous Germans left eastern Pennsylvania and branched to the south and west, along with considerable numbers of Scots-Irish immigrants, becoming the settlers and frontiersmen of western Virginia. Much smaller numbers of Germans landed in Baltimore and drifted west. Some Pennsylvania Germans came south into the valley and then turned east to populate counties in northern Virginia.[4] While the Great Wagon Road, also called the Old Philadelphia Road and later called the Valley Pike, Route 11, or, roughly, today's Interstate 81, was the main route, there were actually four routes taken south from Pennsylvania.[5]

Some settlers, mostly Scots-Irish pioneers, stayed a westerly course across ridges into extreme western Pennsylvania. Today, southwestern Pennsylvania, through which the old National Road passes, remains the bastion of Scots-Irish Presbyterianism and culture in America. Western Pennsylvania and western Virginia became America's original "old frontier" for German and Anglo/Celtic pioneers. The particularly severe winter of 1740–41 helped to provoke a major exodus southward, although for those who reached the higher altitudes of western Virginia's Potomac Highlands, the winter was generally more severe than what they knew in eastern Pennsylvania.

The strong historic connection between the German immigration to Pennsylvania in the New World and the early settlements of the Appalachian back country is easily proven through genealogical research. The Shenandoah Valley, with its Scots-Irish and German populations, was seen as "an extension of Pennsylvania,"[6] a conclusion that holds true for most of the southern Appalachians.[7]

The first white pioneers to settle west of the Blue Ridge were Germanic people. Adam Miller (Mueller) came in 1727, and Jost Hite came in 1730. They established the earliest settlements of Europeans in the Valley, but Pennsylvania Germans were familiar with the Valley passage by that time.

For instance, Michael Wohlfarth of Pennsylvania used the Valley as a route to North Carolina in 1722.[8] Like most early settlers, Miller and Hite had been born in Germany and came to America in the middle to later stage of life. Philip Long, who came to western Virginia by way of Pennsylvania in the mid-eighteenth century, was born in Germany in 1678.[9] Jost Hite, born in the Rhineland in 1685, first came with a large group of Germans to New York. Most of this faction were dissatisfied there and soon removed to eastern Pennsylvania's religiously friendly environs before coming on to the Valley. Hite's son Abraham became an early settler on the South Branch of the Potomac, now West Virginia, in 1751. He married a Van Meter, who belonged to one of several families from Holland who came south with the New York German faction to Pennsylvania, and eventually came to settle the South Branch. The Cunningham and other Irish families came to the South Branch from northern Ireland, via Pennsylvania, at about this time as well. Soon "Dunkers" (Brethren) with ties to that early Pennsylvania church and the mystical community at the Ephrata Cloister, one of America's earliest religious communes, established multiple scores of homesteads in the South Branch watersheds. Their homesteads dotted the valleys of the Cacapon and Lost River, the South Branch of the Potomac and its South Fork, Mill Creek, Loonies Creek, and Patterson Creek (which flows into the North Branch of the Potomac) tributaries, and other arable land in today's Hampshire, Hardy, Grant, and Pendleton Counties.[10] Some Germans used the South Branch as a route through today's West Virginia to populate Highland and Bath Counties in (old) Virginia. Other Brethren settled on the North Fork of the Shenandoah. They had gained their Dunker nickname for their "total immersion" method of baptism.

New hope for a prosperous future drove these diverse religious groups toward backcountry destinations. In September 1745, early settlers and travelers along the Great Wagon Road in the Valley encountered an unusual sight. The road, or path, such as it was at that time, was carrying adventurers away from Pennsylvania moorings into the virtual wilderness along the Virginia frontier. Several German mystics dressed in long, hooded white robes were trudging, single file, in the southwesterly direction of the path. They were on a spiritual mission, though they were not the first religious partisans to probe this colonial backcountry with idealistic purpose.[11]

The white-robed mystic Brethren passing through the Valley included Samuel, Gabriel, and Israel Eckerlin. In many ways, these brothers, pioneers of the Appalachian frontier, were seminal influences on Appalachian culture. They settled with others from Pennsylvania along the New River in today's southwest Virginia. There, Israel Eckerlin and Alexander Mack engaged in study and the making of "esoteric speculations." Samuel Eckerlin, who fancied himself a doctor, looked to the physical needs of other settlers, and brother Gabriel procured food.

They did not last long at their new hermitage, called Mahanaim, now buried by a dam on the New River of Virginia near present-day Blacksburg. After a brief return trip to eastern Pennsylvania, they found their way again to a frontier home near the "Forks of Cheat" on Cheat River. They soon removed farther upstream to Dunker's Bottom, now in Preston County, West Virginia, where they built their new hermitage. On the New River they had abandoned their taboo against taking any life, an aspect of communal life in Ephrata, and resorted to hunting for meat and trading animal pelts.

Israel and Samuel Eckerlin are surely two of the more interesting individuals ever to inhabit the old frontier. Their father, Michael, had been banished from Strasbourg because of his Pietist leanings. Throughout this period, entire sects were setting out for Pennsylvania because of the enormous pressure and discrimination brought upon them by the church and governing authorities. Michael Eckerlin brought up his sons in the mystically charged underground climate of the early Brethren Church at Schwarzenau, where persecution brought constant danger to their door.[12] Although he died in Europe, his family managed to immigrate to Pennsylvania, first coming to Germantown.

The white-robed adventurers attracting notice as they passed through the Valley based their dress on biblical passages in the Book of Revelation (7:13–14). Their costume included a *Thalar, Ueberwurf, Schurtz, Scheler, zugespitzte Monchs-Kappe*, and *Gurtel* (robe, outer cloak, apron, veil, pointed monk's hood, and belt).[13] Israel Eckerlin once wore a more lavish robe he had commissioned in Ephrata, patterned after one described in chapter 28 of Exodus that was worn by Aaron. His personal aspirations, along with a competitive business sense, led to a longing for materialistic gain that got him in trouble with the other spiritual leaders at Ephrata and led to a dispute that was never adequately resolved.

Another Eckerlin brother, Emmanuel, lived for a while on the New River. He eventually led a large group of Sabbatarian Dunkers through the Valley and all the way into South Carolina, establishing a southern outpost of the Brethren faith there that they called Bethabara. The much-loved Gerhart and Margaretha Zinn lived out an amazing life that started in the first decade of the eighteenth century in the Rhineland and took them through a course of various mystical religious factions in Pennsylvania and Virginia. They eventually ended up and died at Bethabara.[14] Spiritual bonds, love, and friendship ran strong among frontier German Appalachians.

During the late 1740s, many Pennsylvania Germans, committed to various religious sects, including numerous Brethren followers, found their way along newly established routes of ethnic movement to the nation's frontier by way of the Potomac,[15] the Shenandoah, the James, and the westward-flowing New River. Pennsylvania Germans were attempting settlement on the "western waters" of the Greenbrier River by the early 1750s, and Scots-Irish settlers penetrated the trans-Allegheny's Tygart Valley at about that same time.[16]

The Eckerlin brothers often passed through the valleys of the Cheat, Patterson Creek, and the South Branch, where they most likely visited with other Brethren as they traveled between their Cheat River hermitage and the Sabbatarian community at Strasburg, Virginia, where they had other spiritual kin.[17]

In the latter half of the eighteenth century, many of the second-generation pioneers kept a southerly course to the westward-flowing Holston River. Others veered off at Roanoke and found their way on the Wilderness Road through the Cumberland Gap.[18] Some arrived in Kentucky by way of the Greenbrier Trace from western Virginia. By the early nineteenth century, adventurous settlers followed the new National Road to Wheeling and used the Ohio River as their route to Appalachian Ohio, Kentucky, Tennessee, and the West.[19]

Early on, Germans were at odds with their Scots-Irish and English neighbors in many ways, and conflicts resulted. In eighteenth-century Pennsylvania, the Penns instructed the land agents not to sell land to Scots-Irish settlers in German-dominated areas, suggesting instead areas farther west. It is commonly believed that the Scots-Irish were used as a buffer between the Indian dangers and the less-adventuresome Germans and English. While Penn's instruction lends credence to that, Germans (most often called "Dutch" from the German *Deutsche*) are found throughout the tales of the Indian Wars on the frontier and were well represented among the earliest adventurous pioneers.

Lewis Wetzel, the pioneer son of a German immigrant from the Palatinate who had come to Pennsylvania, was the white man most feared by Native Americans on the old Virginia frontier. Romanticized treatises exist about Wetzel's life, but by all accounts he was ruthless in his revengeful quest to spill Indian blood. He was well known as a fiddler and was welcomed in homes and rustic taverns for that ability, but his fame lies in his legendary Indian-fighting exploits. Simon Girty, of Scots-Irish ancestry, joined and organized Indian raids on the frontier and, conversely, was the man most feared by white settlers during early settlement. Girty spent his

Settler's cabin, Pendleton County, c. 1800.

life avenging the Pennsylvania provincial government's attack on his father's frontier home in Pennsylvania at Burnt Cabins. The Girty family had settled too far west, where treaties with Indians had not yet been made, thus the government's eviction and destruction of their homestead.

Another generalization, commonly held, is that the Germans were better judges of good soil and had more productive farms than their Scots-Irish and English neighbors.[20] Samuel Kercheval, in his *History of the Valley of Virginia* (1833), supports this claim.[21] Traditional German farming, going back to the Old World in the Middle Ages, drew from successful established forms in which three-field crop rotation was practiced.[22] Everything on the German farm had a sense of order and purpose. This is still evident on old eastern West Virginia farms, another factor that lends credence to the claim.

That German immigrants chose to settle in the lush valleys of eastern Pennsylvania and in the Valley of Virginia on some of the richest limestone clay–based agricultural land in the world bolsters the claim of agricultural acumen. The Blue Grass region (limestone-based area) of Kentucky drew numerous Germans as settlement spread west following Pennsylvanian Daniel Boone and the first hunters and trappers to that area.[23]

Just before the Revolution, the British colonial government attempted to settle a group of two hundred Pennsylvania German families on the Great Ohio Company's land in western Virginia. They proposed to call the colony Vandalia in honor of King George III's German queen, named Charlotte, who claimed Germanic Vandal blood. The capitol was to be at Point Pleasant (West) Virginia, on the Ohio. When these Germans learned that the Vandalia colony would be in Virginia, where there was a government-sanctioned church and where religious tolerance would not be what they enjoyed in Pennsylvania, they pulled back from the plan. This situation did not stop numerous German settlers from coming to colonial Virginia, but they eventually paid a price for the move. Some suffered from enforced tithing because they were not affiliated with the Anglican Church. Still, there was some encouragement from the colonial government for new settlers in the form of limited tax relief.

Chapter 3

The Pioneers

It is the customary fate of new truths to begin
as heresies and to end as superstitions.
—*Aldous Huxley*

Early Dunkers (Brethren) in western Virginia practiced pacifism and in general had good relations with most Indians. Because the Dunkers were treated kindly and even spared by numerous war parties, the "English" suspected them of spying for the French and brought legal actions against them, leading to jail time for some. The pacifist Eckerlin family, while living on the remote Cheat River, was accused of spying for the French because Indians did not molest them.

The Eckerlins, as other early settlers, were nourished by German Pietist and mystical thought.[1] Samuel Eckerlin eventually became an unschooled and self-proclaimed medical doctor at Strasburg, Virginia, and was joined there by another Pennsylvania Dunker, George Keller. Samuel had an herb garden and a distillery and dispensed various cures and tinctures to patients, including a special purging treatment. His treatments were based on his knowledge of herbs and alchemical processes and his experience with occult methodologies timed to astrological activity. Born in Germany, Samuel's life spanned an enormous geographical distance and included a wide experience of eighteenth-century life. He personally knew Benjamin Franklin and oversaw the printing of a Bible, in German, at Franklin's press.

The original Germans who founded Germantown, Pennsylvania, sought religious freedom and spiritual perfection in part by constructing a peculiar tower in which to observe the heavens and watch for signs of the coming of the Lord, an event they thought would take place in the year 1700. There is reason to believe that the Eckerlins used such a structure at their hermitage at Dunker's Bottom in (West) Virginia, where Israel Eckerlin was kept busy making "mystic speculations" through his observation of the heavens. Heinrich Sangmeister and Anton Hollenthal constructed a similar building based on the old Germantown model near Strasburg, Virginia. These German-born mystics had strong ties to the Eckerlins and visited back and forth with them at Dunker's Bottom on the Cheat River, now in West Virginia. The Strasburg structure sat on a prominent hill and is described as having one opening facing the eastern sky. The recluses spent long periods of time within it to obtain "spiritual regeneration and physical perfection." This aroused the curiosity and suspicion of Anglo/Celt neighbors, to the extent that they forced them to disband their *Laura*, their term for these special buildings.[2] We are left only to speculate as to the design and mysterious purposes of these early examples of Appalachian folk architecture. Back in Ephrata, the architecture (much still in existence) may have been influenced by Cabalistic diagrams associated with Rosicrucian thought, whereby one floor plan was laid out on a hexagram pattern. Even distances between buildings and the geometric patterns they formed appear to have been created to conform to obscure religious thought.[3] The actual building work took place during a time period they identified as providential through astrological calculations.

The Ephrata Cloister was an early American attempt at religious communal living using mystical worship practices. The Brethren there practiced otherworldly singing, incense-induced spirit exorcisms, and reconciliation services, as well as celibate living for the most devout. Dynamic astrological/cosmological aspects of their world view were instilled in their sojourn-

Old log church at Smoke Hole, Pendleton County, c. 1800.

ers, who were Appalachian settlers of the mid-eighteenth century. Valentin Bruckman, Martin Kroll, Sangmeister, Hollenthal, Hildebrand Inebinet and others on the frontier kept up a remarkable theological discourse with the mystical religious communities back in Pennsylvania.

Hildebrand Inebinet was a curious frontier character. He threw in with other Sabbatarian Brethren and enlisted their help in a quest to probe the Appalachian wilderness with a divining rod to discover precious metals. Sabbatarian Brethren Jacob Martin and a "Dr. Land" of Lancaster were early Pennsylvania figures who carried out alchemical tests and methods in Pennsylvania. The alchemy practiced by Martin may have involved efforts to produce gold from various basic elements to lighten financial strain on the Ephrata community.[4]

The general movement of settlers to the Valley and into what is now eastern West Virginia was an eighteenth-century phenomenon.[5] While in general the greatest immigration from Germany to Pennsylvania took place in the nineteenth century, it was the eighteenth century's religious groups, influenced by the theology of early Pietists, who established the early Germanic element of Appalachian culture. Evidence of this old infusion is found throughout this work, and the surnames of eighteenth-century pioneer families make up about all of the family names I cite.

During the main eighteenth-century immigration to the Appalachian back country, between 1727 and 1783, three-quarters of the immigrants came as members of a family or a community group, thus better preserving traditional folkways and belief systems. In places such as Pendleton County, where arable land is limited, immigration of mostly German and Scots-Irish pioneers effectively ended by the end of the eighteenth century. Since there is limited arable land in the river valleys of West Virginia's eastern counties, eighteenth-century settlement took up that land quickly, as well as procuring areas for mountain-top grazing on steeper and higher land, which still remains the norm. Because there was no significant manufacturing or extractive industry, there were few additional settlers after the eighteenth century until the timber boom near the end of the nineteenth century. And the work force involved with timbering was mostly transient. With fewer modern influences, older beliefs were retained for longer periods of time among the pioneer descendants of the old "residenters" of the Appalachian agricultural valleys of my study area.

The drier climate in the eastern counties of West Virginia appears favorable to the preservation of folk architecture. Because of a "rain shadow" in Pendleton, Grant, and Hardy Counties on the eastern side of Allegheny Mountain, drier conditions have better preserved log buildings, many from the eighteenth and early nineteenth centuries, as well as miles of rail fence and other wooden structures. These conditions—a drier climate and early settlement—result in a particularly older sensibility within both the cultural landscape and the character of the people.

Germanic and Anglo/Celtic people became more unified in language, religion, social interaction and, indeed, blood, as "Appalachians," but their customs, especially that of the German and Scots-Irish elements, still reflect their Old World heritage. The German sects left a body of occult folklore not allowed within other religious persuasions. All churches dropped these beliefs, especially as they splintered and modernized theology emerged.

Oren F. Morton's *History of Pendleton County* (1910) gives an account of the ethnicity of early settlers in Pendleton County. Morton lists 56 surnames as "English," 31 of "Scotch" origin, 117 of "German" origin, and 20 of "Irish" origin, along with a handful of Welsh, Dutch, Scandinavian, and French surnames. In all probability, most of the Scots, many of the English, and all of the "Irish" families were Ulster or Scots-Irish families, as Morton does not distinguish Irish from Ulster Irish, and many early settlers came from northern Ireland by way of Pennsylvania. He also does not classify African American surnames, although then and now they make up a small minority of the population. He admits that because of the Anglicization of all names, there are probably some mistakes in his survey.[6] Suffice it to say, given these figures and studies in similar county histories of eastern West Virginia, German culture strongly presents itself among the pioneer families in the eastern watersheds of the Potomac, Cheat, New, Bluestone, and Greenbrier River Valleys, which make up the counties of Hampshire, Hardy, Pendleton, Randolph, Pocahontas, Greenbrier, Summers, and Monroe. Further, most of these surnames can be followed westward into later settled areas of the state.

Typical of numerous pioneer western Virginia families are the Puffinbargers. They descend from Johan George Pfaffenberger, who came from Ulmet, Rheinpfalz, Germany, to Philadelphia in 1733. Johan settled and eventually died in Berks County, Pennsylvania. Indians killed his namesake son on the South Fork in Hardy County, and then his progeny settled upstream in Pendleton County.

The family histories of other German pioneers are similar. In Pendleton, these pioneer family names include Arbogast, Bowers, Keplinger, Cogar, Conrad, Crummet, Dahmer, Dasher, Dunkle, Eckard, Eye, Evick, Halterman, Harman, Harper, Hevener, Hoover, Huffman, Judy, Keister, Kizer, Ketterman, Kline, Lambert, Michael, Mitchell, Moats, Moyers, Pitsenbarger, Rader,

Rexrode, Ruleman, Shaver, Stone, Swadley, Waggy, Whetsell, Wilfong,Yankee, Zickafoose, and Zorns.

Along with agricultural interests and the lure of western land and opportunity, it was the pursuit of a spiritually inspired life that brought many to the eighteenth-century Appalachian frontier, a continuation of the migrant quest that began in Europe. Among the early settlers in West Virginia was the Propst family, pioneers to the upper South Fork in Pendleton County. The family descended from John Michael Propst, who arrived in Pennsylvania about 1730 and spent considerable time at Bethlehem, the New World home of the Moravians. Moravians had first settled in Georgia but soon evacuated to the religiously friendly environs of Pennsylvania. A faction then left their New World home and followed the Great Wagon Road with other German countrymen to their North Carolina settlement at Winston-Salem.

While the old German pioneers' folk spirituality included a religio-magical belief system, some modern descendants wrestle with religion entwined with occult belief. Jocie Armentrout of Randolph County drew a line for me where she believed Christianity ended and occult belief began. Regarding the fairly common practice of "stopping blood" (discussed below), she thought God was invoked in the healing of a bleeding person through the Bible verse that is recited. But an aspect of this practice—that the power to stop blood may only be passed from one person to a person of the opposite sex—she believed to be outside the bounds of religion and within the realm of the occult (to which she took exception). The belief that knowledge is passed only to those of the opposite sex is strong in German tradition, including in forms of brauche, or faith healing, still practiced by the Amish.[7]

Chapter 4

Religion

Religion is one way people explain the unknowable.
Superstition is another way.
—Richard E. Wentz

It has been noted that American Christianity was born in a frontier setting of a frontier spirit.[1] As people who practiced various forms of worship headed down the Great Wagon Road, they brought with them a tradition of radical Christianity. The white-robed travelers of 1745 were, at the time, known as Dunkers,[2] Sabbatarians, Seventh Day Baptists (for their observation of the Sabbath on Saturday), or simply Brethren. The early Brethren Church took form after a collision of spiritual thought in Europe about 1708. This blend of anabaptism and radical pietism was first organized as a church in Germantown, Pennsylvania, by Alexander Mack Sr. about 1719. He had founded the church in Germany, and virtually all of his followers came to Pennsylvania. Mack and his followers followed biblical teaching but also paid close attention to numerology, astrology, and the Cabala and adhered to the writings of German mystic Jacob Boehme. Alexander Mack's son, Alexander Mack Jr., a childhood friend of Israel Eckerlin, was also one of the white-robed "saint-adventurers" on the Virginia frontier.

Compassionate Quakers in Pennsylvania, including Thomas Rutter, an early abolitionist, influenced the Brethren. Rutter helped instill recognition of the Sabbath on Saturday as the main day of worship for the old Sabbatarian Dunkers. (They were also called First Day Dunkers or Seventh Day Dunkers.) These Brethren sought a more communal, rather than individualistic or monastic, manifestation of their spirituality.[3] Thus committed groups or communities of people professing various aspects of this faith became the norm, even as they expanded westward to the frontier.

On the frontier, their communal values served them well and were an advantage in spiritual, practical, and political ways. If there ever was a need for people to stick together, spiritually and otherwise, it was on the frontier. With the relative prosperity and social changes of the latter nineteenth century, the Brethren Church experienced major splits, in 1881 and 1883, after which the "plain," or old-time, Dunkers declined in numbers. Only fifty-five old-order Brethren churches are still in existence.[4] There are five different Brethren faiths today, the church having gone through other splits in 1926 and 1939. For Brethren and other German communities, the various churches were their religious, social, and educational centers.[5] The German/Brethren press at Ephrata helped keep ethnic identity intact by publishing various religious, and even occult, tracts in the German language.

It is probable that early Pendleton County settler John Michael Propst personally met Count Zinzendorf, a man of wealth and nobility who took up the Moravian cause in Europe and came to Pennsylvania in 1741, leading to the establishment of the Pennsylvania and North Carolina Moravian communities. It is also probable that Propst's stay in Bethlehem brought about the Moravian visits to the upper South Fork Propst pioneers in the late 1740s. The Propst settlers in Pendleton County took up Lutheran religious beliefs, the Lutheran church being the only accessible church, and their adherence to old German magical occult belief runs strong among descendants yet today.

As early as 1747 through 1749, Moravians held religious services, probably "love feasts" (foot-washing services), on the South Fork in what is now Pendleton County, West Virginia.[6] Moravian leaders, influenced by the peculiar spirituality and mysticism of Count Zinzendorf, maintained efforts to keep a check on Germans living on the South Fork and other backcountry Appalachian settlements during this period. They visited the early German Brethren settlements on lower Patterson Creek in Hampshire County.[7] And they probably visited other early Brethren enclaves in today's Hardy and Grant Counties.

Early frontier settlements in this area of western Virginia included those of the Lutheran, Presbyterian, Mennonite, and Brethren persuasion. However, Brethren churches in western Virginia and Mennonite churches in the Valley were better served in a ministerial way, because ordination of these churches' leaders did not require formal religious training. Some Lutherans considered the frontier Brethren religiously fanatical, but as for tolerance of religio-magical belief systems of the frontier era, apparently they were kindred spirits.

The German Henckle family descends from Anthony Jacob Henckle, a Lutheran minister who immigrated to Pennsylvania in 1717. Some families came right to the frontier, but most came after a brief stay in Pennsylvania, and some had to work off their bill of passage. The Henckel family first settled in Berks County, Pennsylvania. They migrated down the Great Wagon Road to North Carolina, but because of Indian raids there, they came north to Pendleton County (hardly a safe haven at the time). Like the Henkles (Hinkles),[8] the majority of Germanic eighteenth-century pioneer settlers on the Potomac's South Branch and its North and South Forks were born in Germanic Switzerland or Germany.[9] The Hinkle family is now distributed over a wide area and may well have played a significant part in the evolution of the Appalachian dulcimer.[10]

Paul Henkel was a Lutheran minister of eighteenth-century frontier significance. He lived for a time in Pendleton County's Germany Valley, first settled by the Hinkles and where his uncles had established Hinkle's Fort. He learned the trade of coopering there, learned to read and write from a local German woman, and learned proper English and Latin from an "Englishman." Henkel eventually resettled in the Valley, where he made his mark within the local Lutheran church. Paul and his son, Ambrose Henkel, traveled widely and preached at numerous small rural churches that requested that sermons be delivered in the German language. This continued well after English became the established language in mainstream Lutheran churches, about 1825.[11]

Paul Henkel traveled throughout Pendleton County in the early to mid-nineteenth century warning people about belief in witchcraft. In 1851, another Lutheran pastor, Charles Krauth, noted that witchcraft was so ingrained in local German tradition that he deemed it "impossible to dispel."[12]

Radical Germantown Pietist George de Benneville found his way to the Virginia frontier in 1767, where he held large, popular revivals. According to historian Klaus Wust, these were "spiritual assemblies" that were attended by both religious followers and non-German religiously curious frontiersmen. One of the unusual Pennsylvania churches associated with Benneville, known as the New Mooners, held that the main day to worship should be the first day of the new moon.[13] The Inspirationalists and the Neu-geboren (New Born) were other small Pennsylvania German sects with curious beliefs.[14] About two hundred Schwenkfelders, a sect originally from Silesia, came to Pennsylvania from Germany in the 1730s.

The assortment of sectarian revivalists in Pennsylvania included Johannes Kelpius, a late-seventeenth-century German mystic who helped to settle Germantown. He conceived of his radical group, the Society of the Woman of the Wilderness, while living in a cave at their hermitage on the Wissahickon. This group saw themselves as the woman of the wilderness as described in the Book of Revelation (12:14–17). Originally forty men composed this group—by no coincidence, as forty is a biblical number. They came from Germany in 1694; a date aligned with their astrological calculations. These followers and spiritual descendants of Johannes Kelpius led an ascetic, celibate existence on the banks of the Wissahickon. Both they and their beliefs were carried westward to Ephrata and, eventually, the Appalachian frontier.

Baptism within the early group included betrothal to the Virgin Sophia, a representation of God's divine wisdom. This union negated (in theory) any desire or sexual impulse and was made manifest through a celibate existence.

Kelpius, as with many neighbors, including William Penn, a Quaker, entertained the notion that the Indians were the "Lost Tribe of Israel." Thus respected, Native Americans treated German settlers such as the Eckerlins (above) with high regard until the French convinced them to do otherwise.

Some believe Kelpius led his followers to Virginia in 1694 seeking a place to settle before selecting the Pennsylvania site.[15] His letters indicate a mystical cosmology that pervaded the theology of that time and place. His many spiritual descendants followed a course of travel that eventually landed them on the western Virginia frontier, although the older Kelpius remained. He saw westward expansion to the frontier as affirming the ever-growing influence of his particular Brethren philosophy. This excerpt gives an idea of his copious written meanderings:

> Vis. that the Woman of the Wilderness might be carried away by flood. Therefore you, as a Remnant of her seed, long for to see your mother and groan for the Manifestation of her children. No wonder then, if your continual Gazing upon this Supercaelestial Orb and Sphier from whence with her children causeth you to observe every new Phoenomena, Meteors, Stars and various Colours of the Skei, if peradventure you may behold at last an Harbinger as an Evidence of that great Jubelee or Restetation of all things and glorious Sabbathismos or the continual days of Rest without intervening or succeeding Nights.[16]

Ezechiel Sangmeister, a friend of Kelpius, was another saint-adventurer who came to the Sabbatarian settlement at Strasburg, Virginia, in 1752. He made treks into present-day West Virginia to Dunker's Bottom. He was raised a Lutheran in Lower Saxony and kept a journal of his "Life's Description." Published in 1825, it describes a miserable life in the Old World during which his brother was "bewitched by an old woman, and he had to suffer with terrible headaches for a year and a half." He goes on to say the woman bewitched his father in the same way, and he died after two years of this bewitchment at the age of forty-two.[17]

Fully believing in and fearing an evil, occult presence, Sangmeister details mid-eighteenth-century German religious thought on the Virginia frontier in this regard. Jacob Bauman published Sangmeister's other work, *Mystische Theologie*, in 1819, long after Sangmeister's death. Bauman also published and supplied the frontier with Brethren hymnals and occult tracts, along with the writings of Jacob Boehme.

Sangmeister only ate once a day and was said to have been able to reach a trance-like state through prayer. He spent up to six hours a day on his knees. He leaves us a record of how occult belief in Germany pervaded the outlook of early German pioneers on the frontier. The realm of the occult at this time was seen as a stark reality, and it was tightly linked to German theology.[18] This does not hold true for non-German sects, however. Germans commonly attended love feasts and men utilized the "holy kiss," which was intended to signify spiritual affection and mutual love among the fraternity.[19]

While Germans did not suffer from official discrimination in Virginia, they were made to feel unwelcome at times, as when Sangmeister was mocked and jeered by a large crowd when he once happened into Winchester, Virginia, on court day. These old-order Brethren continued to wear the hooded white robes associated with their belief, and thus dressed, they could hardly slip into a crowd unnoticed.

Other surprising German creeds existed on the western Virginia frontier. John Martin, a shoemaker and religious figure, was accused of casting spells on farms and on cattle. He retained his followers, however, and led them from the Valley to westward frontier destinations to what he declared would be the "Last Battle," claiming to have heard the "trumpet call of God" and believing he and his followers would be lifted on a cloud and carried away by "heavenly wings." They never quite found Armageddon, so they returned penniless to the Valley. Martin also predicted that "wild men" would overrun the settlements, a prophecy that came true shortly afterward when Indians attacked the settlements, killing many, including Martin's wife, and sending many German, Scots-Irish, and English families fleeing for their lives.[20]

A later interesting religious figure was George Rapp, born in 1757 in Württemburg. He formed a group known as the Harmony Society. He led about five hundred followers to Philadelphia and on to the frontier, where they eventually established the town of Economy in southwestern Pennsylvania and awaited the Millennium. This celibate society only lasted about one hundred years in the New World.

The Friends, or Quakers, who dominated religious life in the early Pennsylvania settlements and influenced early Germans, also contributed a limited number of settlers in the Valley. They had in their Old World leader, George Fox, a man who was said to have cured 150 victims of witchcraft.[21] Fox, as well as many English Quakers in the Old World, were accused of being witches themselves. This was largely due to their disregard of authority and their radical worshiping practices, which challenged the religious status quo.[22] Unlike their German neighbors, the Friends shrugged off occult beliefs at an early date.

The close encounter on the frontier with fantastic unknown elements of the natural world soon affected the outlook of all Appalachian settlers. The more exotic cosmology and mystical theology of the old German sects affected general religious thought and filtered down to commonly held folk beliefs. Religious settlers began a substantial exodus to the more "in touch," relevant, less structured, and more animated worship practices during the Great Awakening and the camp meeting era in the late eighteenth and early nineteenth centuries. Here, more primal emotions could surface as trademark Appalachian religious worship practices took form.[23] This occurred as distinct ethnicity faded in the face of frontier hardship and a regional identity started taking hold, replacing ethnic differences.

Ancient Germanic cosmology tied to theology is inherent in Appalachian folklore. The relationship of man to the natural world, symbolized in the enigmatic values of German peasant folk art, flourished as the strongest expression of folk art in the New World. The cosmology of frontier Lutherans, Brethren (Dunkers), and other Anabaptist German elements was a stark contrast to the Calvinist teachings of their Scots-Irish Presbyterian neighbors. The latter's adherence to a fatalistic incapacity to control their own destiny left them anxiously awaiting death and its possible verdict of redemption.[24]

Curiously, early Calvinists did put stock in astrology, believing that although their fate was predestined, that fate could be revealed to them through interpreting the movement of the stars and planets.[25] Some Appalachian Scots-Irish gravestones exhibit variations of the heavenly bodies that bear out this thought process.[26]

Non-Calvinist Lutherans and Anabaptist Germans retained a much more active and participatory relationship with their faith and beliefs through daily folkways attuned to cosmological activities, often in the realm of the occult. Witness this ritual from Pendleton County that is used to ensure one will always make the right decision: "Take a herb called skunk cabbage gathered in the month of May while the sun is in the sign of the Lion,[27] wrap a little of it in a laurel leaf add a dandelion to it and carry this on your person and you will have the confidence of all and you will receive the best words."[28]

For the most part, Anglo/Celt religious traditions involving cosmological principles were abandoned in the early to mid-nineteenth century,[29] but German Appalachian occult traditions that exist in present-day West Virginia, as we will see, have withstood modern influences and have had a lasting effect. Today, because of a shift from an ethnically oriented to a regional character, they are correctly considered Appalachian traits.

Some celibate mystic settlers in western Virginia, such as Sangmeister and the Eckerlin brothers, thought that the unknowns of occult reasoning were not that different from the unknowns of the natural world. The frontier was far from what they had known in Germany and the relatively more settled and civilized areas of eastern Pennsylvania. Their pioneer experiences were troubled with unknowns of the natural world, but unknowns of the supernatural world were only a rhetorical difference in their minds, both being connected in their world view. They did not clearly separate matters of the flesh and matters of the spiritual world. They were enamored of astrologic theories and cosmic principles. The natural symbolism in the functionally styled and decorated material culture of the old German settlers of the region brings these settlers' thought processes into two and three-dimensional form.

Curing practices that we realize have a scientific basis today were thought magical in earlier times, simply because the science was unknown. In the twelfth century, strides in literary achievement defined an ecclesiastical view of occult practices.[30] Still today, for many people, the line between scientifically based curing and the body of magical and occult elements that relate to religiously sanctioned curing practices is nonexistent.

In the twelfth century, witchcraft started to take on a more malevolent posture for its detractors, and its grotesque and sacrilegious aspects began to take hold. Popular concepts of witchcraft from the fifteenth century onward were largely a product of the Roman Catholic Church. During the Reformation, when both the Catholic Church and the newer Protestant churches were vying for power, witch-hunts wielded power over innocents to affect political gain and provide a method through which people could be controlled. The belief that witchcraft is the product of an organized cult that included worship of Satan and other specific rituals is a product of the Christian imagination, according to Jeffrey Burton Russell and other historians.[31] Some see the Reformation in Europe as a struggle for control over a hierarchy of visible and invisible worlds.[32] Today, most Christians believe that all forms of magic are inspired, carried out, and made possible by demons or other demonic entities. However, "white magic" had its place, and according to the people I discuss here, magic or supernatural forces may be used in a good way, that is, by carrying out God's work, and this is simply an ancient approach to religion.

Cosmology intertwines religious belief among the esoteric, religious, German philosophers who were stirring the pot of spirituality in the New World. The spiritual/religious figures who first settled at Germantown, later at Ephrata, and ended up in western Virginia left a surprising amount of documentation of their presence. Their belief systems, even from within the religious hierarchy, often encompassed the magical and the occult. Entrenched in folk spirituality, they were more mystical than non-Germans. Their demons were personalized, or at least embodied in *familiars* (creatures that are thought to attend witches) that were consistent with northern European tradition and are commonly found in Appalachian folklore.

Long after most organized religions questioned the reality of occult powers, a leading and founding religious figure at the early German settlement of Strasburg, Virginia, Joseph Funk, engaged in mystical religious speculation. He wandered the hills looking for precious metals that he thought could be used within his pseudo-religious occult rites and rituals. Samuel Eckerlin joined him. It is reported that the French, who were leading raiding parties with Indians, captured Eckerlin's brothers on Cheat River at Dunker's Bottom (West Virginia). Samuel eventually retreated to Strasburg and threw in with Funk, the two no doubt boosted and supported each other's proclamations, astrological observations, and attempts to transcend their ordinary, carnal existence.

The actions of these Appalachian settlers were an outgrowth of Pennsylvania German experiences. The Pietists' spirituality allowed for belief in the occult, especially white magic. At Ephrata, from which some of these early settlers came, the leader, Conrad Beissel, praised "heavenly magic" and viewed magic as a divine power.[33] The relationship to that magic was not seen as evil but as a religious duty. Printing presses at Ephrata distributed tracts containing these unique beliefs to Germans on the frontier.

At the same time as William Penn's denunciation of belief in the occult, religious Germans in Pennsylvania were experimenting with necromancy (conversing with the dead) and hermetic aspects of alchemy and astrology. They were also accused of practicing sorcery.[34] The religiously approved mystical thinking and world view of early German settlers, at that formative period, eventually helped establish a distinctive Appalachian folklore and cosmology that is rich in occultism and magical symbolic elements.

The early Germans, many of whom were influenced by the mysticism of Old World Pietist thinking, were thought of as transcendentalists. Their transcendentalism is often expressed in the somewhat bizarre and wondrous symbolism of their folk art, which indicates a spiritual interchange with nature. They saw the earth, nature, and the cosmos as a spiritual realm. Their liberal outlook differed with Calvinistic thought of the period, and this difference lasted for some time. A Philadelphia newspaper's account of 1856, speaking of German spiritualism, reported that "by comparison, [English clergy] have vagaries of pantheism, and they are crotchety, one-idead, dyspeptic, thin, [and] cadaverous!"[35]

Pennsylvania's diverse religious customs included a hermetic mysticism born of alchemy in the Middle Ages.[36] Various elements, including those who some think may have had ties to Rosicrucians,[37] had come to the Ephrata settlement in Pennsylvania and later dispersed to the western Virginia frontier. Direct connections have been made between European Rosicrucian practice and families who immigrated to eastern Pennsylvania and joined the tide drifting south and west to the frontier.[38]

Outside of prevalent religio-magical belief systems, the old Dunkers, of whom there were many on the old Virginia frontier, also professed simple living and pacifism. Pendleton Countian Robert Simmons, born in 1908, related a story to me about his grandfather, Martin Simmons. He said that during the Civil War, Martin was a conscientious objector, being of the old Brethren pacifist persuasion. When authorities came to force him into conscription, he hid under the house. Someone gave away his hiding place and he was discovered, but he attempted an escape by running across a field. He was shot in the chest as he ran by Armand Hiner, of Franklin, who, I presume, was there in an official capacity. Robert ends this story by saying that the shot never seriously hurt him, as the impact was almost totally absorbed by a small New Testament he had in his shirt pocket. Robert thinks a distant cousin still has the Testament, which "has some bloodstains on it."[39]

Elder John Kline, a circuit-riding Brethren minister who frequented Pendleton County, was not so well protected, as he was shot and killed (some say martyred) in 1864, it is thought, for his refusal of military service and his antislavery campaign.[40] In the early eighteenth century, German Brethren had first formed their abolitionist and pacifist beliefs with the influence of Pennsylvania Quakers at Germantown, where the Brethren Church was founded.[41] Early Germantown resident Daniel Pastorius deserves much credit in this regard. These ideals were brought to the southern upland frontier with German settlers, where they publicly erupted at the onset of the Civil War, when moral choices had to be made.

The family of Robert Simmons, of Thorn Creek, whose oral tradition provided the story above, came from Germany to Pennsylvania, then to Pendleton County in 1753.[42] Just a year after that, the son of the German founder of the Brethren and a leader of the movement in this country moved to just across the county and (today's) state line from where the Simmons family settled. These people were very close to their parents' Old World experiences and New World religion, but the new dilemmas of frontier life quickly demanded their attention.

In the eighteenth century, many Appalachian Germans were caught up in a mystical/occult-centered belief system that was not as common and, in fact, was outlawed in much of the Anglo-Saxon world. This late medieval/early modern outlook viewed the visible and invisible worlds, from the crops in their fields to the weather, to unseen nocturnal demons, to the unexplained advents in the heavens, as forces consistent with God's word and something with which to be reckoned. This outlook contributes greatly to the body of oral literature, tales, and beliefs that we identify as Appalachian folklore. It also guided Appalachians' efforts to cure everything from sickness to ruined crops and bad weather.

Today, some of the early Pennsylvania sites established by the spiritual/mystical groups have become national historic sites. For the legacy of these Pennsylvania groups, however, I suggest looking to the folklore, beliefs, and oral traditions of the Appalachian people.

Chapter 5

Astrology

By what astrology of fear or hope
Did I cast thou horoscope?
—*Longfellow*

Johann Friederich Schmidt, a Lutheran minister who made his mark in the church at Germantown in the late eighteenth century, made astrological almanac calculations between 1769, when he arrived, and his death in 1812. And at least one Pennsylvania German Lutheran minister was calculating and publishing astrological almanacs in the mid-nineteenth century. He was chastised for that by a Baptist minister. Folk spirituality clearly trumped formal religious canon, allowing for a more liberal participation in matters of everyday faith and practice. There was a clear difference of ecclesiastical opinion and disposition between the Lutherans and the Baptists.[1]

German gravestones, especially early ones in Pennsylvania but also ones on the old frontier, exhibit depictions of heavenly bodies, including comets. Comets witnessed by these New World Germans engendered much speculation as to their meaning. Christopher Witt, for example, published a treatise following a ten-week-long comet sighting in 1743. Haley's comet sightings in 1759 and 1834 played a prominent role in the lives of German Americans following Witt's predictions of their announcements of war, plague, and famine, according to early chronicler Julius Sachse.[2] Witt's writings and predictions based on astrologic cosmological principles seem in contrast to his more practical and scientifically based works. For instance, he studied astronomy and he built a tower clock at the women's saal (living quarters) at Ephrata, believed to be the first such clock in America. He was English by birth, but he threw in with the Germans at Germantown and Ephrata.

From afar, we may see distinct differences between scientific astronomy and occult-based astrological theory, but at the time the two were nearly one and the same. Witt, who speculated on the meaning of the movement of the stars and planets, also studied chemistry and medicine. His confidence in healthful choices was based on the zodiac via the "almanac man." This ancient illustration shows the signs that "rule" the various parts of the body and is considered a microcosm of the universe. It was widely expounded in his almanacs and calendars. His cures were all related to the phases of the moon. Being influenced by the theosophy of the old German Pietists, he maintained a liberal adherence to scriptural meaning and a keen interest in a spiritually charged cosmology.

Eighteenth-century Germans ascribed an enormous amount of power to the moon. Astrologic principles involving the zodiac signs and the almanac man were a basis for their cosmology. Louis D. Winkler thinks the Almanac Man to be the most often published symbol, considering that thousands of almanacs have printed it for hundreds of years.

Pennsylvania Germans, who were religiously influenced by European Pietists, embraced astrology. Many apparently even timed their trip to America to coincide with astrological principles and an alignment of the planets.[3] The older European German mystics did not look to astrology so much for what it predicted; rather, they believed the stars could be read in a way that revealed the "inner essences of God's will." They did believe the stars would reveal the time of the Second Coming.[4] Kelpius, Beissel, and other ascetic Brethren hoped, for instance, the heavens would reveal the time of the Millennium and the timing of other Book of Revelation events. A hymn was composed at Ephrata about comets that appeared in 1742 and 1743, which lamented various evils to come.

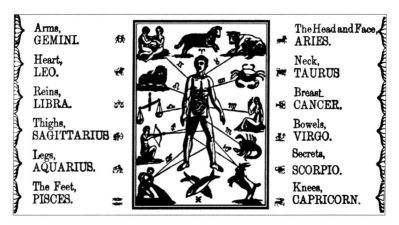

The Almanac Man. Body parts represent the signs of the zodiac. He represents a microcosm of the universe.

Astrology

30

The combination of formal religion and astrology continues to coexist in harmony for many Appalachian people. They have strong ties to a cosmology that guides numerous daily and seasonal activities. Old-time Appalachian Christians I have known find no contradiction in planting by the signs, planning by the moon, and faithfully attending church.

Among early German settlers in West Virginia, religion was thoroughly mixed with not only astrology but also esoteric curing practices tied to cosmic activity. Folk curing bridged a gap between the religious and the secular mind-set. And forms of white magic were not disdained; in fact, they were practiced by the early German clergy. This presents a substantially different historic world view between the Lutherans and Brethren, on the one hand, and the Presbyterians, Methodists, and Baptists, on the other.

It is clear that as Appalachian people became mixed in blood and culture, ethnic identities disappeared and a regional culture emerged. Many Appalachians today retain and embrace a folklore that directly descends from early German religio-magical belief and practice. Appalachian astrological beliefs are much simplified from the original, highly mathematical Greek formulas and today are limited to the "signs" and the phases of the sun and moon. While some still study the signs in great detail, without access to professional astrologers, most of today's practitioners, using an almanac or almanac calendar, are able to ascertain propitious days to go about common agricultural farm chores and domestic activities, with variations supplied by tradition.

Everyday astrology was spelled out in colonial almanacs in both the English and German language. In both languages, the German-style almanacs flourished in Pennsylvania, Maryland, and Virginia. Numerous German writer-calculator-printers, such as Carl Cist, John Gruber, John Baer, Carl Frederich Egelman, Johan Friederich Schmidt, and Soloman Conrad, published thousands of almanacs from the early eighteenth century into and throughout the nineteenth. Over 130 different almanac titles were published in the German language.

In these almanacs, articles, tables, and calculated graphs advise the reader on everything from predicting the weather by the moon to the best days for planting and, in older versions, the right signs for bloodletting. It is a testament to the longevity of German cosmology and thought that almanacs and almanac calendars, descendants of the work of these men, have now made it into the twenty-first century. Almanacs printed at Lancaster, Pennsylvania, and Baltic, Ohio, serve others there and in the Pennsylvania German diaspora.[5] Winkler reports that a German language almanac was published in West Virginia.[6]

Old Ben Franklin, not one to miss an opportunity, printed and sold more than five thousand German versions of his *Poor Richard's Almanac*. Apparently, Franklin was adept enough in astrology to make his own calculations and projections. A curious note in a 1738 *Poor Richard's* indicates that Franklin spent time in "Patowmack," where an "old stargazer lived." Like his fellow astrologers, he was taken by the predicted sightings of comets, especially the 1758 prediction by Haley that fixed that name on that comet and in the books. At that time, Franklin bought into the theory that comets foretold of divine intervention. In later years, and as the science of astronomy advanced, Franklin had a reversal in attitude toward astrological predictions. As scientific principles of astronomy gained sway over astrologic belief, astrology became more identified with the realm of the occult and the magical. The open-minded outlook of spiritual Germans allowed for acceptance and adherence to both. Old astrologers among the Germans counted on "naked eye" planets and "comet apparitions" to govern their predictions. Conjunctions, the alignment of planets, especially during 1683, 1694, and 1743, were of particular notice.

Winkler's studies of Pennsylvania German astronomy and astrology indicate that Germans had the most active role in establishing and perpetuating the large body of Appalachian folkloric belief promoted through almanacs and almanac calendars. Astrologic traditions still exist as more than just quaint curiosities among Appalachian people. It is noted that these practices declined within English society and in New England before the Revolution.[7] New England's almanac makers were under withering attack, religious condemnation, and mockery by the mid-seventeenth century,[8] but over three centuries later, continued folk practice based on this cosmology is still easy to ascertain in the southern mountains, where almanacs and calendars are an integral part of regional folk spirituality.

An ethnological comparative work from nineteenth-century Pennsylvania regarding agricultural practices among Germans, Irish, Welsh, and Scots determined that, as opposed to the others, the Germans "generally have gardens and plant things 'by the signs.' Beans planted in the decline of the moon they do not think will take to the poles."[9]

German-language almanacs were widely distributed on the eighteenth-century frontier.[10] This held secure a distinct occult-centered cosmology in the minds of early German pioneers that went hand in hand with other occult curing and healing methodologies. Lancaster, Pennsylvania–born John Gruber's late-eighteenth-century almanacs, published in both German and English at his press at Hagerstown, still exist. The *American Farmer's Almanac* and the *Hagerstown Town and Country Almanac* provide detailed astrologic data for advantageous times to engage in planting, harvesting, and other rural practices as well as practically every chore that relates to the natural world. They have not changed much through the years.

A comparison of *Gruber's Almanac* with the popular *Old Farmer's Almanac*, of New England Anglo origin, shows a difference in approach. The *Old Farmer's*, now published by the Yankee Magazine group, is bigger, has scores of advertisements for everything from seeds to hair growth enhancers, and seems to play up its quaintness and its age as its selling point. *Gruber's Almanac*, by comparison, has almost no advertising and is a no-nonsense guide to daily astrological activity. While both offer information about the zodiac signs, phases of the moon, weather information, and so on for the calendar of days, *Gruber's* seems wholly concerned with more down-to-earth calendar-related astrology, weather, proverbs, eclipse dates, birth-stone tables, and harvesting secrets along with some recipes and farming advice. In general, the *Old Farmer's* leans toward astronomy while *Gruber's* is more concerned with astrology.

Gruber's Almanac still publishes an illustration of the almanac man, indicating how the various parts of the body are governed by the twelve constellations. This figure, so often referred to by older people, is an essential part of the cosmology of many rural people in Appalachia today. The *Old Farmer's Almanac* also prints the almanac man, but curiously, in its description of the figure—noting that "ancient astrologers" believed in its efficacy—it seems to apologize for its presence and distance itself from that belief. The almanac omits the zodiac signs that are ascribed to each day in *Gruber's* and in the American Calendar Company's Almanac Calendar and only offers the stages of the moon.

Today, Ramon's Brownie Calendars, and calendars that are personalized for rural businesses and banks from the American Calendar Company of Tennessee, supply the Appalachian region with dates to carry out activities in coordination with astrologic principles and traditions. These calendars, with their red and black print on a white background, are a familiar sight in West Virginia homes.

These almanac calendars (first printed at Germantown in the early eighteenth century) have largely replaced almanacs in Appalachia. Banks, funeral homes, and small retail businesses throughout the region distribute them. The daily signs of the zodiac and phases of the moon are illustrated right on the calendar's days, so that this important information is always in view and easily referenced. At the bank where I do business, Mountain Valley Bank in Elkins, West Virginia, you have to request one at least by early December—the demand is that great.

A colloquial vocabulary describes various aspects of the almanac man. For instance, Virgo is the "flower girl" and Gemini is "the twins," or one simply states that the sign is in "the arms," "the heart," or "the secrets," as illustrated on the Almanac Man. Taking a cue from these symbols, farmers try to breed their sheep in "the twins," for obvious reasons. Do not plant your cucumbers during the sign of the "flower girl," they will tell you, as you will get lots of bloom but little fruit. Although zodiacal principals were and are still used by many, some of these elaborate concepts have devolved and become simpler after hundreds of years of practice.

Principles based on the position and stages of the moon, with special importance given its intense waxing and waning stages, are more easily grasped and consequently are more widely known and practiced. But most people who plant and schedule various work duties "by the signs" will base those actions on both the signs and the moon for a double dip of cosmic good measure. These almanacs and calendars are still trusted friends.

Professed Christians, such as a woman I know in Randolph County, see no problem with leading a faith-based life while participating in occult curing traditions and holding to a cosmology that involves astrological agrarian practices. She observes her father's methods, for instance, in planting potatoes. They should be planted when the moon is "near half" and in the sign of the head (Aries). If planted in the fish (Pisces), they will be watery. If planted in the sign of the "flower girl" (Virgo), they will have a heavy bloom that will lessen their yield. "Near half" means that the moon is still a "light moon," or one that is still waxing. If planted in a "dark moon," or one that is waning, the potatoes will go down too deep. If planted in a new moon, they will be too close to the surface and will sunburn. Hay should be cut in a light moon so it will cure well. Otis Rose, an old-time farmer, said that the hay will not only cure out better but also have a different color.[11] People cut "filth" (brush) when the moon and signs are right so that it will not spring back to life. Clyde Case told me that any time the moon shines before midnight, it is in the light phase.[12] A dark moon, according to Clyde, generally rises after midnight.

Clyde gained most of his traditional knowledge from an old German grandfather, and he told me that he is a "moon baby." He said the moon was "ruling" when he was born, and it still affects his sleep in that he has restless nights during a full moon, even though his wife, Lucy, made special curtains to block out all light. He is careful to plant potatoes and corn during the right phase—as corn grows taller when planted in a light moon. Fence posts will be loose if set in a light moon, so they should be set in a dark moon. Even shaving, a daily activity for many men, produces a smoother job when done in a light moon, according to some. Some notice a difference in the size of meat after being fried in a light or dark moon phase.

When the moon appears to be on its back, with the "horns" of the crescent shape pointing up, plants whose fruits or stalks are edible should be sown. When the horns go down, root crops and tubers should be planted. Some regard this as the period when the partial moon will hold water or will not hold water and make weather predictions accordingly. Pole beans and corn should be planted with the sign in the arms. Cabbage and brussels sprouts do best if planted when the sign is in the head, as represented on the Almanac Man. Kraut and pickles should be made in a light moon. Castration, dehorning, or any activity that could draw blood is best done when the signs are not close to the heart. Healing is best advanced in a light moon.[13] As many of these beliefs have advanced within oral tradition, and without benefit of print sources, we now have inevitable variations of belief.

One aspect of the astrological calendar year that is particularly observed by country people is the arrival of dog days. They "come in" about July 3, when the "dog star" (Sirius) appears to rise with the sun. It is the brightest star in the constellation, Canis Major. The weather on this day will foretell the weather for the growing season or the remaining period of dog days, which lasts forty days. If there is even the slightest rainfall on this day, it bodes well for the crops. Beyond this, it is believed that birds and snakes "go blind" during dog days, and that snakes are particularly venomous. At the same time, hawks whistle and the dog star "rules."[14] These beliefs go back to ancient Roman times, when astrology was in its infancy. The Romans believed the dog star was so bright that it brought extra heat to the earth, causing those "long hot dog days of summer." The concept of dog days was of particular interest to Pennsylvania Germans, who believed that if rain fell on your bare head during dog days, it would cause baldness. For the same reason they believed that hair should never be cut during a waning moon but during a waxing moon, and the first Friday of a new moon was a particularly advantageous time.[15]

The evidence points to the folk spirituality of early German settlers as the source of a distinctive Appalachian cosmology that lives on today. West Virginia herbalist and avid almanac user Catfish Gray possesses the unique talent of being able to "job" sticks or small branches of trees into the ground, in the right zodiac sign and moon phase, and have them grow into trees. He showed me through his "nursery" one time in late April. During the previous fall, when the signs were right, he had cut twigs off of various fruit and nut trees and jammed them into the ground in rows.

When I saw them, all were sprouting, and some of the peach twigs were blooming.

For leafy trees, Catfish "plants" them (actually simply pokes them into the ground) in Cancer, Scorpio, or Pisces, during the new moon. For fruit and nut trees, Catfish uses those signs, but planting must be done in the first quarter of the new moon. He says the "neck and knee signs" (Taurus and Capricorn) will work too. For root crops he uses those signs, but after the full moon. For killing dates (for cutting brush or "filth"), May to September is best, and one should cut in a new moon when the sign is in the heart.[16]

Pennsylvania Germans identified a particular day of the year, Abdannsdag, when all things could be easily killed. The day was once identified on almanac calendars, but so much evil was thought committed because it was the "killing day" that publicizing the date was discontinued and the particular date now is a mystery.[17]

Some of the traditions in modern use seem to have taken on simplistic reasoning. For instance, old farmer Otis Rose told me that they never make kraut or pickle beans in the sign of the feet (Pisces), because "you know how your feet smell sometime." He believed the food took on that odor. Many rural women will not can or preserve any food "when granny comes to town," a euphemism for menstruation. This is a taboo of ancient origin that relates to moonlore (menses, from the Latin *menses*, "month-moon") and biblical taboo.

Clyde Case reasons that if the moon has enough power to control tides, it surely has power over other aspects of nature. As a farmer, he noted that cows come in heat every twenty-eight days, in accordance with the moon, that cows and sheep tend to give birth during full moons, and that most plants and animals, in some way, are regulated by positions of the moon.[18] "Red horse," an edible kind of sucker or fish that are "gigged" for food always "run" upstream in spring. The fish time this activity to the new moon. An old man once pointed out to me that you can hear things better, or from farther away, when the moon is full.

These thought processes and beliefs are tied to religiously oriented German pioneers. Their prescientific cosmology and world view lingers. Today, the disposition of Appalachian folklore reflects a strong adherence to the principles practiced since the 1730s, when German pioneers came to the southern Appalachians.

Chapter 6

The Occult

Could I but banish witchcraft from my road,
Unlearn all magic spells—oh, if I stood
Before you, Nature, human without guile,
The toil of being man might be worthwhile.
—Goethe

Elizabeth Von Honing from the Ephrata, Pennsylvania, settlement, the third wife of Christopher Beeler (Bohler), first settled with Beeler in the Valley. They eventually settled at New Creek, near the Potomac River, now in West Virginia, where he lived out his life. Apparitions haunted the woman there in 1761. The spirit of Beeler's second wife appeared to her every night for two weeks, showing her places on the hearth and elsewhere where gold, silver, money, and other treasure might be found in the morning. Numerous witnesses observed various actions of this spirit, including ripping off pieces of the sleeping woman's clothing and throwing objects about the room. The spirit eventually instructed the woman to return to Pennsylvania, which she did immediately, to consult spiritual leaders there. The recounting of her mysterious encounters were published widely and distributed as religious tracts on the frontier, lending ecclesiastical credence to a perceived occult presence.[1] I collected a similar tale/motif in Gilmer County, West Virginia (see chapter 18), illustrating that some eighteenth-century occult motifs continue into the twenty-first century.

In Pennsylvania, the reality of witchcraft was questioned early on when a Finnish woman from Pennsylvania's New Sweden settlement[2] was brought before the chief judge, William Penn, the leading figure of Friends in the New World. Penn dismissed the charge of bewitching cattle and other offenses and suggested (tongue in cheek) that there was no law against "riding a broom" in Pennsylvania. He found her guilty only of having a "witch's reputation" and ordered her to practice good behavior.[3]

Other Swedes/Finns there were defamed and accused of "wizardry" even before Penn arrived.[4] Some early Pennsylvania Swedish influence involving traditional midwinter revelries and methods of log house construction, as we will see, influenced other folkways on the Appalachian frontier.

Irvin Propst of Pendleton County remembered occult cures used by local witch doctors that began:

> Blessed be the day,
> Blessed be the hour,
> Blessed be the day,
> When Jesus Christ was born.[5]

Compare this charm from another Pendleton County source for curing swelling:

> Happy be the Day. Happy will be the Day when there will be no swelling nor boils until Mary bears another son.

Or another:

> Blessed be the day when Jesus Christ was born
> Blessed be the day when Jesus Christ was born
> Blessed be the day when Jesus Christ arose from the dead
> These are the holy 3 hours
> Thus I cure (n.n.) your blood and cure your wounds
> That should never swell or become worse
> As much as Martha will bear another son.[6] +++

The three marks at the end indicate that the "three highest names" (Father, Son, and Holy Ghost) should be invoked. These types of invocations, sometimes called *word magic*,[7] are followed by magical references and directed physical practices through which the cure was thought to take effect. Today's practitioners still invoke the Trinity, or as they would say, "the three highest names," in many of their incantations and "cures." This paradigm is very similar to the practices of honored eighteenth-century German ancestors from whom they learned these methodologies. Practitioners are quick to defend those forebears if they encounter objections to the validity of their methods.

The religion and world view of the various sects accepted the reality of esoteric mystical and spiritual belief and thus retained notions of the occult. These notions supported a faith-based healing system. In Pennsylvania, the equivalents of West Virginia's witch doctors are known as *powwow doctors*.[8] Many are quick to relate German occult belief to the powwow tradition, but in my experience collecting in West Virginia, the actual deed that takes place is called *witch doctoring* and/or *curing*, not *powwowing*. Powwow has a parallel but somewhat different set of beliefs. Both are centered in religion.

In parts of western Maryland, the process of religio-magical curing is called *trying* or *trying for*, and the healer, as in Pennsylvania, is a powwow doctor. In the Ozarks, areas settled largely by Appalachian people, many of German descent, the terms *witch master, faith doctor, goomer doctor, conjure folk,* and *power doctor* are used.[9] In Kentucky, a witch doctor is called a *repeller* and/or a *charm doctor*, and instead of using the word *charm* for the actual deed, it is often called a *ceremony*.[10] The Pennsylvania, the term *powwow* is thought to stem from the early days, when Native American curing was combined with European traditions.[11] In African American tradition, a healer is called a *conjurer* as well as a *root doctor, underworld man, herb doctor, herb man,* and *goofuh-dus man*.[12] In Pennsylvania, a healer is a *braucher* (from the German *brauchen*, "to use"). *Moon doctor* is another term for a folk practitioner I have found in West Virginia.[13]

Much folk curing in Appalachia insists on specific astrological timing along with religious ritual process. As recently as twenty years ago, a Pendleton County baseball team called on the services of a local woman who was known as someone who could cure through what seemed a mixture of occult and religious practice. The team had been successful enough to make the playoffs in their league, but their star pitcher had a serious ankle injury. In accordance with the almanac, the woman "cured for the boy," who then went on and pitched. The fact that he could maneuver and pitch at all seemed a miracle to those who knew his condition and related the story to me.

Occult belief as identified within folk cures and traditions today is, in actuality, rarely encountered. But it may be found if one cares to look and ask. The rise of modern science has affected occult thought in all regions, and what was once common practice is increasingly being relegated to living memory, but the tradition is resilient. While many today have erected a barrier between religion and occult methodologies, the two are clearly seen as entities with which to be reckoned. Part of this has to do with honoring family ancestors who did not make a clear distinction between religion and the occult.

Much of the occult-oriented folklore I have documented ascribes to a particular kind of witchery. Western witchcraft, five hundred years after its heyday, is still an area of intense scholarly study, with regular international conferences devoted to the subject.[14] In anthropological terms, it may be divided into four forms. The first and oldest form was based on attempts to assure fertility of the land. This is well stated by Carlo Ginzburg in *The Night Battles*.[15] His objective view of early European primary source material documenting fertility cults comes from court records in the sixteenth century, but the traditions described are much older.

Until the sixteenth century, when religious pressures brought it under scrutiny, people in the Western world commonly sought to aid the fertility of the crops and the fecundity of the herds through personal actions in the realm of the occult. Remnants of this tradition are present in Appalachian "granny women" or rural midwives and healers, many of whom have been accused of witchery. Other efforts to assist the regenerative process, as in numerous midwinter rituals, will be discussed later.

A second form of witchcraft presents itself in the vast documentation from the Inquisition and the great witch-hunts of Europe and, especially, Germany. In this form, demonic spirit possession is inferred. Accused witches describe fantastic supernatural experiences that lead to the bizarre notions of witches riding on brooms, attending the Sabbat, having orgies with the devil, drying up wells, raising storms, and so on. A significant number of direct descendants of the people most involved with this European paradigm were the German immigrants to mid-Atlantic colonial America and then the Appalachian back country.

A third expression of witchcraft tradition grew out of the first two. This one is the most important to what exists today in Appalachia and concerns causal relationships brought about through social tension. In this form of witchcraft, mishap, misfortune, sickness, and negative forces of evil are not deemed just bad luck or fate, as Calvinist–Anglo/Celtic thought would have it, but are primarily blamed on known people—neighbors, relatives, and acquaintances—who are thought to be in league with Satan. This reflects an evolution of the earlier European paradigm in which it was assumed that witchery was the active directive of demons, devils, or supernatural and otherworldly forces. Although those powers are still thought to be at play, these people, acting in concert with those evil forces, are personally to blame in this thinking. Witch accusations are sometimes made when physical confrontation or legal action cannot be taken.

To people who believe in this third form, Satan is very much an incarnate physical presence. This position is held in regional folklore and Appalachian religion in general. In this category of witchery, those believed to be witches, and their accusers, are motivated by jealousy, spite, and, to a degree, ignorance. The concept of fate is rejected, and curses, spells, incantations, and misdeeds are thought to be evil initiatives of local witches who are bringing harm to "good" people. This form specifically allows for the existence of a counteractive good, white magic, which is most often entwined with religion and combats and counteracts evil, as we will see.[16] An early study of folklore in the southern Appalachians notes that the distinction between white and black magic is clear.[17] White magic, as part of accepted religious practice, surely arrived on the old frontier with German people, both clergy and lay people, and it survives in regional Appalachian folklore today.

The final form of witchcraft is the "new age" or neopagan variety that has gained popularity in recent years. While the first three forms here interact with one another in many ways, this modern form has no real connection to historic forms. New age witchcraft and occult practice, despite claims of ancient Celtic birth or other romanticized notions, is a twentieth-century British-American phenomenon that is clearly the brainchild of a few individuals.[18]

Modern science has made breakthroughs in understanding the reasoning behind some of the older European beliefs that have come down to us through the course of early Appalachian immigration. For instance, Johnny Arvin Dahmer of Pendleton County told me that "rye coffee" was common as a substitute for real coffee in leaner times in the area, and his mother was quite good at making it. He recited a little rhyme that is a statement about the tradition of rye bread, as a staple, that came with his ancestors to the region:

> Rye bread is rough,
> Rye bread is tough,
> Thank God we have rye biscuits enough.

The rhyme declares that rye may not be as desirable as wheat flour or cornmeal but certainly is a staple grain for which we should be thankful. Because of rye's Germanic association, there is a plausible theory that the rye plant was a factor in the witchcraft tradition of northern Europe, which had its strongest manifestation in Germanic areas. The rye plant hosted the ergot fungus, especially in the Palatinate along the Rhine River and in other river valleys in southwestern Germany, the area from which and through which most early German Appalachian families came.[19]

Ergot-contaminated grain, when consumed, would cause serious mental imbalance, "spells" or "fits." To an unscientific society, this could easily be blamed on the forces of witchery with the subject being thought under the influence of a spell or possessed by a demon.[20] There is a strong possibility that the disease, ergotism, is connected to German witchcraft tradition. Cold, wet springs brought on the proliferation of the ergot mold. In years that cold springs can be ascertained through tree-ring analysis, the following fall and winter show an increased amount of witchcraft accusations. In areas where rye is not a prominent food, witchcraft accusation is almost nonexistent. Neither did witchcraft exist where hot, dry climates eliminate the fungus altogether.[21] The biblical *darnel* is thought to be the ergot fungus.[22]

Witchcraft was on the minds of Germans, in both the old country and the new. The ergot-poisoning theory would be suggested, through science, much later. The end result of this fungus theory, however, could easily be present in West Virginia, even though we can not blame the perceived existence of witches in West Virginia on ergot poisoning. Since people of that region began immigrating to America in the late seventeenth century, the ergot/spirit possession tradition and the resulting perceived reality of witchcraft was firmly established in their collective mind before they came. We should never sell tradition short. It acts in the present based on the past, and the rye-ergot-witchcraft theory may illustrate its powerful effect through time.

The unknowns of frontier life played into this world of spirits and demons, invocations and incantations, and a more connected cosmological view of the natural world as it relates to life's mysteries. Spiritual musical expression on the frontier during the Great Awakening was saturated with images of heavenly signs, wonders, natural phenomena, and their prophetic meaning, much in a wilderness setting.[23] It was also during this period of religious revival that Scots-Irish and German settlers lost a substantial part of their own ethnic identity. Their identity had been centered on their religion, but a natural shift toward a strong regional identity was assisted by the religious conversion of the Great Awakening, and a regional identity gained strength.[24]

Witchery occupied the minds of early progressive religious leaders in Pennsylvania, such as Henry Melchior Muhlenberg, a Lutheran. He warned against belief in the supernatural and the occult, conditions that he found common in the legions of immigrants arriving from Germany.[25] But Muhlenberg's historic mentor, Martin Luther, was ambivalent on the subject. The older Luther got, "the more witches he saw." At one point, Luther chided followers, saying that witchcraft was forbidden and so was the belief that witchcraft was real. Only half a dozen years later, however, Luther was preaching that these "devil's whores" could "steal milk, raise storms, torture babies" and conduct other despicable acts. He later would personally approve the executions of accused witches.[26]

In the mid-eighteenth century, John Wesley was agitated because the English had given up belief in the reality of witches and witchcraft. He complained that, to the English, witchcraft and apparitions were relegated to "old wives tales," and this contradicted the Bible. His ranting in the Methodist journal, the *Arminian Magazine*, revived old fears, and he succeeded for a time in reinstating a belief in the reality of witchcraft among his followers. After Wesley's death in 1791, Methodists, in their attempt to gain popular respectability for their church, were not long in again distancing themselves from belief in the occult.[27]

Immigrants among various spiritual perfectionist groups, influenced by the esoteric German mysticism and the pietism of Johann Arndt, Jacob Boehme, and others, came to Pennsylvania in the late seventeenth century and through the eighteenth century. For the most part, Appalachian Germans are almost solely the products of the earlier eighteenth-century movement.[28] This preserved older Germanic folkways in this region. While religion dominated life though this period, for Germans, it also harbored a belief in the reality of witchcraft, magic, and the occult. The tradition of witchery was so strong, especially within concepts of witch doctoring or occult curing, that it continues to this day.

Gravestone bearing a pediment with a tree of life, compass stars, and an inverted heart in the old Propst church cemetery.

43

Chapter 7

Folk Art and Material Culture

Spirituality is expressed in material forms
as well as in oral and ideational forms.
—Richard Wentz

Unusual forms of polyphonic singing were developed at the Ephrata Cloister in Pennsylvania. Some who were of Anglo and Anglo/Celtic background found this unusual polyphonic singing mystifying.[1] An Anglican minister who witnessed this singing in 1771 at Ephrata, wrote this description:

> The music had little or no air or melody; but consisted of simple, long notes, combined in the richest harmony. . . . The performers sat with their heads reclined, their countenances solemn and dejected, their faces pale and emaciated from their manner of living, their clothing exceedingly white and quite picturesque, and their music such as thrilled to the very soul. I almost began to think myself in the world of spirits, and the objects before me were ethereal. In short, the impression this scene made upon my mind continued strong for many days, and I believe, will never be wholly obliterated.[2]

The singers at Ephrata, early on, had perfected a style of harmonic singing developed by Conrad Beissel, a central figure at the commune. His compositions included two men's parts and three women's parts. The singers wore white robes and followed Beissel's instructions, which included a specific sparse diet and long practices and performances. He was convinced that a life-style of purity and wholesomeness would bring them to musical perfection.

Ananias Davisson, a Presbyterian teacher, published *Kentucky Harmony* at Harrisonburg, Virginia, in 1810, and is credited with bringing the Pennsylvania-born "shape note" singing system to the valley.[3] As with other aspects of Appalachian culture, shape note singing was harbored and nurtured by both

Anglo-Celt and German people.[4] Joseph Funk's German-language hymn-book, *Choral-Music*, was first published in Pennsylvania in 1815. Funk became an important publisher and printer of shape note hymn books in his own right, including the popular *Harmonia Sacra* (1832), having established his own press at Singer's Glen, near Harrisonburg, Virginia. Just up the road from Singer's Glen, in Pendleton County, West Virginia, a shape note singing tradition continues.[5] The large Funk clan, of which Joseph was a member, had immigrated from Germanic Switzerland, were on the Virginia frontier by 1735, and, according to Wust, had moved "within the fringe of pacifist sects."[6] If Joseph Funk was related to the Funks of the Ephrata community who joined the Sabbatarian Brethren community near Winchester in the eighteenth century, interesting musical ties could be made, as musicologists have not yet established a strong musical connection between the Ephrata group's ethereal harmonic forms and the German music traditions spreading to the frontier.

During time spent in Pendleton County, I met fiddle players Tyson and Stanley Propst, in their eighties and nineties, whose family fiddling tradition goes back many generations, possibly to John Michael Propst, who came to Pennsylvania from Germany in 1733. By 1748, after fifteen years,

Sorcerers dancing at the Sabbat to a violin. Francesco Maria Guazzo, Compendium Maleficarum, *1608.*

he showed up on the Virginia frontier on the South Fork. Old fiddler Melvin Wine (1909–2003), a National Heritage Fellow, was of old Pennsylvania German stock in the Valley.[7] Melvin held his fiddle vertically against his upper chest, instead of under his chin, exactly the way a viol is held in a 1620 woodcut from Nürnberg, Germany, and generally the way the oldest traditional Appalachian fiddlers play.[8]

West Virginia fiddlers of German background, such as Clark Kessinger, Woody Simmons, Ray Sponaugle, and Lefty Shafer, who are/were talented folk artists, represent a rich tradition, but they do not fit in the Appalachian Anglo-Celtic box of dubious construction. Old "Uncle Jack" McElwain (originally, the German Mucklevane) may have carried the torch of Appalachian fiddling farther than any other in the state when he won the fiddling contest at the 1893 Chicago World's Fair.

The German influence on music is particularly strong regarding the instruments themselves. All of the earliest documented American violin makers were German. The Appalachian dulcimer was originally a Germanic instrument in the zither family that came to Pennsylvania. As an evolved folk instrument, its new provenance is the southern Appalachians. An interesting example of an early dulcimer is in possession of the Dasher family, pioneers

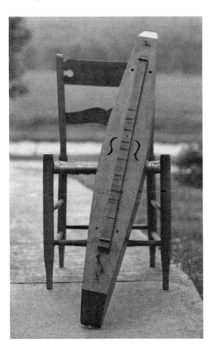

Dasher family dulcimer.

who came to the South Fork near the Hardy-Pendleton line. This dulcimer-like instrument, as old as anyone can remember, seems to be a transitional example, a so-called missing link, fitting somewhere between the straight-sided instruments of Germany and the evolved hourglass- or teardrop-shaped instruments of the Appalachians The Dashers came to Pennsylvania in 1737 from the Palatinate and moved to the South Branch in 1757.[9] Zithers are documented as accompanying fiddles at Pennsylvania German dances,[10] just as dulcimers played with guitars for dances in West Virginia.[11]

Unlike music, most old Germanic folk art presents itself as

Several dozen houses in Pendleton County have copious interior decorations, including vining, finger-painted designs, and stenciling.

two- or three-dimensional constructed forms. They are expressions of values held by this particular group of people over a long period of time. I have photographed numerous examples of German decorative folk art in Pendleton County. The tradition of interior decorative painting credits two local men, Saul Thompson and Austin Fleischer, who painted the interiors of dozens of farm houses and churches. Their work includes trompe l'oeil effects on church walls and false clocks on mantles, as well as folk art scenes and murals on doors and walls, faux-painted doors, trim, and marble lintels, and even classical architectural designs in several churches. Their farm-house work included potted flowers on doors, free-hand and finger-painted ceiling borders, wonderful vining floral designs in hallways and bedrooms, and stenciling.

Numerous forms of decorative folk art use traditional German motifs, and they are widely disseminated. Largely naturalistic, the motifs are tied to a cosmology that stems from an older world view couched in spirituality. Some of the motifs have been traced back from Germanic countries through the medieval period and to the Near East.[12]

Germanic decorative folk art reached its creative peak in the early nineteenth century in this country, before the industrial revolution greatly influenced rural life. The folk spirituality represented in the symbols and motifs are mnemonic devices connecting the creators and owners to the natural world and signaling good fortune. They have a history within the old peasant life of medieval Germany. Still today, collectors consider the heavily Germanic-settled areas of the Valley and eastern West Virginia prime territory for finding folk art treasures.

Birds, including peafowl (peacocks), parrots, and goldfinches (or distelfinks, literally "thistlefinches"), are common, as are "double eagle" motifs. They are considered lucky, and the various birds are often seen in matched pairs. Stars, moons, barn symbols or "hex signs" (most commonly the rosette), compass or cocalico stars, hearts, inverted hearts, the tree of life, and tulips, or "holy lilies,"[13] are found on both utilitarian and decorative items. Spiritual Germans longed for the "time of the lily," when God's peace would descend upon the earth, thus the tulip or holy lily, is favored in decorative designs.[14] Doves and unicorns are also found, as Germans considered them life-giving images.[15]

The motifs are commonly found on regional pottery, grave markers, tinware, coverlets, quilts, samplers, forged iron work, cast firebacks, barns, butter molds, kraut cutters, and furniture (often painted chests) made in the region. All indicate an awareness of a cosmology in the province of a spiritual world. German Pietist Jacob Boehme, who was held in high esteem by early Pennsylvania German religious figures, taught that God reveals Himself through nature. This is confirmed in all of the natural symbolism of Pennsylvania and German Appalachian folk art.

German illustrative fractur design was probably first brought to western Virginia by Samuel Funk in the mid-eighteenth century.[16] Funk learned the art at the old Ephrata community in Pennsylvania, where this art form reached its zenith in the eighteenth century. Appalachian examples by common working people, who could not devote nearly as much time and effort to the artistic expression, are generally simpler and cannot compare esthetically or in depth and meaning. However, the mind-set regarding the deep underlying meaning of the expression and its purpose is there.

Family Bibles with varying degrees of hand-illuminated printing carefully noted signs of the zodiac under which children were born. Older Pennsylvania birth records, often sporting intense fractur illumination, carefully placed birth information within a framework of natural symbols in an astrological context. This tradition goes back to sixteenth-century Germany, where birth records included detail down to the very minute of birth so that astrologers could cast accurate horoscopes.[17]

Eighteenth-century German clockmakers, living just across Shenandoah Mountain from Pendleton County, are noted for including the advancing stages of the moon on their clock faces, as well as numerous symbols of German peasant folk art.[18] These clocks directly tie cosmological principles to folklife activities through functional objects in a decorative way.

Samuel Eckerlin discovered a seam of clay along the Shenandoah River that he proclaimed was of an excellent consistency for pottery. He sent word back to a Pennsylvania friend and potter Simon Siron to bring a complete pottery workshop down the old Philadelphia Road. Thus in 1761 the substantial pottery tradition in the Shenandoah Valley began. Strasburg became known as "Pot Town." In the 1780s, German potters established themselves in Jefferson and Monroe Counties, now in West Virginia. Potter Jacob Foulk left Pot Town and brought his trade to Morgantown, West Virginia, in the early nineteenth century. From early German potteries in the lower Shenandoah Valley, especially Strasburg, the trade spread south and west to distant Appalachian areas and beyond, in much the way German Appalachian culture of all kinds became dispersed.[19] Unmarked pieces of redware pottery, a pottery commonly associated with Pennsylvania German tradition, have shown up in the South Branch Valley, my main study area. Some believe redware was made there.[20]

An old outbuilding on Thorn Creek, near Moyers, has a cast fireback nailed to it, dated 1769, that exhibits Germanic folk decoration. It probably originated in the Valley, where German craftsmen from Pennsylvania established forges and foundries. A fair amount of magical belief surrounds iron and fire, dating back to pagan times. An old Swiss-German blacksmith at Adolph in Randolph County once told me that if you hit cold iron with a hammer, "the devil would get you."[21]

Occult belief, oral tradition, folklore, and material culture collide within the presence of a "feather crown" or "death crown." The belief is that a person, who is about to die, is dying, or has died will cause a metaphysical effect within the pillow on which their head lays. A portion of the feathers inside the pillow will clump or form into a circle or "crown," which is seen as a token or sign in some way representing the death or its consequence to the pillow user. The motif is widely distributed throughout the United States.

Johnny Arvin's belief, which old community sources taught him, is that the pillow of a deceased person should be examined. If there is a feather crown inside, "we can be pretty sure they've gone to heaven." Alas, if it is not present, Johnny Arvin says diplomatically, there is "a doubt in our mind."[22]

Eighteenth-century fireback, near Moyers, Pendleton County.

Sylvia Cottrell O'Brien reported that the presence of a crown is certain in the pillow of a person who has died. She noted that after the death, the crown would be burned. "I've seen Mam do that," she said.[23] Another Pendleton woman reports that the crown precedes death and is, in her experience, an omen: "If the crown forms, that person is to die."[24]

Material objects such as feather crowns tie together the scientifically proven existence of a tangible object and an intangible belief or product of the psyche. To people who readily accept a spiritual connection to a material object, there is no difference between the two. Herbalists and folk healers easily move from the scientifically explained phenomena of plant chemistry that affects one's physical being to an occult or occult-influenced process of healing. Similarly, people move from a belief-oriented tradition to a material object without notice, from the subjective-imaginative to the objective-tangible.

One of my disappointments doing field work in Pendleton County is that I did not get there soon enough to document some wonderful folkways that are now apparently gone. The African American folks at Moatstown contributed to my collection of occult beliefs, but they had a strong tradition of basket making, coopering, and playing old-time string music, all of which had died out by the 1990s.

This rural community, which uses the surname Moats, descends from early female German settlers (Moats) who bore children fathered by a slave, a reverse of the more typical white father–black mother interracial offspring. Black folks in this neighborhood, well into the 1970s, were playing on old-time fretless banjos, fiddles, and guitars. Their frequent "frolics" included many house dances. Some individuals were known for their step dancing, and an important aspect of the evolution of old-time Appalachian string music could have been better understood had someone documented these traditions.

I was able to determine that ash baskets were made in this community by African Americans, a tradition that is common in New England but rare in the southern Appalachians. Many black families made white oak baskets of various traditional designs. It was claimed that a prominent Pendleton County German basketmaker, Levi Eye, produced seven thousand baskets.[25] People of Pendleton also made "rod oak" baskets. A member of the large Simmons family made a beautiful example. This style of basket traces to Germany and the tradition of willow basketry.[26]

Surprisingly, people in this neighborhood who worked hard at making white oak baskets, which I take to be an industrious activity, were considered to be on the lazy side. Perhaps this is because they were not directly

Ribbed basket credited to Clay Eye.

"raising their living" but making baskets to trade or sell to pay for their living, a notch below farming, which was considered the noble endeavor in traditional agrarian thinking. Farming was the way of life in Pendleton County, but however one's livelihood was obtained, the home and the workplace were one and the same to the family.

The craft of coopering was, until recently, common among both the Moatstown folks and within the white community. Tyson Propst was a master of this craft in his later life.[27] Local coopers made wooden buckets for maple sugaring, still a common practice in the area. They also made churns, and Propst made some other styles of wooden vessels.

Overshot weaving on handlooms was common in Pendleton County, and many examples of fine coverlets are extant. Only a few of the older traditional hand weavers and spinners are still living. This area of the Potomac Highlands is still a sheep-producing area, more so than any neighboring county. There was a water-powered carding mill in Franklin, and apparently local production of wool supported its existence.

Pendleton resident Johnny Arvin Dahmer has a large collection of vernacular horse-drawn farm implements, homemade plows, tools, and other objects of local production or interest. He has many wonderful examples of material culture that came from the old Pitsenbarger place, the closest neighboring farm. He spouts folk wisdom continually, as he did one time

Tyson Propst at his shaving horse.

when he was unlocking an outbuilding to show me some objects inside. He said that locks do not stop thieves, but "they will keep an honest man honest."

For distinct material culture with old German folk art motifs, it is hard to beat the old cemeteries in the South Fork Valley. The Old Propst Church at "Propstburg" is a prime example. Most German folk motifs exist within the stones that date from the late eighteenth to the mid-nineteenth century. These grave markers, carved in stone, are a lasting testament to the South Fork's Germanic heritage.

Whoever was carving the stones in this neighborhood was skilled and thematic but not professional. Numerous selected field stones here display a designed pediment, sometimes with supporting sides in a houselike design. One nineteenth-century stone was probably made by a later maker, but in the earlier pediment-house motif. This mysterious stone has unusual stick-like figures that appear to be escaping through a gable roof.

Several early stones indicate the ethnicity of the maker and the community he served. There are numerous hearts, both upright and inverted.

Gravestone with a pediment-design decorative flower, Old Propst Church.

There are several tree of life motifs. I also found classic hex signs or cocalico or compass stars, but it is unknown whether they were intended to be apotropaic or not. While some scholars discount that probability concerning these symbols, others do not, and there are occult symbols inside houses and barns in this neighborhood (see chapter 22) that have been proven to be apotropaic.[28] There are also moons, sunbursts, and beaded edges among the distinctively Germanic decorative designs.

Gravestone with a houselike design and stick (soul?) figures, old Propst church.

German motifs were carved into furniture and painted on chests and barns and the like, including many painted and decorated "Pennsylvania" or German-Swiss "bank barns." The most common are ones painted red with decorative white bordering, and some have "devil doors" (painted arches over the doors) and white stars painted on the doors.

Unlike barns in and around Berks County, Pennsylvania, which traditionally bear hex signs, a study of barns in the Germanic-settled areas of the southern mountains found that stars and horses are the most common decoration, and this is the case in eastern West Virginia. The tradition of decorated barns seems an old and lasting one in all of the old German-settled areas. The oldest barn style in the area is the double-crib log barn, but because of its uneven, rough sides, it can not be decorated with paint at all.

Early twentieth-century Swiss German bank barn with a star on the forebay, Pendleton County.

Double-crib log barn, Pendleton County, late nineteenth century.

Folk Art and Material Culture

Chapter 8

Johnny Arvin Dahmer: Family Curing Traditions

Imagination is more important than knowledge, for knowledge
is limited while imagination embraces the entire world.
—Albert Einstein

One time I was asked to speak to the Pendleton County Historical Society about folk art in the area. The meeting was held at a small schoolhouse–turned–community theater not far from the county seat of Franklin. At the time, I was documenting interior decorative paintings in many of the old farm houses in the area. I like to participate in such events because, as in this case, I glean knowledge about local affairs. This was an opportunity to acquire information about the painters whose work I was documenting. I showed slides of the painted farm houses, spoke about the tradition, played a few old-time fiddle tunes, and learned much from the residents in the discussion that followed.

Afterward, I talked for a short time with Johnny Arvin Dahmer, whom I had only briefly met before. I refer to Johnny Arvin by his first and middle names because it is common to refer to a person by both names to distinguish them from others in the community with the same first name and surname. Johnny's father was also a John, so Johnny Arvin became the distinguishing name of his son. This method of distinction, as opposed to saying "junior," is common in much of rural West Virginia.

Johnny Arvin remembers parties at the home of his grandmother Dahmer. She liked to dance, so neighbors, the Blizzard boys, played fiddle and banjo music. Lizzie Rexrode Dahmer was his grandmother's name. He remembers that she drank a little cider (meaning hard cider) and she would just laugh and laugh. Johnny Arvin says that unlike the Dahmers of Dry Run, the Dahmers of Deer Run, although related, were known for a "sour laugh." Johnny's daddy laughed happily like his grandmother, and his branch of the family came to be known as the "laughing Dahmers."

This fun-loving grandmother, who lived in the neighborhood, smoked homegrown tobacco in a clay pipe, a common habit among old-time Appalachian women. Unfortunately, in her case, she got cancer of the mouth, but it did not deter her enjoyment in her last years. Johnny Arvin said that smoke could be seen coming out of the surgical hole in her cheek as she puffed.[1]

Folk wisdom seems to acknowledge the dark side of tobacco use in this West Virginia rhyme:

> Tobacco is an Indian weed,
> The Devil himself sowed the seed;
> Robs your pocket, burns your clothes,
> And makes a chimley out of your nose.

While Johnny Arvin's middle name is used to distinguish him from other John Dahmers, nicknames are also used to make name and family distinctions. Johnny told me stories about "Captain Bill" Propst. His father's name was Jake, so they took to calling him "Jake Captain." There was also "Rocky George" Propst and "Bill in the Run" Propst, whose names indicated where they lived. After telling me about "Stiller John" Propst, Johnny Arvin said that there were nine John Propsts in the neighborhood that he remembers.

Johnny Arvin is an exceptional source of good information concerning the folklore and folklife of his area. He is considered to be the county historian. His knowledge is from oral transmission, and he takes into account the folklore surrounding the societal aspects of whatever history is being discussed. While, like the African griots of old, he can rattle off local genealogy, genealogists rarely take advantage of the other truly important knowledge he retains, the folklore and oral history that pervade all of his memories and stories about people who he can place genealogically.

Johnny's stories are about his ancestors, local historic figures, neighbors, and friends. What may make Johnny Arvin different from people who pursue the study of culture in a formal sense is that he does not seem interested in other people's culture, only that within his own community. This specificity is to his great advantage, as he is an expert on local traditional life.

Because he is well known in the county, doors open quickly to Johnny Arvin wherever he goes. Befriending Johnny, I should add, opened many doors for me as well. Johnny Arvin is an intuitive ethnographer. He unconsciously started doing field work and taking notes as a child. His child-

Johnny Arvin Dahmer.

hood memories are full of cultural information. Johnny remembers that old people fascinated him, but as a child he was bashful. He told me that because of shyness he would not ask direct questions of the many visitors to his childhood home, but he would remember what was talked about and he would "ask daddy later on."[2]

Johnny Arvin is to the professional field of folklore as a folk artist is to the fine art world. He is self-motivated by inquisitiveness and he is scholarly in that he is concerned with representing his information in a truthful way, whatever the consequence. He found it important to note information and document folk culture, although he has never used that term. He learned to use his box camera to photographically document items and neighbors of interest. Johnny quickly points out people whose accounts may not be based on truth. As an old fiddler said to me one time, speaking about a questionable source, "I wouldn't believe him if his tongue was notarized." But the same fellow also said, "Now if I tell you a certain goose rubs snuff, you look, and you'll find a snuff can under its wing!" His way of attesting to his truthfulness.

Johnny Arvin is known to be good at dehorning cattle. A dehorning seems to have been somewhat of a social event as well as a gathering to get important work done. People dehorned cattle so they would not be dangerous to work around. One time, Johnny Arvin recalls, a cow was dehorned but was bleeding profusely. An old woman in the community, known as one who could "stop blood," was contacted. Through her actions, the blood was stopped. Johnny Arvin noted the common rule that governs transmission of this seemingly miraculous ability: a woman can tell a man how to do it, or vice-versa, but the knowledge can not be passed between members of the same sex.[3] Another blood stopping cure comes from an old Dahmer family "cure book": "Three happy hours have come into this world. In the first hour God was born, in the other hour he died. In the third hour He was become part of us. Now I name the three happy hours and I put to you n.n. so that your limb and the blood heal against damage and wounds."

Johnny Arvin has a lot to say on matters of oral history, and he comes by his knowledge honestly. His father apparently had similar interests in local stories, legends, and lore. His grandfather was a folk healer, and his great grandfather was known locally as a witch doctor. His great-great-grandfather, a Lutheran minister from Baden Baden, Germany, brought the family's occult curing tradition to America in the hand-written German-language cure book mentioned above, which is full of occult methodologies for curing sicknesses. It contains a mixture of herbal remedies, religious invocations, and occult methodologies.

Johnny Arvin's great-great-grandfather was John George Dahmer. He arrived in Pendleton County about 1790 with the cure book. Family tradition says that he was a prisoner who was being persecuted for his religious beliefs, and that he was captured and was slated to be executed before making his escape. Details passed down through oral tradition explain his capture and escape. At some point, John George bolted into a swamp. He

Johnny Arvin Dahmer on his shaving horse.

Johnny Arvin Dahmer

hid out in the water with his head up under a skunk cabbage–like plant, where he could breathe. He injured his leg in his escape, an injury from which he never fully recovered. Even rough translations of the songs he overheard soldiers sing while in the swampy area looking for him are included in Johnny's narrative. He eventually got to North America on a ship, although the family does not know the port of entry. Finally, he made his way to Pendleton County.[4] In all probability, despite his forced Old World evacuation, he joined the westward expansion of Pennsylvania Germans and arrived in Pendleton County in much the way his German and Scots-Irish neighbors did.

This refugee-immigrant was a Lutheran preacher who was well educated and spoke several languages. His occult manuscript was passed down through the family and was put to use by the family and the community.[5] The book contains many occult methods for curing, and contains some additions made to it in the 1880s. It also contains magic number squares and the rotas-sator square (to be discussed), as well as symbols and references to cure various illnesses, living conditions, and social situations.[6]

An analysis of the cures in the eighteenth-century Dahmer manuscript, also known as the family "cure book," shows that an old text, often called *Egyptian Secrets* (among other titles), lent a significant amount of theory to the cures in its pages.[7] The Dahmer manuscript has little in common with the widely known Pennsylvania German powwow book, the *Long Lost Friend*.[8] While some of the remedies in the Dahmer manuscript seem based on scientific principles, as in herbal cures and the like, many others are totally in the magical and occult vein. *Egyptian Secrets* was used as a source for numerous broadsides and pamphlets that were printed in the Valley at the early German presses there. Many of these tracts showed up in eastern West Virginia counties.[9] Various printed occult references found their way to the frontier. Another curious tract, the *Gospel According to Nicodemus*, was known to be in the possession of another early frontier pioneer, Abraham Hackman, of the early Brethren Brotherhood.[10]

The cures in the old Dahmer manuscript are not very different from sixteenth-century German liturgy. Consider this prebaptismal Lutheran exorcism directive from Nürnberg: "Flee from this child, unclean spirit, and make room for the Holy Spirit." About half of the incantations found in the old Dahmer manuscript use Christian references and are in the religious realm. For instance, one states that on the first Friday in the new light, before sunrise and with no food inside you, you invoke: "Welcome, Princely Friday, Jacob: Behold the 77 fevers, whether cold or hot which our Lord God knows well (then invoke the trinity and say this three times)."

Belief-oriented publications are ancient. In 1652, a manuscript was discovered in the Vatican that dated from 743 C.E. Its title translates to "Letter Concerning Superstitions and Pagan Practices," and the manuscript was written at a time when Germanic tribes were converting to Christianity.[11] An even earlier document of German folk customs, *Germania*, written by the historian Tacitus, dates to circa 100 C.E. If modern Pendleton Countians of German extraction still harbor curious ways, it may be said that, as in the old expression, "they came by it honest." Theirs is a tradition that goes back centuries, and this prescientific outlook will not die easily. The old Dahmer manuscript is a prime example.

Johnny Arvin's immigrant ancestor, John George Dahmer, had a son, Joel, who was known locally as a witch doctor.[12] Just when this title was pronounced on local curers is not known, but to Johnny, it is not a pejorative term. Johnny Arvin and his neighbors call people who render cures for ailments brought about by the suspected supernatural efforts of evil people witch doctors, doctors, or sometimes just curers.

We may think of some of Johnny Arvin's narratives as folk tales—for instance, one about the devil appearing in the flesh—but he seems not the least embarrassed to present them as they were originally presented to him, as literal truth. In these stories, he relies on the strength of his sources to validate their worthiness. He always offers a qualifier—"they said," "he said," or "she said"—near the beginning and throughout his narratives.

Johnny greatly respects some of his sources. When mentioning other sources, however, because of his prior knowledge, he makes a point of questioning their integrity. With some examples of occult lore I have collected, the narrator's attitude varies. There is sometimes skepticism, sometimes guarded belief, tacit acceptance, or actual first-person practice—but always the stories involve witch doctors, that is, those on the side of working good or white magic against evil or black magic. Referred to as *doctoring* or *curing* in this region, witch doctor practices depend on a belief in the reality of witches, who have become evil antagonists. The accounts themselves fall within the "social tension" arena discussed earlier.

Be that as it may, almost without fail, when I have identified a trait or motif in eastern West Virginia that alludes to the old beliefs of witchcraft, sorcery, or magic, I am usually able to find a precedent within German or, at least, Continental witchcraft tradition. I am of the opinion that this is significant to folkloric origins here. There is no question that Anglo/Celtic traditions contribute as well, and many beliefs span all of northern Europe, including the British Isles, but in most of the examples I have documented, it was an influx of eighteenth-century German settlers, such as the Dahmers, Propsts, and Pitsenbargers, that contributed exceptional occult traditions and beliefs.

Johnny Arvin can relate detailed accounts of his great-great grandfather's experiences. His stories begin in Germany and end yesterday. His mind is a repository of genealogical information, landmarks, local property corners, unusual and/or older dialect, animal paths and Indian trails, historic public policy, and the folklore and folklife of people in the Dry Run, Thorn Creek, South Fork, and South Branch watersheds of Pendleton County.

Johnny Arvin related incidents of public flogging carried out by an ancestor who was a public official. On one occasion he was ordered to flog a local woman a specific amount of lashes for a certain indiscretion. He did this with great delicacy and care, after which the woman turned to him and said, "Mr. Dahmer, you are a gentlemen, indeed." While carrying out a punishment of lashes to a black man who had committed some offense, the man turned and said, "Mr. Dahmer, leave a little piece of the liver!"

Johnny recalled an incident at hay making time. A man was on top of a stack as the "tramper," making sure the hay was compacted, and as the stack got to its full height, the man said that this would probably be the closest he would ever get to heaven. Just then, the stack fell over.

He also told me about *serenading* or *belling* one newlywed couple. A man people thought would never marry actually did marry an "old maid" of the community. After much noise making and many valiant efforts to get the couple to come out of their tightly locked house, someone broke in through a window and got the couple to the door. The troublemakers said they would leave peacefully if the old fellow would kiss the bride. He said, "I've never kissed a girl yet and I'm not about to start!"

Belling, a practice sometimes known elsewhere as *shivaree*, from the French *charivari*, is still practiced in rural West Virginia. The word *belling* refers to the common use of cowbells to make a disturbing racket. All kinds of mischief is involved, most predicated on the effort to disrupt the new couple's wedding night. Grooms are commonly rode on a rail and brides are set in a tub of ice water, practices with sexual connotations. A Tucker County family has a rail on which is carved the initials of all the grooms who have been ridden on it. I was told of cables being stretched tight between a tree and the house, the cables rosined and played with a board, causing the whole house to vibrate with an unearthly noise. Clapper boxes are cranked with a handle creating an annoying racket. At a house burning coal or wood, if the couple fails to make an appearance, a sack of feed is put on top of the chimney and the couple is "smoked out."

Johnny Arvin's neighbor, Robert Simmons, was serenaded on his wedding night. And, among other things, pranksters drove his truck into a swamp. Robert, an easygoing man who could appreciate good clean fun, said, "Now I didn't like that much."[13]

Johnny Arvin told me of his earliest memory, that of breaking an arm as a small child while chasing and catching chickens for market. Johnny explained that his grandfather rubbed his hands over the broken arm, "mumbled some words," and put the arm in a handkerchief sling. It healed with no permanent damage. When he underwent a physical for the armed forces, an x-ray showed his broken arm had healed perfectly, without ever being set, which seemed like a miracle to Johnny Arvin and reinforced his belief in family tradition.[14] This experience allowed Johnny Arvin the ability to entertain the possibility of success in traditional curing. While he does not necessarily believe all of the supernatural occurrences handed down within the oral history of his family, he thinks that faith is enormously important to outcome regarding cures. He clearly honors, respects, and has confidence in the traditions of his ancestors.

Johnny Arvin explained an occult symbol to me, one found in the cure book brought to Pendleton County by his great-great grandfather: "What this was used for, they believed those magic squares, and you have to use those letters, what they stand for—you have to believe it, then that'd do the trick."[15] This seems Johnny's way of dealing with subjects that may be beyond his scope of belief: the old people had more faith and that provided for their success.

Johnny Arvin said that some old people can "conjure the bees," indicating that they have magical powers over them. He said that these people work their bees with no protection at all from their stings. People use various methods to entice bees into a hive if they have swarmed. They bang on pots and pans, say charms, or engage in other seemingly mysterious practices. Since science can not explain how they are able to control the bees, it is said that they are conjuring, and these hiving practices, bordering on the occult, are widespread in West Virginia.

Meeting Johnny Arvin and learning of his vast reservoir of folk wisdom and traditions, and his experience with traditional magical belief and folklore, was my main motivation for putting these oral traditions into print.

Chapter 9

The Pitsenbargers

But I'm afraid, though you are clever,
Time is too brief, though art's forever.
—*Goethe*

Of all his neighbors and associates, Johnny Arvin Dahmer was most taken by his close neighbors, the Pitsenbargers. Mention of the Annanias Pitsenbarger farm, just down the run and across the road from Johnny's farm, brought an unending litany of stories and anecdotes to our conversations.

The Pitsenbargers included Annanias, his wife Susan, and their three children, James Alben, John Gilbert, or "Gilly," and Sarah Elizabeth, known as "Sis." The children lived out their lives on the old farm and did not marry, much to Annanias's despair. According to Johnny Arvin, Annanias often said that what he wanted was to hold a grandchild on his lap, but "the boys won't ever go out" and "Sis won't breed!" The family also raised a girl, Mable Helmick, who was from the "poor farm" (Johnny implied she had minor mental disability).

The Pitsenbargers were a typical Pendleton County family who came in the eighteenth century from Germany via Pennsylvania. Annanias's family was the fourth generation in America.[1] Alben was a fiddler of some renown in the neighborhood, a worthy talent in that Johnny Arvin describes the Pitsenbargers as extremely clever people. He uses "clever" in the old Appalachian sense, meaning they accommodated, were generous, and entertained any and all who happened through. The Pitsenbarger farm was on an old, well-traveled path that went from the South Fork to the South Branch, so their visitors were many.

Alben played the fiddle but also "had to have a little drink" and would, from time to time, "act the fool." Johnny Arvin's cousin, Bill Dahmer, said people called the Pitsenbarger place "Loafer's Glory," for its slow-paced reputation and the rollicking good times to be had there. The Pitsenbargers

The Annanias Pitsenbarger house.

made as much as thirty-two barrels of cider every year. I suspect that having fun, playing music, and enjoying hard cider, even while operating a big subsistence farm, did not live up to most community standards. However, neighbors and travelers were attracted to the gatherings there because of the congeniality and endless storytelling sessions, music, and cider.

Most people who remember the *frolics*, or work parties, in the neighborhood, remember that banjos and fiddles were almost always present and that square dancing usually ensued. (This English word *frolic*, like the German cognate *frohlich*, is common in eastern West Virginia as a term for these affairs. Anglo/Celts in other areas of the state commonly use the word *bee* for workings.) Robert Simmons clearly remembered apple-butter boilings, wood sawings, and corn shuckings. Occasionally, among younger people, singing games were played. He remembered a game called buttons in which they would sit in a circle and pass (or pretend to pass) a button from one to another, then try to guess who ended up with it.[2] Hard cider was the drink of choice, at least for the older folks. The fiddle was the instrument of choice for dancing among Pennsylvania Germans, and this continued on the frontier and into Robert's day. Robert himself had two fiddles he had made by hand.

For the Pitsenbargers, as with most families, both the family institution and the home existed in much the same way as it did in the preindustrial era. Despite the fact that there is virtually no industry in the county,

Pendleton regularly has the lowest unemployment in the state, usually at 2 to 3 percent. Timber has always been harvested, but since the virgin timber was cut, only small, sporadic timbering operations continue. No train tracks currently exist.

Tradition says that when the first steam engine was brought into the county, they blew the whistle when they got to the top of Shenandoah Mountain and were about to cross today's state line into Pendleton County. A local resident, Katie Hoover, heard this unearthly sound and rushed through the neighborhood declaring that she heard Gabriel's horn and the end was at hand.

The Pitsenbarger farm hosted a constant stream of travelers. Johnny noted that it was hard on Susan Pitsenbarger, who would dutifully feed and comfort the travelers upon the orders of her husband. In this sense they were proud of their "cleverness." Johnny Arvin says that Annanias was "a rough mountaineer" and "cussed a lot," but Johnny appreciated his verbal skills. One time he told Johnny that he had a cow that was "as old as the North Star!" He used the adjective "old" before almost any name or object, as in "that little old baby." "He wasn't two faced," Johnny told me, and "he wouldn't go around a bush to talk about somebody!"

True to local tradition, Annanias Pitsenbarger always went fishing on Ascension Day. Pennsylvania German tradition had it that the fish would migrate up (ascend) the rivers and streams on this day.[3] It is a tradition, such as domestic animals bowing down and speaking on Christmas Eve (see chapter 23), that seeks to show that the natural world is cognizant and observant of Godly activities.

Annanias loved his hard cider, and the family was famous for making it. Cider making was an important fall activity. The alcoholic content of the cider energized many a winter night's fiddling and storytelling session. The cider would "get the bugs in," meaning it got strong in alcoholic content. Once, when Johnny went to the Pitsenbarger farm for a "dehorning," they warned everybody who was drinking to "be careful and not drink too much, it has the bugs in."

The Pitsenbargers always kept three grades of cider on hand, according to Johnny Arvin. He said the common stuff was offered to travelers they did not know. The next best was for visitors with whom they had some acquaintance, and the best was saved for their close friends and neighbors. Annanias may have been "a very rough mountaineer," in Johnny Arvin's words, but his cleverness earned him great respect.

The Pitsenbargers distilled apple brandy at their stillhouse before the Valstead Act of 1917. They ground their apples at an old wooden cogged mill[4] driven by a horse. They had a large willow tree with a hole in it about six feet off the ground. It served as the fulcrum for a pole, which, when pushed through the tree and raised, forced the cider from the pomace. This tree stood near to their "apple house," a place for storing apples, within a grouping of outbuildings. They also buried apples, to keep them from freezing, by sandwiching them between straw in a hole in the ground then covering the straw with dirt.

The Pitsenbarger farm had separate outbuildings for every job, twenty-six in all, beside the log house. The log springhouse sheltered an excellent cool water source for the various food and drink products. This included live fish that swam around among the crocks of milk and butter set in the cool water. Further along, the spring water was used at the washhouse for clothes when the weather was too cold to wash outside on a "beetling" bench. The spring water continued down a light grade to a place where it provided drinking water for farm animals.

The farm has a large double-crib log barn, the most common older style in the area. Log structures are built in squares, called *cribs*, so the logs support each other. Two cribs placed near each other with a passage between form a "double-crib" structure. This main Pitsenbarger barn is on a slightly raised, well-drained area, and there are barns in all of the various meadows to store hay. Most of the oldest barns in the South Branch watershed are of this double-crib log type. In the nineteenth century, when sawn boards became available, Swiss/German, Pennsylvania, or bank barns became popular. Just how this style of construction, known to seventeenth- and eighteenth-century immigrants in Pennsylvania, was "put on hold" until lumber and timber frame construction became possible is not clear. I have not found a bank barn in the South Branch Valley made of logs, although I have looked. They do exist in other places where Pennsylvania German settlers located; in fact, there is one not too far away in the German-settled area of western Maryland. It is possible that early, large wooden bank barns over in the Valley sustained and provided the pattern when sawn lumber became more available to barn builders in backcountry areas like Pendleton County. Many of the older framed barns I have noted are framed and built in the double-crib log style, even though the length of logs and their maneuverability were no longer deciding factors in the design. The double-crib log barns and dogtrot houses are forms brought from Pennsylvania with both Scots-Irish and German settlers.[5]

The log house on the Pitsenbarger farm is a two-story dogtrot, or saddle-bag, affair, with the central opening sealed and used for a pantry and clapboards covering all. Now uninhabited, it was built by the German Evic (originally Ewig) family, who migrated farther west in the state. There is a "summer kitchen" and a cellar house out from the main house. A dinner bell near the porch was for summoning hands to dinner at midday. Johnny Arvin said that while they had a dinner bell, the rule of thumb in the neighborhood was that if you could step on the shadow of your head while out in the fields in summer, it was dinnertime.

One time I visited Tyson Propst, Johnny Arvin's cousin, an old fiddler of the Propst line of fiddlers[6] and the only traditional cooper I have ever met. He was over ninety at the time of this visit. I thought it interesting that Tyson and his brother Stanley had reroofed a small barn on their farm fairly recently with wooden shakes, even though modern roofing materials were easily obtainable. Apparently, a combination of tradition, self-sufficiency, and economics led them to use the wooden shakes. They are very practical people, and nostalgia for doing something in the old way or for an old effect did not influence their actions in reroofing the barn.

Tyson told me about his walks from "Propstburg" (the rural area where many Propsts settled and live) to Dahmer (a one-time post office where his relatives, the Dahmers, lived), a distance of perhaps ten miles by path. On his way to visit his Dahmer relatives, he would walk through the old Pitsenbarger place. He told me that over the years he noticed that some of the outbuildings there had unusual roofs, that they had built their roofs there "without any nails."

It seemed a long wait (actually only a week) before I could get over to Johnny Arvin's to ask him about those roofs. I guessed he would know all about them. When I brought up the subject, Johnny concurred with what Tyson had told me. He took me over to the old Pitsenbarger place and showed me around—my first visit there.

The outbuildings Tyson talked about, as late as the early 1990s, were still in use and sported weight-pole roofs, a frontier building technique (but older than that). Entire log structures were raised on the Pitsenbarger place, complete with a rainproof roof, without using any nails or metal fasteners of any kind. Some buildings on the old place still have their original wooden hinges. Even when nails were available, as they easily could have been in this case, folk tradition trumped convenience and cost. This type of roof construction on the Pitsenbarger farm lasted almost to the end of the twentieth century. Now, in the early twenty-first century, they have finally "gone to rack."[7] Johnny Arvin told me that he had always taken notice of those unusual roofs on the Pitsenbarger farm, and in the 1970s he took some photographs of them with his box camera.

He then produced an old photo album with black and white photos of the Pitsenbarger farm in all its glory. It included shots of a blacksmith shop, a wood house (for storing firewood), a wagon shed, a carpenter shop, and a loom house, several of these structures with weight-pole roofs.[8] The

A recently collapsed hay barn in a small meadow on the Pitsenbarger farm, October 2000. It may well have been the last original building in the United States with a weight-pole roof.

granary, another log building, has a threshing floor. Johnny said that when they were "thrashing" buckwheat there, they could clearly hear it up at the Dahmer farm.

The old Pitsenbarger farm used a large "sweep," a long pole mounted on a fulcrum, to raise hogs high enough to submerge them in a barrel of scalding water before butchering. Using only his own weight on one end, a man could easily lift a four-hundred-pound hog with a sweep. There was a hog house or meat house for butchering and a smokehouse. In earlier days, the hogs were set loose in the woods to fatten. Later they stayed in the hog house, which sat above the garden. Any runoff from the hog lot would end up in the garden, where it was used for fertilizer.

Their unique chicken house has roosts above a large hopper that funneled chicken manure into the box on a large sled. A horse was hooked to the sled when it was full. The manure was taken to some area of the farm that needed fertilizer, saving the tedious job of loading the manure. The family never owned a tractor. Traditional Appalachian-style horse-drawn sleds with hickory soles were used year-round for all hauling around the farm.

Johnny Arvin once told me that it was 1885 before a frame house was built in his neighborhood. Until then, all the houses there were built of logs. This information, which was from his father, illustrates how Johnny

70

Arvin retains oral information passed to him. His father passed on specific dates of such events, and he remembered.

Johnny's neighborhood oral history begins before the Pitsenbargers moved there. The old double-crib log house was "built by frolic" in 1845. House raisings were a common reason for frolics, but log rollings and snitz stringings, among other events, were also popular. Older residents tell me that chicken pot pie was always the fare of choice at these occasions.

In the most recent frolics that I was told about, string music was provided by the neighborhood musicians, the Blizzard boys, and dancing followed the meal after the day's work. When "loafers" would try to come late, arriving barely in time for the food and festivities but after the work was done, they would be "rode on a rail."

The Pitsenbargers were both clever (in the hospitable sense) and cunning (in the occult sense) in their ways. Johnny Arvin particularly noticed these traits. They were caught up in the old German witchery that runs strong in the neighborhood. One resident ended up with the Pitsenbargers' "witch ball" (to be discussed later). They were "fantastic people," in the words of a local resident, meaning they could do things in almost supernatural ways. For instance, they kept orange and lemon trees that bore fruit.

Outbuildings with weight-pole roofs on the Pitsenbarger farm. Photo courtesy of Johnny Arvin Dahmer.

The Pitsenbargers had their own ginseng patch. Sis had a large herb garden and practiced healing and curing with "teas" (herbal plants). According to Johnny Arvin, they had a large collection of old-time flowers and could name them all. They had large numbers of fruit trees, mostly apple, but also peach, pear, and persimmon, as well as grape and berry vines. Gilly Pitsenbarger liked to chew, and they raised their own tobacco.

The Pitsenbargers kept peafowl, and Johnny Arvin notes that at one neighborhood frolic the neighbors made the traditional pot pie with this bird's meat. The peafowl is a revered luck symbol and often shows up in German folk art designs.

While the Pitsenbargers were not witch doctors themselves, they often sought them out for help in occult affairs, especially to battle personal illness. Two perceived witches in the neighborhood even engaged in an occult free-for-all, known locally as the "witch war" (see below). Numerous witch doctors over the years, including Johnny Arvin's grandfathers, practiced cures in the neighborhood and vicinity.

Chapter 10

Dovie Lambert

Here supernaturalism is universal, and affords an
explanation for everything that is not understood.
—Hampden Porter

I am a flea market junkie. In most of the United States, especially near working-class populations, flea markets are the closest thing we have to public market spaces of the kind found all over the world. Such markets are where fair trade is established within cultures that have market spaces and time allotted for their use. While not a great substitute, outside of some older established cities where good indoor-outdoor markets exist, flea markets and farmers' markets are the best we have, and for the most part they exist without any governmental support. Even Wal-Mart, one of the wealthiest companies in the world and a very poor substitute for a public market, is often awarded tax incentives to build within the boundaries of local governments. True markets maintain their status as the result of natural forces that create such spaces and activities wherever humans reach some level of critical mass. You can buy goods at discount shopping marts, but you can not sell there, and a good reason why public (flea) markets are resilient is because you may sell or trade there as well, thus establishing fair market value. Although bartering is illegal because it isn't taxable, it continues. It remains to be seen how eBay and other online shopping venues will affect future public markets.

One day at the local flea market near Elkins, West Virginia, I noticed an older woman who was selling hand-cracked black walnuts, hand-embroidered dish towels, and some hand-sewn quilts. Having cracked a few black walnuts over the years, I knew the amount of time she had put into the one-pound bags she was selling. It takes considerable time to hand crack them and pick out the goodies. These are local black walnuts, much superior in flavor to the English variety, and much harder to obtain commercially. They are even the subject of a West Virginia riddle:

> High as a house,
> Low as a mouse;
> Bitter as gall
> But sweet after all.

Dovie was the old woman's name. She sold her quilts for fifty to seventy-five dollars each, and I would guess she had put hundreds of hours into the making of each one. I struck up a conversation, bought a bag of walnuts from her, and told her I wanted to come to her house with my wife. She said she had more quilts there, and I thought my wife would want to see them.

Dovie Lambert.

Local mores dictate that it is improper to visit a woman, even an older woman, for a first time without another female. So the two of us had a good visit and I got to know Dovie a little bit. That little time spent was enough to know I wanted to know her a lot more. My wife and I bought a quilt, on Dovie's way-too-cheap terms, but later I was able to help her out a little by regularly paying for her table at the flea market. Dovie is "poor as a church mouse" in economic terms, but her mind is a vast treasure trove of astounding thoughts.

During that first brief visit, we talked enough that I knew she was knowledgeable about herbal cures and remedies. I thought it would be good to interview her at some point about her experiences in that area. A few months went by until a work-study student working at the Augusta Heritage Center at Davis and Elkins College was thinking about writing a paper on home remedies and herbal medicine for her sociology class. She came to me to ask about any people she could interview. Shortly after, Betsy Morgan and I headed up Stalnaker Run, a Randolph County hollow, to visit with Dovie.

Dovie agreed to let me turn on a video camera while Betsy asked her prepared questions about traditional herbal medicine, edible plants, and home remedies. I chimed in with a question here and there when something came to mind that I thought should be asked. There are several cures, such as *granny grease* (see below), that are widely known and used, so I asked for her recipe to compare it with others I had collected. We were amazed at Dovie's knowledge of the local flora, and at the same time we were puzzled by some of the vernacular names she had for local plants, illnesses, and preparations.

Thus the interview proceeded until Dovie, without changing gears, started talking about cures that sat squarely in the occult vein. She talked about a disease she called "wildfire" and went on to tell how it could be cured with the topical application of blood from a black chicken.

Dovie talked about "stopping blood," curing something she called "sweeny,"[1] and other cures and potions that reached beyond the scientific to the metaphysical, or was backed up by what Don Yoder identifies as a "pre-scientific world view."[2] At one point she talked about a grandbaby she had to "doctor" because it had a "spell" on it. I glanced down at the video camera several times—was it still on? in focus? recording audio? I hoped I had gotten the shutter speed, white balance, and aperture settings right. Sometimes when talking with older people, I get anxious when the subject matter of their narrative turns in an incredibly profound direction. This was such a time, and the camera was ticking along. Dovie eventually moved onto other subjects and territory, but I was continually hung up on things she had just said. Did I hear it right?

Often, with older people, their first-time delivery of a narrative is their best oral performance. They do not comprehend or they give little importance to the idea of documentation, and when they tell the story again, they know it is a reiteration and so it does not measure up. While involvement with witchery and witch doctoring is a more or less taboo subject for many, Dovie was openly speaking about it.

Some informants will skirt around certain aspects of the occult, especially concerning the use of certain words, showing they are aware their thought processes are unique and publicly not acceptable. Dovie does not. She calls what Johnny Arvin refers to as "curing" simply "witch doctoring" or "doctoring." She calls the effects that witches have on her and her family "spells." And she believes the people "have to keep it a-going [even] if they have to put it on their own family." Unless it is used, she suggests, witchery will die out and be impossible to revive, but she does not expect that to happen any time soon.

Dovie showed exasperation and consternation regarding her efforts to protect her family from witchcraft. She explained some traditional beliefs, including the notion that if a witch gets something out of your house, she can lord some power over you. She says that if she "doctors" a baby and then various people come in her house, one could be the trouble-causing witch and cause more trouble. All the witch would have to do is get a drink of water to reactivate the spell. She notes that there is no way she can tell which visitor is the culprit. She says, "You can accuse them, but is that right or is it wrong?"

The word *spell*, which Dovie often uses, implies magical thought in the sinister vein. Spells are used to vary nature. They are negative formulas, words, and phrases of power that can control or spellbind you. They are thought to address and invoke pagan deities, demons, spirits, and supernatural forces.[3]

As with Germans of old, Dovie's religious beliefs do not conflict in any way with her witch-doctoring practices. During our first encounter, she revisited some incredible experiences about subjects and methods that no older person, at that time, had ever told me. Occult beliefs had always been, in my experience, taboo subjects for open conversation. But to Dovie, the transition from herbal cures to belief-oriented curing to occult methodology and back to herbal curing and predicting the weather was natural.

Dovie predicts the weather using some traditional methods. One of these uses a bottle of an old patent medicine called "Save the Baby." She keeps it on her windowsill. When there is going to be rain or snow, it becomes cloudy, while for good weather it remains clear. She says that a pint of moonshine with a piece of camphor gum dissolved in it will do the same thing.

In Pendleton County, an old weather predictor allows that if the sun goes down cloudy on Sunday, it will be ugly before Wednesday; if it goes down cloudy on Wednesday, it will be ugly before Sunday. Old Wilkie Dennisen told me that the nearer to midnight the moon changes, the better the weather will be. This adage is spelled out in an 1833 German almanac within an article concerning predicting the weather by the moon by a "Dr. Herschel," but it was formulated about twenty years earlier than that.

Old people have told me that a warm day in the cold season is a "weather breeder." But Johnny Arvin's grandmother complained that "the old signs don't seem to hold true anymore," and Johnny agrees, indicating that modern life and ways are affecting all aspects of life in the natural world.

Like most rural older people, Dovie knows quite a bit of weather lore and has many theories about predicting weather. But it is her occult beliefs, hard to link to any one source, which captured my attention. She apparently was raised in a Mennonite church, but I do not think that particular faith went back far in her family. When I asked her if her ancestors believed the occult practices she described, she said, "They all done it. Ever since I knowed any of them, they all done it." She has some Anglo ancestors, but most of them are German, and she has a Swiss/German grandfather (Flubarger) who arrived in Randolph County during the local nineteenth-century Swiss/German immigration.[4] Since her many descriptions of occult thought and belief are found among others in the region, I strongly suspect that her ancestors, from the early Pennsylvania German immigration, are the source of her practices.

From this profound discussion, Dovie went on to talk about butter making and how she missed good homemade country butter. Country butter, in West Virginia, is made after the cream has been allowed to sour or has become "bonnyclabber,"[5] as Dovie would say. Then it is churned into a white-colored sweet butter with a bit of a cultured taste to it. I love it. Dovie would later tell me that even though she misses country butter, her cow was what she "missed worse." She had kept cows all her life, but when she approached the age of ninety, living alone, she could no longer take care of them and had to give them up.

Betsy had plenty of material with which to work when she wrote her paper on herbal medicine. And I had found a person of phenomenal traditional experience and a rich source of occult lore. When Betsy formulated more questions while she was working with her notes and I had started to put some of Dovie's occult practices into some frame of reference, we decided to go back for a visit. It was about three weeks later that we visited again. Dovie was "proud" to have the company. I was better prepared to steer the conversation in order to answer numerous questions I had when Betsy's questions about herbal medicine were complete.

Dovie's little house sits on the side of a hill. A steep path leads up to the house from a spot where vehicles can go no farther. She has a flat patch of land for her garden, a few outbuildings, and a small pasture. She heats with wood and coal. She has a spring that is gravity fed into her house and through the kitchen sink. It flows continuously, so you always hear the tinkling of water, something fairly common in backcountry homes.

Betsy went through her lists of questions. When I steered the conversation back to the subject of witchery, Dovie surprised me by offering information about how a person becomes a witch. Again I was astonished by what she was saying, so I became acutely attentive, again, to the camera. I knew I could listen to and replay the tape later and deal with the content, but this conversation had taken a dramatic turn. Later, when I tried to get her to repeat things she told us that day, they were never again told with that spirit, verve, or detail.

Most methods of witch doctoring do not deal with witches directly but deal with witches' spells or their effects. The spells might be curses or other forms of *hexing* (German for witching) put on innocent people by witches. Dovie's methods are forms of imitative magic. A "ticket," for instance, is prepared and harmed in some way, and this, through this thought process, causes harm to the perpetrator. (A ticket is simply a piece of paper on which a certain Bible verse is written along with the accused person's name, if known. It is always finished with an invocation of the Father, Son, and Holy Ghost.) Ancient Teutonic (and other) sorcerers took an effigy of their enemy, raised it in the air, burned it, stabbed it with needles, or plunged it in water.[6] Richard Wentz has observed that people will sometime turn to "extra-ecclesial repositories" found in new religions or ancient occult practices when standard church doctrine or "the normative tradition" does not fulfill their needs.[7]

Dovie explains her ticket method of dealing with witches and witchcraft:

> Now, the best way to get rid of a witch is to write you a ticket and go to a white oak tree and bore you a hole. Put that in there and take an iron rod, push in there and [slaps her hand on an imaginary rod]. It'll hurt 'em. If it don't kill 'em, it'll hurt 'em. Now that's what [a man] done to [a baby]. And [a woman's] daddy was the one puttin' the spell on the baby. It wasn't, I think about three days, he died. [The man,] just [by following this formula,] knocked him flat.[8]

A similar method to dispel witchery was found among Pennsylvania Germans.[9] Harm is caused on the supposed perpetrator by damaging the ticket in some way. Describing a particular incident in which a child had become bewitched, Dovie offered the following:

[She] wrote him a ticket and he went to a white oak tree. There's a big white oak tree right behind the house. And he bored a hole in that there tree and put the ticket in there, and put an iron rod in there, and took a hammer . . . hit the iron rod . . . hit the ticket. That's how he doctored [the child]. And [she] done [another man] the same way out on a big oak tree out here. But with [him] we never did find out who it was. [She] claimed it was her Daddy. And up 'til she had kids, she didn't know he could devil you. Her own Daddy![10]

This, and most of the bewitchment documented here, falls in the category of the "psycho-dynamic, social tension theory"[11] of witchcraft. This largely deals with jealousy and spite among acquainted people, neighbors or relatives, and for the most part places women in the guilty role.

If someone bewitches a cow, Dovie indicated, a ticket would be tied in her tail to direct the cure. Other methods include placing amulets in the barn (see below). Sometimes the tickets are sewn up in rags and carried by people for protection. Historically, bits of parchment holding quotes from not only the Bible but also the Koran and the Torah have been considered to have protective powers. The practice of wearing amulets for protection is similar to the practices of ancient pagans who wore figurines of their gods.[12] This religio-magical custom is carried on today by those who use the cross and figures of the Virgin Mary, Jesus, and the saints as "amulets."

German-Swiss farmers in Randolph County hung a small cloth bag containing certain specified items in their barns to protect their cattle.[13] In sixteenth-century Germany, a lock of baby hair that was present at birth and/or dried umbilical cords were common talismans, and a wolf's tooth was sometimes worn for protection.[14]

A ticket, in this sense, is a magical item used as an amulet. Carrying the object on your person transfers its power to you. It can ward off disease or trouble, and when used with a talisman (good luck item or something used to enhance one's fortune), it bestows a double dip of good fortune and benevolence.[15]

Dovie's sister said that tickets were used in this way. She said of some witches that lived nearby, "[They] put the witches on everyone. [But] they never got Mom and they never got Dad, because they always carried a ticket."[16]

The ticket is akin to the German *Himmelsbrief*, literally "letter from heaven," which is thought to be written by God himself. An Irish monk carried the tradition of the *Himmelsbrief* to Germany in the seventh century,[17] and it is carried for protection. Examples have been documented among Germans in the Shenandoah Valley, and German American soldiers carried them in both world wars. The belief is that no fire or bullet will come near to the person who carries it. Broadside copies hang in German American homes for protection.[18] In the nineteenth century, England had a similar tradition using something called the *savior's letter.*[19]

In West Virginia, the ticket is carried or even placed over a door to guard against evil that is psychologically personified in the form of a witch. Dovie said that her mother put a ticket over their door at home. If a witch came in, she would have to "back in," meaning she could not come in forward "like you or me do."[20] Witches represent the *other,* something different from normal, and as such, they may be forced to do things in the reverse—or backward.

Another occult cure similar to Dovie's was used by the Dahmer family and involved boring a hole into a fruit tree. Johnny and his cousin Bill Dahmer recounted what Bill called a "sign cure," because it had to be done under the right sign of the zodiac and/or position of the moon and planets. The cure is for hernia. The inflicted person is taken to a fruit tree before daylight and without speaking, where a hole is bored into the tree. A small piece of cloth from the subject's clothing is taken from the area closest to the hernia. Some pieces of fingernail and hair from both the upper and lower parts of the body are put into the cloth. This is tied up and pushed into the hole. Then a wooden plug is driven into the hole in three blows while reciting, "In the name of the Father (first blow), Son (second), and Holy Ghost (last)."[21]

Wooden plugs inserted in holes in trees and buildings and trapping some carefully chosen materials inside are thought a cure for various physical ills. Dovie's sister, Mary Cottrell, in describing the practices of a local witch, said, "She had a tree above the house. She called it her pin tree. . . . She'd drive pins in that cherry tree. Whenever she wanted to bewitch someone she'd put a pin in that tree."[22] In this case, this is done as an evil action rather than a curative action, showing that the methodology can be either defensive or offensive.

Sometimes nails are driven in trees at the height of a child for curative purposes. Stanley Propst of Pendleton County told me of a cure for phthisic (pronounced *tisic,* a pulmonary condition) in children. The child is taken out of the house before daybreak without speaking a word. He is walked toward sunup (eastward) to a tree. A nail is driven into the tree at the height of the child and an incantation is spoken. The cure takes effect when the child grows higher than the nail.[23]

In the old Dahmer curing manuscript there is a cure for toothache that uses this transfer methodology:

Take a new, unused nail, stick the tooth with it until it bleeds, then take the nail and hammer it on the rafter in the basement, towards sunrise, at a place where neither the sun or moon shines. The first time you strike the nail say: Toothache flee. The second time, Toothache go away. The third time, Toothache you have gone in the name of the Father, the Son, and the Holy Ghost.

In southern West Virginia, Kent Lilly described a method of removing a curse from a farm through a magical procedure. Several cows on a local farm got the "hollow tail," a condition in which the tail goes limp or flaccid. Kent said they tried to cure them by a method I have documented elsewhere as "wolfin' the tail."[24] The tail is split open and has salt and pepper poured into it. However, in the case Kent described, the cure did not work. The offended party decided there was a curse on the farm. A moon doctor was consulted after reading an almanac (to determine the right day), and a hole was bored into a log in the barn and some sulfur was put into it. Then a hickory plug was driven into the hole. When the peg rotted off, the curse was removed from the farm.[25] Sulfur is the biblical brimstone, and it shows up again and again in magical belief in West Virginia.

This particular curing practice, also with Dovie's ticket curing method (see chapter 8), is in the German powwow tradition in Pennsylvania. Although best known in Pennsylvania, powwow books were widely known and were even sold through Sears Roebuck's catalogs at the end of the nineteenth century.[26]

A Pennsylvania German in Lebanon County concluded his farm was "ferhexed," so he sent to the next county to a powwow doctor for a cure. The witch doctor (as he would be called in West Virginia) told him to look on one of the foundation timbers of his barn for a wooden plug. He said there would be hair of his variously cursed animals inside the plug. When the plug was found, removed, and the hair taken out, the animals recovered and the curse died.[27] In this case, the method seems to have been for causing a curse, while the most of the examples I have collected are for removing a curse, except for the one in Dovie's case. There the spell is removed but reversing the curse through imitative magic also harms the perpetrator.

Aside from using an oak tree in which to place a ticket in this particular method of witch doctoring, Dovie describes various ways in which a ticket can be used to deflect and deter the actions of witches. In two cases explained to me, they resulted in the significant effect of causing the demise of the perpetrators. Dovie and her sister believe these tickets are powerful tools, and both give God the credit for their power. Most often these tickets are used in cases in which witchery is suspected to have caused harm. The perpetrator is thought to be in league with Satan. However, Dovie also described instances in which tickets were used as a preventative measure. In these cases, a ticket is written and sewn up in a cloth pouch and worn around the neck or, for cows, tied up in the tail.

Dovie says that to make a ticket, one need only have a scrap of paper on which you write a Bible verse: "Get thee behind me, Satan: thou art an offense unto me: for thou savourist not the things that be of God, but those that be of men" (Matt. 16:23). Then, she says, you write the person's name and "Father, Son and Holy Ghost," referred to as the "three highest names." Once written, some physical harm is done to the ticket. Among the various instances recounted to me by Dovie and her sister, the ticket was burned with fire, "jobbed" full of holes, or cut with a knife. To cure cows giving bloody milk, a ticket is put into the milk and mixed with kerosene and burned. The ticket may also be pushed into a hole in an oak tree in which an iron rod is inserted and hit with a hammer, thus smashing the ticket inside. Dovie's offspring use this practice to "doctor" babies, so a younger generation is carrying on this tradition into the twenty-first century.

In each case of witch doctoring with a ticket, within an amount of time ranging from minutes to hours to a few days, someone proving to be the witch shows up exhibiting the physical abuse that matches the damage done to the ticket. One time Mary's mother cured a cow with bloody milk by pouring the milk into a hole in the ground. To this she added her prepared ticket and then she beat the milk with a thorn. In no time, a local witch, who lived just over the hill from the family, showed up with her legs "scratched full of holes."

Dovie believes witches go to certain springs at a certain advantageous time to perform an initiation ritual in order to have the power to curse another. Her curing methods are similar to that of the ancients who used *defixiones*, very thin lead tablets bearing written curses that were placed in places such as graves, wells, doorways, springs, or other places of magical significance.[28] These curse traditions spread throughout the Western world and are likely to have been early precursors of the Appalachian traditions documented here. Most witchery has been relegated to simple oral tradition through the folk process, but for some, as in Dovie's case, and with her children, it is still a practice that involves physical actions and, in her mind, direct results. Malicious spells and the reversing of spells are ancient in origin. Archaeology has shown that ancient uses of spells of this type existed throughout Europe.[29]

Various curses in the Bible are similar to the defixiones found at ancient sites. Examples include Judges 17:1–2, a confusing curse involving money and theft; Zachariah 5:2–4; Jeremiah 51:60–64; Ezekiel 4:1–3; and 2 Kings 13:17–19. Judging by these verses, the Hebrews were familiar with this written curse tradition. Recovered objects studied by scholars reveal that the curses are intended to bring harm to those to whom they are directed. They go back to ancient Mediterranean culture, and over fifteen hundred examples have been excavated on the Continent as well as at ancient Roman sites in Britain.

The ancients believed that there are some specific places in the cosmos, certain magical sites or places, where the spirits of supernatural beings abound.[30] Some of this thinking exists today. Dovie's tradition chooses an oak as the species of choice to invoke a powerful charm directed at a perceived witch. Ancients held the oak sacred, especially in Westphalia, but also within mythology concerning the God Thor and among the Celtic druids.[31] Fruit trees were also important.

While today's anthropologists easily debunk the reality of witchcraft, they acknowledge that many cultures do believe in its efficacy, and many anthropologists adhere to the reality of spirit possession.[32] Witches are thought to be devil worshipers, pagans, heretics, magicians, and social misfits. Many people today claim to be possessed by the Holy Spirit, and this is widely accepted and praised. It is only the reality of non-Christian spiritual or "demonic possession" that seems to be questioned by the literate masses.

It seems the psychological aspects of occult-related social interactions have been around a long time. Within the ancient Greek uses of defixiones, one tradition is to roll or fold the lead sheet into a small object, sew it in a cloth, and hang it around the neck as an amulet.[33] This is exactly the method Mary Cottrell described her parents using to keep off witches in West Virginia.

Dovie described sewing a ticket in a pouch and hanging it around the neck of a baby to guard it against witchcraft. A common cure throughout West Virginia was to put some asafetida in a pouch and wear it around the neck to ward off sickness. In this case, it seems that the asafetida is used in a way that is common to occult methodology. Fumes from the asafetida would rise to the child's nose, and perhaps this effected the cure. It was used as an amulet against witches in Europe and in the Valley, where it was called *Deivelsdreck*. In Germany, it is called *Teufelsdreck* (devil's dung).[34] *Dreck* (dung), symbolized here in asafetida, is commonly used in German

Appalachian folk medicine. Dovie knows of five or six methods of curing that her mother used involving various kinds of animal dung.

The origins of the asafetida cure were in a traditional occult vein, not within the scientific realm. All of the methodologies of warding off the power of witches described by informants seem to have a continental European, especially a German, precedent.

Chapter 11

Witchery on the Farm

The most beautiful thing we can experience is the mysterious.
It is the source of all true art and science.
—Albert Einstein

Farm and rural agrarian life provides a backdrop for much of the folklore found in this book. Traditional rural life touches on many misunderstood natural and biological laws and forces, providing unlimited opportunities for abstract occult thinking. Folkways and methodologies develop through the use of magical methods to negotiate various concepts. Luck is not an arbitrary entity; good fortune is assisted through adherence to a cosmology and magical thought process that has stood a test of time.

Johnny Arvin Dahmer lived at least half of his life during a time when horses were commonly used for power on the farm, and he described to me several instances in which witchery was believed to have caused work horses to lose their energy. Witch doctors were called in to restore them to health through removal of the spell. In a conversation between Johnny Arvin and an old neighbor, Eva Simmons, the two talked about a peculiar old custom involving a woman in the neighborhood:

> Johnny Arvin Dahmer (JAD): Did you ever hear about whipping the toads?
>
> Eva Simmons (ES): Wasn't that some of the Pitsenbargers up here above Moyers? They'd whip the toads in the ash corner.
>
> JAD: I bet that was [a man named] Pitsenbarger up there.
>
> ES: I think it was.
>
> JAD: Because I heard [a man] say that [he] said to him one time, he said, "He married a damned old witch." I bet that's who you're talking about.
>
> ES: Well [a woman] was one of them.
>
> G. Milnes: What did you say they did?

JAD: What about those eggs again? Whip the toads?

ES: I used to hear my mother tell it, she said that they whipped the toads in the ash corner to make the chickens or the ducks lay more eggs. Wasn't it?

JAD: Well, it probably was. They got more eggs.

ES: Yeah, they got more [eggs] than [they had] hens.

JAD: They got more than they had hens to lay, I reckon, didn't they?

ES: Yeah.[1]

Johnny Arvin recalled a local story about a family suspected of witchery. A young girl went out to gather the eggs and she asked her mother, "Hows come you get more eggs than you have hens?" This simple fact, to those who are familiar with small-scale egg farming, automatically points to the occult, as it is beyond the natural course of egg production since hens only lay once a day.

Johnny recalled a similar story about his old neighbor Annanias Pitsenbarger's perception of this curious practice. Annanias described l ow people could "whip the toads" and make the hens lay more eggs. He said he had witnessed it one time down at the old Pitsenbarger house, where he also saw someone milking a dish towel.

These old traditions might have something to do with the imaginary German paradise, Schlaraffenland. This old concept is a predecessor of the American Big Rock Candy Mountain concept in which numerous kinds of foods grow on trees, whiskey comes trickling down the rocks, hillsides are covered with cakes, and rivers flow with brandy. Schlaraffenland is prominent in German lore and many expressions of West Virginia and American folklore trace to this and other similar European sources.[2]

View of Shenandoah Mountain from Moyer's Gap.

Since Pitsenbarger's knowledge of how people had power to produce milk from an ax handle or dish towel (below) is an old Germanic motif, similarly, whipping toads probably has an Old World precedent. This is especially true because toads are very common in all aspects of witchery and magic. An old and slightly different belief, apparently collected almost a century ago in the vicinity of Pendleton or Rockingham County, Virginia, is that a witch would keep toads instead of chickens, and those toads would supply their eggs. Such eggs would be known by their hard shells.[3]

Proof that toads are thought to have magical properties was known to a Brushy Fork man in Pendleton County who carried a certain bone of a toad in his pocket to keep a goiter from growing.[4] On the European Continent, witches were accused of keeping toads as familiars.[5] Some toads have tiny flesh horns on the top of their heads, perhaps causing them to have an association with the devil. Witches are said to baptize toads.[6]

A tale about a child and a snake collected in Germany by the Brothers Grimm is well known in West Virginia, although sometimes it is a toad instead of a snake in the Old World version. I have found four versions of the tale. Essentially, a little girl feeds a snake daily (usually with bread and milk), but when her parents find out, they kill the snake, and the little girl dies. A teller of this tale told me that because the little girl fed the snake, she was immune to its poison, but when her parents killed the snake, her immunity was lost, causing her demise.[7]

Other curious snakelore among country people concerns the native hog-nosed snake, often called a puff adder or, in West Virginia, a "blowin' viper." This is because, like toads, it is thought to blow poison. People believe that it can not bite you because "God locked its jaws."[8] It flattens its head like a cobra and it hisses and blows at you when you get near it. If that does not scare off what it perceives as danger, it rolls on its back, plays dead, and a red syrupy liquid flows from its mouth. I would not have believed this had I not witnessed it. Later I was assured by a qualified naturalist that these snakes indeed do that.

Toads were thought to have an evil eye; its very glance could cause evil. Toad entrails were used in divination.[9] Secretions of some toads, apparently a hallucinogenic substance, along with their bodies and excrement were used within the popular notions of witches for potions in their cauldrons and for their nocturnal flights.[10] Sometimes the devil would appear to witches as a toad. In these instances, witches would kiss the toad in an act of homage.

Producing eggs in a magical fashion, as above, is known to others in this region, as Dovie explained in telling this story about a suspected witch:

He's the same one that came to my grandma's house. And he told my aunt, he said, "Let's bake a cake today."

Aunt Mint said, "We ain't got no eggs to bake a cake!"

"Oh yes," he said. "We'll get eggs." He sent her down to the chicken house; she came back with six eggs! The chickens hadn't laid an egg all winter!

They went on and baked the cake. They was natural eggs. Well grandma couldn't believe it. She said, "Wes, how in the hell did you get them chickens to lay them eggs? They ain't laid all winter."

He said, "I got my ways." Well he got the eggs all right. Well if I hadn't a-been at my grandma's house and seen this go on, I wouldn't of knowed it, but I seen it go on. Her chickens hadn't laid one egg all winter and that was along in . . . towards spring, either in March or April. They hadn't got an egg all winter. And grandma's raised chickens just like me and Mom raised chickens. Now generally when it goes to get real cold your chickens quits laying. And you keep them all winter for nothing. . . .

I told Grandma, after he left, I said, "Grandma," I said, "I didn't know we had the devil in the home."

She said, "I knowed it," and she said, "I don't like for him to come back here either." She didn't like him. It's like she said, he'd a caused her or my aunt anything according to the way he got them eggs. He did not go to the chicken house and get the eggs hisself. He had my aunt go down to get them.[11]

Older farm life proved a breeding ground for folklore like this. People had a keen awareness of natural laws. Accusations of witchcraft, where scientific cause and effect is relegated to random happenings determined by good and evil, magic and sorcery, position of the moon or alignment of the stars, are complicated. When something goes amiss, a human being is needed to personify the event. Even if no particular person or force is obviously responsible for the problem, curative methods in the occult realm, when practiced, will put minds to ease, as in the following narrative from Dovie:

We had an old hog. She was ready to have her babies and when she had them, she had them and she had them and they all died. Mom said, "What in the world happened to all the babies?"

I said, "Don't know Mom." I said, "Maybe the Devil's got her." Sure enough—she did. She doctored the old sow and she had two after Mom doctored her and them two was alive. She had six dead ones.[12]

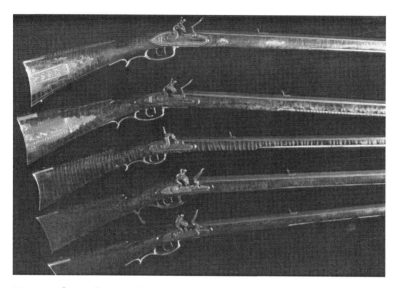

Mountain rifles, another Pennsylvania German contribution to Appalachian culture. Made by Bill Mullenix, Randolph County, West Virginia.

Dovie does not specify the methods her mother used to doctor this sow. She equates witchery with the devil here. Although not always spoken, her verb *doctor* means "witch doctoring." In this case, it most certainly alludes to her ticket methodology, which combines religion and the occult to work imitative magic on the perpetrator.

Mary Cottrell remembered when a neighbor woman, known as a witch, wanted to buy her father's "buck sheep" (ram). Sheep farmers normally only keep one ram to breed their ewes, so it is a very important possession on the farm. Her father refused to sell it. Mary said that the witch did not want to take no for an answer, but she finally went home. The next morning, when her father went to check on the stock, the ram was dead. When I asked if the witch had gone to the field and killed the ram during the night, Mary said no, she did not even have to leave her house. She just said a curse that would "take its breath away." She also noted that this woman had gone to a spring, running from the sun, to become a witch.[13] Mary believes that witches are combated effectively through using the Bible verse on the ticket. "They won't bother that, that's God's work," she says. "If you believe in God the old Devil is not going to bother you."

Robert Simmons told me that his buck sheep was missing one time. His search led to a neighbor who was known to practice witchery. He found the ram there. Though it clearly had his mark, RS for Robert

Simmons, written on him with tar, the man refused to relinquish the buck, claiming he owned it. Robert said that he could have rightfully taken the sheep, as it clearly belonged to him, but he decided not to do it because he thought the man would then put a curse on his farm. Typically, Robert lends credence here to a belief in and a fear of witchcraft. However, when asked directly, Robert, a devout Christian, denied any notion of power over people supported by witchery. While he believed his religious faith would protect him from witchcraft, he did not deny the existence of witchcraft and in fact feared it. Like others his age, he still harbors a traditional belief in witchcraft that, in effect, rivals religion and causes him to be cautious and careful around the "devil's work."

Eva Simmons of Pendleton County remembered that lambing time was a favorite time for farmers to engage witch doctors. When they would have stillborn lambs or other natural occurrences that lowered the percentage of lambs living after birth, they immediately suspected neighborhood witches. As Eva put it, "They'd call these old witch doctors" to make things right. Eva remembered that many people traveled to someone on Broad Run near Brandywine in Pendleton County to consult a witch doctor.[14]

Johnny Arvin told me that there was an "old cross sow" in the neighborhood that had her pigs in a hog house but would not let anyone get near them. Young pigs are often sold at the market or to individuals who fatten and butcher them, providing cash for the farmer. Sows can get mean and dangerous, however, when you try to take away the piglets. In this case, "Old Jake" Propst, who had occult ways, was called in to do something about it. Johnny said he went to the hog pen, "mumbled some words to conjure the old sow," then went right in and gathered up the pigs with no trouble, a phenomenal occurrence as far as Johnny was concerned.

Because the Potomac Highlands is a rugged region, no farms are far from forests and every farm contains some woodland. While farm life lends itself to the traditional occult thinking documented here, a knowledge of woodslore is especially present and extends the natural world even further. Native plants, both edible and medicinal, and their usage are a part of the traditional folk spirituality practiced by people of the countryside in this area.

Chapter 12

Folk Medicine

Medicine is older than the medical profession.
—Bruno Gebhard

In colonial times, a German-language herbal treatise, *Neue Kreuterbuch*, first published in Switzerland in 1543, was widely read by ethnic Germans and used by German doctors in Pennsylvania, as was a herbal published by Swiss/German Leonhart Fuchs.[1] As the number of German-language readers decreased, many of these published herbal remedies entered oral tradition. This contributed to the vast store of folk wisdom regarding the curative uses of plants that I and many others have found in present-day West Virginia.

Early generations of Appalachian settlers held distinct herbal and occult traditions and suppositions that were very real to Old World generations. These early settlers witnessed the emergence of pseudo-scientific cosmological theories that grew out of principles of alchemy.

It was religion that defined life during this period, and any attempts to use astrology, cosmology, alchemical belief, or folk curing practices were held in a religious context. Influenced by Old World Pietists, John Martin's mystical attempts to obtain a perfect union with God were sought through alchemical processes. Even earlier remnants of alchemy were practiced on the old Virginia frontier, where early Brethren sought precious metals with a divining rod.

All of the old German Brethren with ties to Germantown and Ephrata who made their way to the Appalachian frontier were acquainted with the works of Christopher Sauer and Christopher Witt of Germantown, if not the men themselves. Both men had an interest in astrology, astronomy, and herbal medicine. Witt maintained an extensive herb garden, and Sauer built some of the earliest clocks made in America and operated one of the country's first printing presses. In 1768, Sauer published America's first herbal guide (*Concise Herbal*) and a serial calendar in almanac form. Some of the myriad Appalachian folk cures that involve treatments attuned to astrologic principles are likely to be the legacy of these unique individuals, especially Sauer because of his published herbals and almanacs. Sauer also printed collections of supernatural ghost stories as related by the faithful, promoting the belief among the Germans that the reality of these apparitions strengthened spiritual well-being.

Elder John Kline was a nineteenth-century Appalachian herbalist, a German American Brethren minister and herb doctor living in the Valley who frequented Hardy and Pendleton Counties in the mid-nineteenth century. Kline collected his wild plants in the western Virginia mountains, and he carried his supplies on his religious rounds for treating the sick. He was also an advocate of a "Doctor Thomson," a New England herbalist who had many followers.[2] Kline averaged over four thousand miles per year on horseback, serving a wide area, spreading the Gospel and caring for his subjects through his herbal cures and knowledge. His travels were legendary.

Until recently, the positive motives of herbal healers of this kind were generally looked upon with skepticism if not outright suspicion, probably due to the rise of the medical establishment. Today, enlightened people are taking another look at holistic health, including the use of herbal medicines. At the same time, there are herbalists in West Virginia, descendants of generations of herbalists, who maintain curing traditions and have never discontinued their use.

Most people who know folk remedies have come from families who practiced this type of curing for many generations. Phoeba Cottrell Parsons described numerous medicinal and edible plants to me, although because she uses many dialect words for them, it was not always clear what plants she was talking about. For instance, for food she suggested eating "snake tongue," "juglehorn," and "groundhog greens," along with the better-known locust bloom, wild beet, dandelion, nettle greens, and cress. She also uses snake tongue for medicine, along with yellow root (goldenseal), catnip, and other more common plants.[3]

Catfish Gray, another herbalist I interviewed, ate creasy greens, wild carrot, wild beet, sweet anise, white wild lettuce, yellow dock, lemon balm, and winter cress and drank sassafras tea. He used "soap plants" for washing hands. For medicine, Catfish commonly sold white yarrow or foxtail, slippery elm, joe pye weed, lemon mint, goldenseal, cohosh, sweet anise, tansy, pennyroyal, bergamot, boneset, chamomile, peppermint, sassafras, and horehound, among other plants and herbs, as well as his "bitters," which contained many plant extracts. Catfish claimed to have dealt in as many as nine hundred different herbs and plants that he collected in the region and sold through his lifetime. Some of his recipes and cures, including his bitters, were advertised and sold through the Penn Herb Company of Philadelphia, the largest business of its kind.

I think that someone with a botanical background needs to do a comprehensive study of the lesser-known plant names in West Virginia, before they are forgotten. These dialectal names for edible and medicinal plants and their uses, unless identified in the field, will lose their relevance. Some examples of these names are thimble weed, God's candy, coon-root, compass weed, shad flower, dame's violet, seven sisters, kraut-weed, spider

Catfish Gray with his chart of astrological advice.

flower, stick weed, white top, broom brush, St. John, creeping charlie, camel root, snakeroot, old mother schoolcraft, wafer ash, princess weed, bull plantain, cow weed or heal all, blue devil or frost weed, pepper grass, shepherd's purse, sand grape, shoo fly, hive vine, thimble berry, sinkfield, Indian hemp, beggar's ticks, alligator wood, wood astor, tar weed, horse mint, red root or wild sage, swamp root, and seed-box.

Although there are fewer species of trees, they too are important. Yew pine, round wood, ironwood, cucumber, bam-a-gilly, wahoo, and hickory poplar are just a few vernacular names known to old-timers. Some names have simply changed through mispronunciation. For instance, many

Folk Medicine

older people use bam-a-gilly for medicine. It is a tree sometimes found in yards of older Appalachian homes, brought there by salesmen who would come through the country selling young trees to be planted for their medicinal properties. The term comes from "balm of Gilead," itself a colloquial name that comes from the Bible. It is so named because the milky sap of its buds has a pleasantly sweet fragrance. It is actually balsam poplar, or *Populus tacamahacca*.

Emogene Nichols Slaughter of Braxton County inherited a family tradition of healing with herbs that came down on both sides of her family, showing that men, in this case her father, had knowledge as well:

Painted door on a Pendleton County farm house.

He mostly showed me all the different kinds, the horehound and the licorice. We'd go out and get that to make tea along with coltsfoot. We had to get 'em before frost, you know and have it dried before winter. I make cough syrup now. I use coltsfoot and horehound generally, and if I can't find the horehound, I get that licorice that I showed you. The sweet anise, I think some people call it. I make a broth and cook it down real strong and add honey to it. My daughter swears by the cough syrup.

We always have spring tonic of sassafras tea. The red is the best. It makes the best tea.[4] It's the same thing but in different localities the roots are different because of the soil. I get mine generally over here along the river and it's the red roots but I can go back up here against the mountain on the north side of the hill and it's the white roots. The old people always said that it (spring tonic) thins your blood after the wintertime you know. Cleared out the blood stream. Just makes you feel better. I really feel that it does.

And in the spring you always go out and pick greens. I found some the other day. I found the Indian lettuce, and white top, and plantain, potato top and wild beet, touch-me-not, and nettles, and poke. One that we call rock salad. It's the purple milkweed. It looks like milkweed only the vein in it is purple. I pick that, and one that we call bear's paw, and rattleweed. The only one that I eat raw is rock salad and the wild lettuce. We have a good mess of ramps in the spring, and that helps you feel better. Takes all the germs away, they can't stand the smell!

We used to always make our own soap. We used to dry berries. We'd dry apples and berries and peaches. The pennyroyal, we used to put it in our straw tick to keep out gnats and fleas. It's in the mint family and it makes a good tea also. My Dad always swore by it for asthma. He'd have Mom to brew him up some pennyroyal tea. We used leaves of spice bushes, but they aren't as good as the bark. Occasionally Mom made tea from the leaves. We used the catnip. If you couldn't sleep, that's what it was for. It's a relaxant. Give it to babies for colic. Feed it to 'em by the spoonful. I still dry the pennyroyal and peppermint. Peppermint's for upset stomach—and the spearmint. I pick the catnip on up the crick up there. I grow comfrey too. Comfrey's real good for all kind of things. We always had it. Mom always had it and my grandma. It's good for tea, and it's good for poultices.

When I was a kid I bruised my heel one time. I was squallin' and hollerin' and Mom said to go out there and put your foot down in that cow pie and stand there for a while. I did it.

There's a little blue flower that grows right out there. My family always called it "old mother schoolcraft." It was always used for childbirth. Pipsisewa is for kidneys and bladder. I can stop blood with a Bible verse and I can also take out burns with a Bible verse. My Dad taught me that. My son can do it too. I can also take off warts.

Boneset is for pain. You know what we always done for headaches? Willow bark—chew it. I was reading in something that it's a proven fact that it has acetaminophen in it. [It actually contains salicylic acid, the active ingredient in aspirin, whereas acetaminophen is the active ingredient in Tylenol.] That's the active ingredient in it. My grandma, after she got older, I'd go and get it for her She'd just chew It.

This rock up here, there's a substance that forms under that rock and it'll bubble up out of that rock and you can rake it off and it's white and powdery. The old people called it alum. My Dad said when he was growin' up that if they got the toothache they always would use alum from that rock there.

I have a time a-findin' yellow root. And I have trouble finding snakeroot. The snakeroot the leaf grows clear around the stem. And the pipsisewa, it's just scattered you know. Pipsisewa is for kidneys and bladder. It has a healing effect. There was an old lady that lived up here on the hill. She lived to be ninety-six years old and when she was ninety-four, she was in the hospital with kidney problems. Kidney failure is what they called it. They sent her home to die. So she had her son-in-law to go out in the woods and get her some pipsisewa. I was up there and I said, "Bill, I want to go with you," 'cause I didn't really know it. So I went with him and we got the pipsisewa and I helped him make the tea and gave it to her, and she lived two more years. And she didn't have to go back to the hospital either.[5]

Emogene explained to me her philosophy about the use of herbs: "I believe there is something out there to heal everything. In fact, the Bible tells us there is. If we just experimented enough. I think there's a cure for everything. I also feel though that a lot of the cure is within yourself."[6]

As Emogene noted, boneset is a widely used herb. Among other things, it is said to help "break" a fever. Rhymes were created to help people remember to use it. In Johnny Arvin Dahmer's neighborhood there is a little rhyme: "To bring a sweat, / Use a tea of boneset."[7]

Mary Cottrell knows numerous local plants used for cures. She uses peppermint tea for stomach pain, spearmint, pennyroyal and "bee weed" (bee balm) for fever, peach bark for worms, and catnip for nerves and for a baby until the mother's milk flow was adequate. Her father always chewed yellow root for a sore mouth and kept chamomile in his pocket for upset stomach.

Mary was raised using granny grease and mustard poultices for flu and cold symptoms. Her mother used red clover and cherry bark with rock candy and corn whiskey, boiled down "thick," for coughs. They used chestnut leaves boiled into tea to make you vomit, which eased whooping cough. Sheep "nanny tea" (manure tea) was used for measles. Corn silk, dried, was made into tea for kidney trouble.[8]

Besides nanny tea, Johnny Arvin remembered another particularly off-putting cure. He said that to cure his sister of a sore mouth or thrash (thrush or oral candidiasis), his grandfather took a straw and drew it through the manure pile in the barn, then drew it through his sister's mouth. Did it cure her? Well, Johnny said that she is now eighty-nine years old, so "she must have got better!" Numerous other cures that make use of excrement and urine are documented in Pendleton County.[9] Johnny's sister's cure is similar to an ancient one found in *Romanus Büchlein*, an old treatise that contains cures from western and southern Germany. A longer but similar one is from Pennsylvania:

> Job lay among the dung
> As our dear Lord Jesus came along
> "Job, why dost thou mourn?"

"Why should not I be weeping and mourning be?
When my lips and tongue would rot for me?"
Take three straws out of the dung,
Draw them through your mouth along,
And your lips and tongue will again be strong.

> The sick one lies upon the dung and takes three straws out of the manure and draws them through the mouth and says the words about and draws each one through three times until the above words have been spoken. Then he ties them together and hangs them in the chimney.[10]

As a youngster, Johnny Arvin noted a similar cure in his notebook.

Old-timers talk about cow manure poultices. In German folklore, not only cures but also oral traditions—sayings, jokes, rhymes, legends, and songs—are filled with references to manure.[11]

Perhaps the most curious excrement cure, widely documented in West Virginia, is the use of sheep manure tea (sometimes called nanny tea or sheep-nanny tea). It is and was commonly prescribed for curing measles. The folk belief is that measles first break out on the inside of your body and "sheep nanny tea" will cause them to break out on the outside, the important first step toward recovery:

> Jack Mayse: I had big measles. My mother was awful finicky about that stuff. Uncle Steve said—Pop had sheep—to go up and get some of those fresh sheep pills and make a tea out of it and give it to me. I was just a kid and had them big measles and they went back in on me. Oh, my mother, [to her] that was a no no. Anyhow, we done it, and I drank that tea. I was a little rascal. I ain't a-kiddin' you, those big measles, I was welted with 'em.
>
> Waneta Brown: And they come out on him, just thick, and Geraldine had a few up and down her backbone and they settled on Jacks liver and he couldn't play or nothin' all summer.
>
> Jack Mayse: Otherwise, I'd a-died because they went back in on me. Sheep tea now, believe me, nanny pills, brought that out on me.[12]

How these folks know that Jack's measles "went back in on him" and "settled on his liver" is a mystery, but is stated as fact. Folk etiology, the effort to ascribe a reason for an unknown cause of sickness, is at play here. A similar logic is applied to the effect of getting a bump on the head. When the bump swells out, it is believed that the person will be okay. If it does not, it is thought that it may be swelling inward, thus causing damage to the brain.

One Pendleton County man joked that he was given so much sheep manure tea as a child that he "got the habit—had to have the stuff after I got well!"[13]

A *plaster* is a cloth soaked with a home remedy, often granny grease, that is placed on the chest to break up congestion and colds: "Granny grease, it was lamp oil and turpentine and camphor and hog lard and you mixed it all together you see and you get it good and hot and put it on you and put a flannel on him. Get it hot and rub with it."

A granny grease or salve remedy from Pendleton County uses rosin, beeswax, mutton tallow, linseed oil, and camphor.[14] A Randolph County recipe from Dovie Lambert calls for castor oil, soap, elder bark, red clover, timothy, and mutton tallow. She notes, "It would beat any of the store salve." A West Virginia rhyme indicates two of the main ingredients used in these salves or plasters:

> Beeswax and mutton tallow
> Make a good plaster;
> If you rub it in
> It'll work a little faster.[15]

Some people have used bear grease plasters for colds and croup. Another widely known ingredient used by itself or in a plaster is skunk grease—fat that is rendered from a skunk.[16] Mary Cottrell said her mother would rub skunk grease on her nose to reduce stuffiness.[17] Dovie used skunk grease for curing. The use of skunk grease was widespread among Pennsylvania Germans. I believe the skunk replaced the badger for Germans in the New World, as badgers do not naturally occur in Pennsylvania. Although smaller, the skunk favors the badger in appearance with the stripes down the back. In German, a badger is called a *Dach*, the animal for which the dachshund was bred to hunt.[18]

In Germany, people used many parts of the badger for healing and magical purposes, including the fat, in the same ways that skunk grease is used in West Virginia. The badger was also used as a weather predictor in Germany, but in the New World, Pennsylvania Germans substituted the groundhog for this role because skunks, unlike badgers, do not hibernate.[19] February 2 is Groundhog Day, or "Candlemas." Candlemas comes forty days after Christmas and was substituted for Imbolc, a much older northern European, Celtic-related festival that was observed on February 1. The day signaled the end of winter in much of medieval Europe. The Catholic church substituted Candlemas for the old pagan day as the observance of the baby Jesus' presentation at the temple after the forty-day period of purification for mother and child under Hebrew law. German Protestants brought the old weather-predicting tradition to Pennsylvania, where it is still actively observed in some German communities. Groundhogs were substituted for the badger (and bear) traditions of Europe. Now the hibernating groundhog has their supposed powers to predict the weather.

A Braxton County woman I interviewed seemed to invent a new species of parasite in her use of skunk grease and her attempts to make sense of her child's ailment:

> One time, my oldest boy, oh, he must have been seven or eight, maybe nine years old and over at home, Alvin and me got up and oh, he was coughin'. He's just carryin' on high. And that's all I had was skunk grease. See, I'd get skunks and take the inside grease and render it out good. It didn't have no smell about it. So we got him up to the fireplace and got him good and warm and warmed that skunk grease and bathed him in it and kept givin' it to him, and it made him sick. And he threw up a croup-germ that long [indicates over an inch on finger]. It was just like joints, you'd stick two joints together, you've seen them bugs, looks like they're jointed. And you couldn't stick your fork in that![20]

Whatever a "croup germ" is, I do not want any, but it is just one example of an amazing amount of folk interpretation of what in modern times has become medical science. How much good comes out of the more amazing curative actions above is unknown. I am sure the placebo effect comes into play, but with most herbal remedies there have been many generations of trial, error, and use to back them up. More and more, science is determining that traditional cures have some scientific merit. Still, among some older people, puzzling diseases caused by bacteria and viruses remain unexplainable. I am reminded of the Braxton County woman who said she was glad "I got my children raised before all these germs came in fashion."

Magical or metaphysical cures are not all that different from the use of medicinal plant curing in some minds. People have explained the use of medicinal plants to me by naming various cures that involve the use of herbal concoctions, local plants, and home remedies. But as with Dovie and Emogene, without being prompted, these people will go on to mention cures they know about that are beyond any scientific knowledge and are in the realm of the magical or the occult. They regard it as religious practice.

In Pendleton County, a woman who described the use of herbal teas for treatment of various sicknesses also said that a piece of red yarn, worn around the neck, would prevent and cure nosebleed. Another described how a midwife would always bring an ax to a birthing. She would place the ax on the floor under the mother's bed in the belief that it would cut the pains of birth.[21] The color red and the sharpness of the ax are a part of the sympathetic magic in the thought process behind these beliefs.

Johnny Arvin Dahmer noted that his curious neighbors, the Pitsenbargers, often called on witch doctors to cure for them when they had ailments. The Pitsenbargers strongly believed medicinal plants and their usage were related to, not apart from, cures in the magical and occult vein. The traditions involving these plants evolved before scientific explanations were available, but also, to some extent, during the period when that science was becoming known.

Dovie Lambert discussed how to cure the skin disease "wildfire" while talking about the use of herbs for various symptoms; the cure involved killing a black chicken and rubbing its blood on the infected area. I suppose the use of a chicken in this way might be construed as having a possible scientific purpose, but when the color black is specifically introduced and stated in this way, it surely shifts the cure into the realm of the occult. We can not prove that the blood of a black chicken is basically different than the blood of a white or any other color of chicken, and so, if it does not make practical sense, it must have magical usefulness. Color adds a level of importance throughout traditional occult belief, and the color black is often tied to magical methodologies.

Another black chicken cure is used for snakebite. The intestines, not the blood in this case, are used as a poultice. It is believed that the intestines of a black chicken will draw out the snake poison. Otis Rose said the color black was of particular value in this belief as well, although a different body part is used:

> [My brother] got bit with a copperhead one time. He's a-rakin' up hay. Got bit on the arm. Back at that time there wasn't very much that they could do. The older people told him to kill a black chicken, and put it on that, and it would draw the poison out. And they done that. But he was sick for quite a while. And I don't know whether that there black chicken they put on there helped draw it out or not. But now that's what the old people said to do.

Otis said that they also used the breast of the chicken, that they bound it on the wound, but it had to be from a black chicken. This falls under the general heading of "sympathetic magic" described by Frazer as consisting of two forms, homeopathic and contagious. Contagious magic adheres to the law of contact.[22]

Black is an important color in some of the old Pendleton County cures. A charm used to "be liked by other people" instructs, "Take the heart of a black raven or wolf, put it in a frame. Tie it around you, that is good. It is also good when you carry the heart of a dove or swallow with you."[23]

Another cure of contagious magic instructs that the color black be used for atrophy: "Take a knife on which there are three crosses. Take as much bread as can be put into the knife. Then place it under the head of the patient so that he can sleep on it over night. Then take the bread and give it to a black dog to eat. The dog is going to die but the patient is going to be cured."[24]

A widely known belief is that if, during a drought, a black snake is killed and hung over a fence, belly side up, it will rain within three days.[25] Otis Rose told me:

> Once it was so dry, you know, we'd mow the grass and it'd just turn brown—and I killed a black snake. One of the boys was workin' there, and he said, "I'm goin' to hang this thing up."
> I said, "Okay." And he hung it up. In about two days, we had plenty of rain! Now I don't know whether it was the snake that done it, or whether it was just the good Lord seen fit to send it to us.[26]

It seems to Otis that either way, it was a supernatural event.

I once saw a dead crow hung from a long bending pole over a cornfield in a backwoods area in central West Virginia. I am not sure if it was simply to deter other crows from stealing corn or if it had some deeper purpose involving the color black. I could not find anyone to ask.

Dovie noted that the disease wildfire starts as a small red spot on the skin and increases in size:

> It'd start just in a little red place and it just starts keepin' a-goin', getting bigger and bigger, bigger and bigger, bigger and bigger. And old people claim—wildfire—they claim if it got big enough to cover your heart, it'd kill you. And we'd take a black chicken and cut its head off, and smear that blood on that there . . . and it'd kill it. But it has to be a black chicken.[27]

Wildfire is the skin disease erysipelas, a streptococcal infection characterized by inflammation and redness of the skin in round or oval patches. In Germany it was also known as St. Anthony's fire, or *Das versegnt*, but also *wildfire*. Dovie's Randolph County cure specifies that a black chicken be used. In Pendleton County another clearly magical cure for erysipelas/wildfire was known. The afflicted person had to strip off all clothing, kneel down in front of a fireplace, and face away from it. Nine matches were struck in groups of three and then thrown over the shoulder into the fireplace while the afflicted person said, "In the name of the Father, Son, and Holy Ghost" for each group of three.[28]

Painful "shingles" can often appear on a person's waist. Dovie Lambert believes that if they go completely around the body and join, they will kill you. We have to guess that in people's minds, being afflicted in these various ways is more complex than the simple bacterial, viral, or chemical reaction causing the skin problem. The cause of the disease is probably placed in the occult realm, within the province of evil, with witchery suspected. William May once told me that there are one hundred ways for a witch to put a spell on you, but there are only ninety-nine ways to remove the spell.[29] Emogene Nichols believes that God provides a natural cure for everything, if only that cure can be found. Others attest that the cure is not limited to the scientific sense, but may be in the occult realm as well.

Of all the cures that fit into the vein of magical belief, stopping blood is the most common in West Virginia. Emogene Nichols hints that belief or faith is an important ingredient in any cure. Besides stopping blood, she also mentioned belief-oriented cures for "taking out burns." These cures exist alongside herbal remedies, explained almost in the same breath. I really do not think there is a difference in Emogene's mind. Whatever scientific principle governs the beneficial effects of a herbal cure is just as mysterious as a belief-oriented method. In cases in which biblical verses are used to "stop blood" or "take out" burns, the power is attributed to God. Some German American curers claimed they could "blow" the fire out of burns while invoking Scripture.[30] A man from Sugar Grove in Pendleton County was known to cure poison oak by quoting a Bible verse.[31]

Stopping blood is quite common. Many elderly rural people know of the cure, have been the recipient of the cure, or have the knowledge themselves to cure others. The Bible verse that is invoked in the cure is Ezekiel 16:6. The cures for stopping blood, taking out burns, taking out frost (frostbite), and so on may only be passed to a person of the opposite sex. Several women have given me knowledge of the verse as a gift, because I am a man (and I was curious about the cure).

Mary Cottrell explains her experience with stopping blood:

> I can stop that. In Ezekiel. It's right in the Bible. "When I passed by thee and you was polluted in your blood, I said live!" And you say the person's name, and say that nine times.
> I had a boy fell at school and cut his tongue [and it was] bleeding. And I said that and the blood just stopped right now. If you say

it too fast it makes you sick. But if you're out someplace and someone cuts theirself and you say that, it stops the blood. I can tell a man . . . and she can tell a man, or he can tell a woman, but you don't say it for the same sex.

Blood stopping has made the transition into today's technological world, as some blood stoppers perform their cures over the telephone, as was explained to me:

> Now [a woman] called in here at eleven o'clock one night. And she said, Waneta, [a woman] is a-hemorrhaging to death, would you stop blood? I said, well can't you do it. She said, I ain't got that much faith. So . . . I knew her all my life . . . so I asked her her name and all. I can't remember anything, I read it off. I carry it [the written verse] with me all the time. I read it off two or three times. The next day at two o'clock [she] called. That was unusual. [She] said Waneta, she said they called back and they said that [she] was just fine that she stopped hemorrhaging right now. But she said, "I didn't have the faith."
>
> I believe in all that stuff. I could tell you but I couldn't tell her [another woman]. Now the first I used that, Leroy was here and he had a pup. And I wouldn't let him keep it in the house, so they went up to the shed to sleep, and he cut his leg like this [slashes at her leg]. The blood was just a-streaming, all over the place. That's the first time I ever tried it. Well, I thinks I better try to stop that. I got that much faith. I'm no Jehovah['s Witness] or nothin', but I can help that with faith. When they got him into the hospital, Doctor Hoylman said to him, he said, "I don't understand." He said, "It's cut that there artery and the blood's just a-layin' there."
>
> Leroy said, "I don't know, it just quit all at once." Well, I never told a soul.
>
> We was out here on the ridge past High Knob at a homemakers meetin'. And they said they wanted somebody to come and give [a neighbor] some blood, she's floodin' to death. And I thinks well, good Lord, I can stop that. I just got that piece of paper and held it up in front of me like I's readin'.
>
> And they called back and said, "She done quit—she's perfect now, a miracle happened, but they didn't know how."[32]

An examination of Johnny Arvin's great-great-grandfather's "cure book" or manuscript brought from Germany[33] shows that most of the cures are akin to those found in the ancient text *Egyptian Secrets*. It was translated to English from German in 1856, long after some of its occult cures, as in the Dahmer manuscript, came to the New World and made it to the frontier.[34]

Only a few cures found in the Dahmer manuscript show up in the German powwow book, the *Long Lost Friend*, well known in Pennsylvania.[35] Many Pennsylvania Germans were opposed to the use of this book and because of its occult methodologies refused to touch it. They proposed the curious notion that if this book was kept in one's house, crows would congregate nearby or on the roof. One in the flock would be a disguised witch.[36]

The first cure in the Dahmer cure book is dedicated to removing evil spirits:

> When man or beast is attacked by evil spirits, follows
>   how they can be helped:
> Arch sorcerer (witch) you have attacked the n.n.
> Go away from him in your marrow and in your bone
> So go back where you come from
> I conjure you for the five wounds of Jesus, you evil spirit
> I conjure you for the five wounds of Jesus
> I conjure you for the five wounds of Jesus at this hour
> Keep this n.n. healthy again
> In the name of the God, the Father, and the Son and the
>   Holy Ghost.

The eleventh and twelfth cures are for wildfire, showing that Dovie's colloquial name for the disease has its origins in Germany:

> Against wildfire on people or animals, wildfire, gangrene, fles [sic], pain, rushing blood, and mortification. The Lord encompass you. Beware! The Lord is the highest. In spite of you, he will draw you away, wilfire [sic], gangrene, pain, rushing blood and mortification. +++

The twelfth cure reads:

> Against wildfire. Go away wildfire, gangrene or mortification. Leave your burning. God keep you, n.n., your flesh, your blood, your marrow, your leg and all your veins, that should be guarded and kept safe from gangrene and mortification.

This is followed by these instructions:

> blowing To be said three times with the name of the three holiest names and every time over the wound.

The three crosses at the end of this cure indicate the invocation of the Father, Son, and Holy Ghost. These names are often referred to as "the three highest names."

Albertus (c. 1200–1280 c.e.), from whom, evidently, many of these old cures descend, was a Dominican monk. His *Egyptian Secrets* affected folk cures that transcended time and space and are to be found today in Pendleton County. He also wrote treatises on the magical properties of minerals and plants and was a supporter of what has come to be known as *natural magic*, or the folk magic described herein.[37]

Several people told me they can cure *sweeny*, a word not found in most dictionaries. The *Oxford English Dictionary* associates the word with German dialect and gives its meaning as "emaciation" or "atrophy." I have heard it used most often in reference to an affliction of horses, but Dovie knew a cure for people:

> There's a verse in the Bible where you can, ah, say you have sweeny.
> You know what it is? Well, if you have sweeny in your knee, your
> knee will just—sweeny away, nothing but the bone and the skin.
> There's a verse in the Bible that you can—rub that person. They call
> it sweeny, that's what it's named, sweeny, in the Bible. And there's a
> verse in there you can stop blood. And there's a verse in there you can
> doctor the devil. It's all in the Bible.

Dovie says that you "rub that person." This and similar references elsewhere in this book refer to the Christian practice of laying on of hands. This is very common in German folk cures.

With "doctor the devil," Dovie is describing her method of writing a ticket, her religio-magical (witch doctoring) way of blocking and cursing an offender through imitative reversal. In her mind it depends on faith to make it work.

On Brushy Fork in Pendleton County, horses were cured of sweeny through the following charm:

> Sweeny, I want you to leave,
> Out of the marrow into the bone,
> Out of the bone into the flesh,
> Out of the flesh into the hide,
> Out of the hide into the hair,
> Out of the hair into three quarters of the earth
> In the name of the Father, the Son, and Holy Ghost.

The three highest names are to be repeated three times, it being no accident that the number three is a powerful number.[38] Among Pennsylvania German folk practitioners almost this exact charm was used, but it had to be done in a waning moon, early in the morning, and without speaking to anyone.[39] Silence is necessary to the efficacy of many cures I have found in Pendleton County. Perhaps it adds to the solemnity of the charm, ritualizes it in a sacred way, and shows a reverence for the invocation itself. The same might be said of the more rare insistence on nakedness.

In 1975, I befriended an old couple in Randolph County, Leonard and Blanch Brake (Anglicized from the German Brechtel). I questioned Leonard about how people made apple cider in that neighborhood. I had seen a large old oak tree in the neighborhood with a twelve-inch hole pierced through it about six feet off the ground. Leonard said the hole was used as a fulcrum to put a pole through for leverage to press the juice out of apple pumice. But Leonard went on to tell me that the tree had another use in the community. Sick babies were taken there and passed through three times to cure them of various illnesses.

Leonard had been struck directly by lightening while working in a field in his younger days. He was actually pronounced dead at the time but "woke up" and was okay, except for having slurred speech for the rest of his life. No doubt this event caused him to be of some status in the supernatural folklore of the neighborhood, to the extent that his help and participation in passing the babies through the hole in the tree was deemed significant. An old-timer, in later life when he and his wife acquired a television, Leonard was convinced that anyone on the screen could see him. He never even walked through the room in his underwear because of this, according to his wife.

There is something considered magical about certain natural and unnatural places and objects, as in the instance above where babies or children can be passed through objects to their benefit. In Pendleton County, babies were passed through a horse collar to be cured of livergrown. As I understand it, livergrown (Awachse) is a supposed ailment whereby the liver attaches itself (or grows) to the ribs. It was thought to strike when young babies were taken in carriages over rough roads. As with sensing when measles go "back in" on people, this seems a case in which people have some sixth sense to discern internal abnormalities. Babies were put through the wooden hopper over the burrstones at the old Mitchell (Mischler) Mill while they were grinding. Johnny Arvin remembers they had to be put through the hopper backward, three times. It was also thought that the fine flour powder or dust in the air would help cure whooping cough.

Curious notions about the body abound among older country people. A woman told me that a friend scratched his eye with a thorn and "all the sight leaked out of it." An old man in Braxton County told me his grandfather died of "heart leakage."

Another Pendleton County health concern was undergrowth. A flax thread was used to measure certain distances on the body (around the head, etc.), then a loop was made of the entire thread and the child was passed through it nine times. The thread was then placed some-where where it would rot or

Mitchell Mill, Pendleton County.

decay (usually under the eaves of the house). When the thread decayed, the undergrowth was overcome.[40]

In many documented cures in German folk culture a child is passed through some unusual object to effect the cure. The object could be a horse collar or a hole in a tree, as mentioned, or even a hole under a berry vine that had bent down and taken root.[41] It is thought that when a natural object grows or is shaped so as to make a hollow passage in an unnatural way, this passage will magically affect those passed through it (usually three or three times three times).

In Pendleton County, attempts to cure a child of a hernia involved a process in which a white oak sapling was split while on the stump, the split spread apart, and, early in the morning, the child was put through it three times.[42]

Dovie mentioned other situations in which a verse in the Bible is used in occult cures. She connected her "doctor the devil" cure with witchery. Indeed, Dovie's invocation of biblical passages, not only for specific cures but also as a literal text infused with occult methodologies, has a great bearing on her folk spirituality and her relationship to the occult. No doubt the many magical and supernatural references in the Bible—Moses parting the water, Joshua's destruction of the walls of Jericho, Jesus multiplying the loaves and fishes and changing the water into wine—are to Dovie magical occurrences that prove meaningful within sacred text. She states that whatever unusual happenings occurred "in the Bible" surely still occur in the present.

I do not underestimate the power of thought, faith, or trust. For that matter, we need to recognize that science can not answer every question. Perhaps one day it will, but until then, if holding a belief supplies any relief or positive energy to an afflicted person, so be it. This is the reasoning given for the continuation of dubious folk cures. Faith and folk healers of occult or religious persuasion do not need results to justify their means. Their faith makes them believers, and belief, in their minds, is enough to justify their actions.

Chapter 13

Healers and Granny Women

That all good minds would grow keen
To serve thee alone;
Holy virgin, mother, queen,
Goddess on thy throne!
—Goethe

Belief in instances of women taking "night flights" to secret gatherings have been documented back to at least the tenth century. At that time, however, there was little or no mention of evil, black magic, Satan, or the profanity associated with these occurrences in the later phase of witchcraft that was induced by the Inquisition. It was believed these early gatherings were presided over by a feminine deity who was variously known as Diana, Herodias, Holda, or Perchta.[1]

Scholars have numerous theories regarding the European origins of American witchcraft. Traditions I have found in Appalachian West Virginia favor central European/Germanic sources, which have grown out of the whole gamut of the European experience. A strong case is made that witchcraft in central Europe originated within a fertility cult that was largely feminine in nature and reached back to well before the eleventh century. Russell says the shift from the essentially positive practices of the early fertility cults that encouraged fruitful and plentiful agrarian practices in the Middle Ages to the classical, diabolical witchcraft of the fifteenth through the seventeenth centuries was unconscious and without structure and organization.[2]

Witchcraft in the Middle Ages sprang from older pagan belief, the definitions of which were solidifying by 1232. At that time, Pope Gregory IX, in a letter addressed to Henry, king of Germany, cited numerous trappings and fantastic concepts that even today are generally found in the popular image of the witch. Frogs, toads, black cats, shape-shifted animals, familiars, animistic versions of the devil, obscene sexual practices of witches, and the blaspheming of accepted Christian practice are found in this letter.[3]

Familiars are usually represented as black cats in Appalachian folklore.[4] These creatures, and other diabolic beliefs of classical, Continental witchcraft, like nocturnal gatherings, are rare among the Anglo/Celts.[5] Even before these entities were documented in the German king's thirteenth-century letter, it was believed that while the Norse god Odin lay asleep, various deeds were accomplished by his soul in the form of a bird, animal, fish, or serpent, perhaps an early explanation of the concept of familiars.[6] Circe, the sorceress of classical literature, was widely depicted in fifteenth-century illustrations transforming men into beasts. This is a prominent scene in Homer's Odyssey and in the works of other classical writers.[7] This, too, is evident in Appalachian folklore and beliefs regarding magical revelations about toads, black cats, and serpents.

Acceptance of magical phenomena and the existence of "cunning" people continues today, despite the fact that modern science debunks such powers and beliefs. In the past, most unexplained phenomena were accepted as magical occurrence. Today they might have rational explanations. Many of the "witches," so named in hundreds of Appalachian folk tales, were no more than herbalists, curers, or the equivalent of Appalachian granny women.

The existence of magicians, diviners, sorcerers, cunning folk, and other such occult practitioners was a generally accepted fact of life going back to the Old Testament. Many Appalachian folkloric methods of divining one's future (who you will marry, etc.) involve rituals that use the Bible. Sometimes a random page was selected for clues or the Bible was placed under the pillow, revealing the suitor's name in a dream.[8] Here, the Bible is not only a sacred book but also, because of that power, is used in magical ways, quite apart from any established church practice.

Roeber closely ties the practice of healer/midwives on the frontier to German tradition. He tracks the practice in Pennsylvania, where he finds a sustained medieval religious paradigm prevalent among women who struggle to maintain conjuring, divining, and curing traditions in the face of rapid social, legal, and scientific advancement.[9]

There is a need to put a face on evil, so it is sometimes humanized and personalized in order to confront it and make it better understood. With men in all the powerful positions of authority and a tradition of misogyny in the church, it was convenient that women should fill that need. Especially sought were those who were thought to be in touch with magical powers, as were the herbalists, granny women, and curing agents of the countryside.

The patriarchal system of the inquisitional period brought about the universal association of witches with women.[10] Before acceptance of a male-gendered Judeo-Christian God, paying homage to and having ties to goddesses was widespread in the Western world. Later, this threatening scenario led to the popular notion of the witch as an old and ugly hag like the Greek Stringla,[11] not the beautiful goddess of earlier times. Today, among the masses, the stereotypical witch is relegated to Halloween custom and costume. But some, as my sources outline here, still have a more serious and traditional notion of witchery. They recognize witches not by their (often comic) stereotypical pointed hats and black clothes but by their presumed actions. They regard witches with a fearful deep respect and often avoid dealing with them.

Throughout history women have first made breakthroughs in obtaining equality, or at least a higher status, through the arts. Perhaps the magical arts were such a threat to the male domination of church and state that women were singled out for retribution. Germanic cultural traits put the onus on women as the witches. They became the prime suspects of this "scourge" on society. Inquisitors searched their bodies for "witchmarks," moles and skin blemishes that when pricked, did not bleed—sure proof of a witch.

Commonly, the European and, in particular, the Germanic tradition is that women play the leading role in witchcraft. It was women, according to men of the church, that made pacts and had sexual relations with the devil, who then forced them into their nocturnal roles of doing and spreading evil. Originally, night rides were believed to be taken by both sexes to positive effect regarding agrarian pursuits.[12] Night rides by the benandanti, people who opposed harmful witchery, well documented in court cases from Italy, protected the crops against the evil forces. In a sense, it was the "green," good, or white magic, practiced by women in these early documented European cases, that has been twisted to represent evil and the dark side of occult belief in the thinking of men. During the Inquisition, possibly the only recourse for tortured women in terms of gender was to implicate men at their confessions, which they often did.

Of all the regions touched by the great witch-hunts and panics of the Inquisition, it was the Germanic areas where women, as opposed to men, took the huge brunt of the blame. This was true in the New World as well. Johnny Arvin Dahmer concludes, "It seems women are accused more of being witches around here than men. But men could be too, you know."[13] This tendency to accuse women more than men is the result of a longstanding practice of misogyny in Germany and in Christianity as a whole,[14] and it has filtered down to traditional Appalachian belief today.

In Europe, midwives were often thought to be witches. Some suppose that it was convenient to blame failures in delivery on the witchcraft practiced by the midwife.[15] The fifteenth-century text *Malleus Maleficarum* (*The Witches Hammer*), which was commissioned by the pope in 1486, aided this thinking.

Dana Keplinger, a Pendleton County woman of German descent, notes the existence of many herbal healers and granny women whom she feels were unfairly considered to be witches by the public there. Had they lived in a different time and place, these women would have suffered considerably more than the relatively mild injustice of name-calling and ostracism. While including herself, Dana says,

> We dealt with the green side of life. Nanny Yankee [from the German, *Jenkje*] lived there on the south side of Petersburg, in a little house, and it was said that she cured warts and cured people. She delivered a lot of babies and cured people of diseases, and they called her a witch, but see to me—that's not the way you should look at it. She was a healer.[16]

When Dana says she and other herbal healers "dealt with the green side of life," she is explaining what is now being understood about the origins of European witchery. It had its beginnings in the agrarian or "green" realm of the early Middle Ages. Fertility and the powers that controlled fertility were the great positive force of nature. Through the efforts to support fecundity and fertility, crops and livestock would increase and be protected from evil forces. This view of life has been reinvented today in various new age movements.

Fifteenth-century literature such as the *Malleus Maleficarum* denounced witchcraft and stirred the great witch-hunts of Europe, especially in Germany. The Inquisition affected the tradition and world view of early German immigrants to Pennsylvania. These settlers brought distinct ideas and folk variants of occult traditions with them. In Europe by the late seventeenth century, skepticism about witchcraft was increasing among the educated classes, but witchcraft was firmly established in the minds of country folk. German peasant immigrants brought it along with their folk art and traditional agrarian background to the New World.

Through time, printed works offering information on how to recognize witches, become witches, and combat witchcraft through both religious and secular methodologies were widely disseminated. Even on the frontier, settlers of German descent had access to occult tracts offering methods of combating evil forces through religio-magical means. It has been observed that the nonliterate descendants of German immigrants not only took up and preserved occult lore through oral tradition but also added variety through the folk process and produced their own magical incantations and evocations of remarkable poetic power.[17]

With the change in language from German to English, much of the literary aspect of folk tradition dissolved and oral tradition became the predominant means by which folklore was disseminated and preserved. I propose that this shift to oral tradition is a factor in the amount and depth of the folklore from Germanic sources that I present here.

Chapter 14

Women and Witchery

Enmeshed by superstition, we're forlorn:
For things will happen, and forebode, and warn.
—Goethe

Magic played an important role in the lives of our ancestors. Erotic magic was widely believed and understood as a form of binding magic during the Renaissance. At this time, it was thought that love was a form of natural magic,[1] not just a biological attraction. A magical term still used (lightly) in this sense is *charm*, as when people to say that a member of the opposite sex is charming. The same term can be used in a more serious way, as when someone says that a snake can charm people or make them act in an unnatural way, a widespread belief in West Virginia folklore.[2]

Love charms, in the sense that they are spoken to invoke some power that will reveal or influence one's future love, may still be found, as in this West Virginia example:

> Walk to the garden in the light of the first quarter of the new moon. Take a white cotton handkerchief or a piece of cloth with you. Spread it out on the ground and squat down, positioning yourself so that the new moon is visible over your left shoulder and say:
>
>> New moon, true moon,
>> Pray tell unto me,
>> Who it is my true love shall be.
>> The color of his eyes and hair,
>> Show me in my sleep tonight.
>
> As you say this chant, scoop three handfuls of dirt and place them in your handkerchief. Tie the handkerchief into a bundle and walk backwards to the house without speaking. Put the bundle under your pillow and go directly to sleep. That night you will dream of your true love. The next morning untie the bundle and sift through

the dirt with your fingers. There you will find a hair from the head of the man you will marry.[3]

Aspects of this love charm, as in keeping the new moon over your left shoulder while going through the ritual, hearken back to veneration practices associated with the goddess Hecate. Hecate was the Greek goddess of the moon and of crossroads who was associated with witchcraft. The "Hecate cult" is even older and is believed to have originated in Asia Minor.[4] Some think that the word hex may be derived from the name Hecate.[5]

Some of the erotic and sexual aspects of witchcraft, and there are many, may have their beginnings in the repressive psychological mind-set brought about in inquisitional Europe. At this time, any open expression or acceptance of such behavior was driven underground. Some think that among the New England Puritans, and others, the revelation of bizarre sexual conduct was a projection of the questioning official's repressed libido and twisted puritanical mind. It may well be the case, as this allowed for open expression of hideous desires, achieved vicariously through witches by witch accusers and persecutors.[6] The Inquisition originally was undertaken to root out heretics; perhaps witches were just the logical next step in the effort to rid the world of the ungodly. The pious zealotry of the religious leaders of the period surely begat many of the bizarre beliefs attributed to innocent "witches" of the period.[7]

Johnny Arvin Dahmer's description of an instance of late night debauchery in which the devil made his appearance (although he did not want to go into great detail) fits the mold of nocturnal witch gatherings where unspeakable activity went on:

> Hell-bound parties, he called them—at night, you know. He was a Lutheran preacher and he didn't believe in that stuff. And there at that house they were having a great big time that night, a-way late in the night. I don't know what they was a-doin' you know, you'd have to guess. It must have been . . . not nice! And, ah, all of the sudden— they must have all been up—the door opened, and the devil walked in! They said he had chains . . . rattling chains. And he had horns! They said he didn't say anything, he just walked in and looked at 'em, and walked back out. Oh, it scared 'em powerful! And they said you could smell sulfur a-burnin' too! Smell sulfur a-burnin'.[8]

The descriptions made by accused witches under the influence of torture went into great detail about the lewd behavior of witches. Johnny's modesty perhaps prevents him from a more detailed explanation here. He

116

said, "It must have been . . . not nice," implying something despicable. The old abandoned log house where this event took place is still well known in the neighborhood as a place where witchery went on.

Johnny describes the devil in a folk-related animistic physical form here (with horns, rattling chains, etc.). Renaissance artists rendered the devil using such a caricature in attempts to artistically capture this complex antagonist. Medieval theologians developed his elaborate multifaceted existence in their attempts to portray and embody evil. The devil incarnate is commonly found in Appalachian folk tales as well as in Pennsylvania German lore.[9]

Inquisitors demanded to know the sexual nature of the accused witch's actions at the trials. They were able to torture accused witches into confessing to just about anything they could dream up and suggest in the way of indecent behavior. In doing this, authorities were also responding to demands of the lower classes to root out a perceived evil within society.[10]

The early Middle Age agrarian origins of witchcraft, with its many examples of fertility rites encompassing a sexual interchange with nature, suggest positive origins for much of this behavior. Later, however, this was seen as lurid and negative. In these earlier times, the sexual aspects of life assisted nature and were not seen, in the religious sense, as unrestrained evils of the flesh but as a strong, positive, natural force that provided a legitimate reason for existence.

Fertility rites were important events on which life depended. Early practitioners were not thought to be lewd or obscene; they were seen as the protectors and promoters of the general well-being. The main reason for these early nocturnal gatherings, so they thought, was fertility in general, and the rituals, in fact, precisely coincided with the agricultural calendar.[11] May Day observances provided an opportunity to claim victory over darkness and celebrate life. Well into the mid-twentieth century, maypoles were erected in numerous communities around West Virginia, festive events celebrated Mother Nature, and "May Queens" were chosen.[12]

As late as the early to mid-twentieth century in this country, folklorists were documenting ancient fertility traditions believed to have Old World sources. People engaged in the sexual act in newly planted fields and gardens in order to ensure a fertile environment and a productive harvest.[13] Native American women sometimes encircled a newly planted field, while naked, to assist germination. A similar practice was documented among Pennsylvania Germans. A young, pubescent girl and boy encircled a newly planted field together, and, it was said, it soon rained and the germination was vigorous.[14]

Inevitably, the remnants of ancient fertility rituals surfaced at the witch trials of the later witch-hunting period, giving them their negative aspect when held up to biblical scrutiny. A common example, in the seventeenth century, caused inquisitor Ignazio Lupo to assert in a circulated treatise that witches commonly gathered on certain days on a certain mountain to "adore the devil and indulge in orgies."[15]

During the Inquisition, women being questioned commonly described how, or affirmed the suggestion that, they flew through the air on special nights to join in the Sabbat with the devil, engage in sexual licentiousness, and fly home before daybreak, so as not to arouse suspicion. Since these confessions all came after or under the threat of torture, it is hard to believe that the church's inquisitors could not discern that these fantastic tales of indiscretion were illusory flights of fantasy. However, today it is hard to realize the full extent of a literal, prescientific world view. While the term witch-hunt is casually thrown around these days, the brutality of the actual historical event is unthinkable.

There is an ancient but well-documented belief that witches can render a man impotent through magical means. This was a prevalent belief in seventeenth-century Germany.[16] The spell often involved what is known as ligature. Usually, a symbolic knot is tied in some lace during a marriage ceremony, and thus, through imitative magic, it renders the groom impotent.[17] Ligature is common in historic witchcraft, and belief in it extends back to before the Christian era. Virgil, the Roman poet, writing in the first century B.C.E, speaks of this symbolic knotting method of affecting copulation.[18]

Johnny Dahmer remembered an event in his neighborhood concerning his great grandfather, the witch doctor Joel Dahmer, that seems connected to these ancient practices. Whatever the exact cause of impotence was in this instance is unknown to Johnny, however, it was believed to be an instance of witchcraft: "A man came one time and said his penis wouldn't stand. He [Joel Dahmer] said he could help that. What he did I don't know, but I do remember talk about that. It worked."[19]

Joel apparently cured for a wide variety of ailments, according to Johnny Arvin. Another man who "couldn't make his water," which was most likely a prostate problem, came to him to be cured. Joel went through his magic, "said some words," and cured the man, whose yell of relief upon the start of his urine flow could be heard a long ways off.[20]

Johnny Arvin's great-great grandfather had the following cure for incontinence in his cure book: "Take a talon of a buck, burn it to a powder and give it to him (the afflicted person) to drink as a beverage."

Dovie Lambert told me a story of a supernatural occurrence in which a cousin, thought to be a witch, was accused of sexual lewdness. Before this man arrived at an aunt's house one day, a "hairball," thought to be an omen of evil (see below), was seen. Dovie said that when that happened, she said "some words" under her breath. Only minutes went by before a man came to the house. (This belief, that by performing, saying, or invoking some words of power, the witch, devil, or perpetrator will magically appear, is common in both New and Old World occult tradition.) Dovie said that the man showed up and asked her aunt if she would like to "go to hell with me."

Her aunt asked, "Where in the hell are you going to take me?" To which the man replied, "I want to take you out into the woods and sex you all day!" The aunt kicked him out of the house but wondered why he had come at that time. Dovie then told her that she had seen the hairball, had said the verse/cure (words of power) under her breath, and that he had shown up within minutes—a common response that provides a way to break the spell.[21] She later said that she thought they had the devil in the house (in the person of the man who came in).[22]

Mary Cottrell reported an instance of contagious magic, sexual in nature, involving a man's spouse and some local witchery: "His wife was running around. She said, 'You get me a lock of her hair and I'll stop her.' So [this man] took a scissors and got a lock of hair from [this woman] and give it to his mother. She never went out no more."[23]

This story supports an old belief that if one can get possession of a person's hair or fingernails, they can, through sorcery or magic, have control over that person. Dana Keplinger reported the common practice of burying all hair and fingernails, especially from her babies, so "the evils couldn't get a hold of it." She said, "It's a spirit thing."[24]

Conversely, there is a love charm in West Virginia whereby a witch instructs girls to get a piece of hair, a piece of fingernail, and a piece of the shirt the one she loves wears, then to sew this in a heart-shaped bag and wear it under their clothes. This will charm the boy, but he must never discover it was done or the resulting marriage will fail.[25] These uses of fingernails, as with hair and so forth, are clearly forms of contagious magic that are also widely found in the black conjure tradition.[26]

Brooms are almost always involved where witchery is present, and often in sexual ways. There was an early example of accused witches claiming to apply a special magical salve or "unguent" to a broomstick. The naked witches in early depictions fly off to their nighttime meetings or the Sabbat. The salve entering the female body was thought to provide the supernatural wherewithal to make the flight.

Brooms are still important to those on guard against witchcraft in West Virginia folk magic. The most common belief is that a witch cannot cross over a broom.[27] A householder would leave a broom lying across the doorway. If a person picked up the broom upon entering, her secret would be revealed. Dovie recalled her mother using this method: "She always laid the broom down across the door. And she always claimed if that one was a witch, when they come in, they'd pick the broom up."

People in Johnny Arvin's neighborhood remember that a superstitious neighbor always kept a broom across the path to his door or at the doorway. Some remember a broom over the door as well. In Pendleton and Randolph Counties, brooms were used to prevent or at least single out witches as they entered a house. The brooms themselves are often considered magical objects, as when witches ride them or when they are used as amulets to ward off witches. They show up in various forms of folklore relating to love, as in this rhyming play-party I heard in Randolph County:

> Here comes the old chimney sweeper,
> He has but one daughter and he can't keep her;
> So join your right hands and this broomstick step over,
> And take a sweet kiss from your own true lover.

Jumping the broom is a euphemism for getting married, and lore about brooms (sometimes called *besoms*), is found in both black and white traditions.

Gravestone with a tree of life, South Fork, Grant County.

Women and Witchery

Chapter 15

Witch Doctors

Life is a battleground.
—Carl Jung

Sometime before 1950, a Pendleton County farmer experienced a rash of bad luck. Thinking his farm was under a spell, he called in Charlie Moats, the son/apprentice of renowned witch doctor, Ben Moats. Charlie felt the farmer was compelled to make a serious sacrifice. Under Charlie's direction, they hog-tied one of the farmer's young calves, which they thought bewitched, built up a sizable bonfire, and, after "muttering" some incantations, burned the calf alive.[1]

The concept of sacrifice goes back to prehistory, is prominent in the Judaic roots of Christianity, and is still a part of primitive culture and religion the world around. Consider the widely known tradition of selling your soul to the devil in order to become a masterful fiddler.[2] African American blues musician Robert Johnson sang about going "down to the crossroad" to make a pact with the devil.[3] The German figure Johannes Faustus made his deal with the devil and paid with his soul, according to (re)writers, who based their work on the Faustian legends, widely spread throughout Europe. Scotland produced the legend of Dr. Fian, their Doctor Faustus, who gave his soul to the devil but only confessed this under torture.[4] Faustus gets credit for a German pamphlet, attributed to a Dr. Fausti, the title of which translates as *The Black Raven; or, Good and Bad Spirits Appearing in the Spectre of Raven*. It made its way to this country with early Germans and was eventually translated to English.

Sacrifice was foremost in the mind of Pendleton County witch doctor Charlie Moats. He had decided, based on traditional practice, that the sacrifice of a calf was the only way to "burn the witch off," as Johnny Arvin puts it, and rid this farm of an oppressive evil curse.[5] The calf was thought to be bewitched, because of acting curiously, and in effect was thought to represent the general curse under which the farm was being controlled. In Johnny Arvin's words, burning the calf was the same as burning the witch. It is an incredible example of medieval thought processes at play in a mid-twentieth-century Appalachian community.

Within these traditions, the sacrificial concept is used to remove a curse on animals or, in Moats's case, a whole farm. A similar event in which cows were thought bewitched because they were giving "ropy milk" is recorded in Pocahontas County, West Virginia, from the late nineteenth century. A calf was burned alive to cure the witchery and stop the curse.[6] Other early similar reports by McWhorter of sacrificial actions on the Virginia frontier include the burning of a pig and a horse.

There are underlying reasons why Charlie Moats and other witch doctors decided to destroy a valuable animal for the betterment of a farm. Sacrificial practice is all through the Bible, both Old and New Testaments, and is commemorated through the sacrament of Holy Communion. It is still known today in various ways in folk and conventional wisdom. Proverbial sayings tell us, "You reap just what you sow" or, with a more modern twist, "No pain, no gain." When burning the calf, Moats acted out of respect for local tradition, acceptance of a traditional response, and, perhaps, with an ignorance of scientific understanding but within a frame of mind whereby he had no doubt that what he was doing was a positive thing. If the curse on this farm was imagined, this cure, based on traditional knowledge, could easily remove that imaginary curse.

Many of the occult folk healers in Pendleton County insisted on a small amount of money in exchange for their witch doctoring. Johnny Arvin stated that this payment was very important to effect the cure. He described an encounter he had with "Gilly" Pitsenbarger:

> I had to take him to Franklin. He wanted to see a doctor. I took him down—I was going to take him down—and I asked Mabel, "What's wrong with Gilly? Why does he want to go to a doctor?" She kind of shuffled her feet and didn't want to tell me. "Well," I said, "it's something, what's a-bothering him? He looks all right. Why does he have to go to the doctor?"
>
> "Oh," she said—see he's taking back after his Daddy—she said, "This old thing across the hill is a-riding him." The witch was a-riding him—the old thing across the hill.
>
> I took him to Franklin, and you know who he wanted to see— to go to the doctor? He wanted to see one of these Moats up here in Moatstown. He didn't call him Moats. It was someone come in there. He is a kind of peculiar looking man. I could tell you his name but I won't right now. I asked [Gilly] about that.

"Oh," he said, "he went there, and he had to place a little money in his hand first." He placed a little money in his hand. Then he mumbled some words, and he had strong enough faith, it helped him. He didn't go to a doctor. See, it come down in the family. See how it was brought down in the family? I just questioned him a little about that, you see. See I was getting to an age . . . getting curious about this. I could drive a car then.[7]

Once again, Johnny's interest in local folkways and belief drove him to inquire about local occult practices. His inquiry demonstrates his exceptional perception and appreciation of local occult experiences. Johnny carefully stressed that money is involved in the "cure business," though the actual amount of money is irrelevant. What is important is that some small sacrifice is made.

In Europe, there are documented cases in which people who believed they were bewitched offered the suspected witch money to heal them, thus effecting a method of blackmail.[8] In another account recalled by Johnny Arvin, the witch doctor specifically requested payment be made in order for the cure to work, as in this recollection about his great grandfather:

George Van Devender came from Smith Creek up for him to cure for him. He's a poor man, didn't have any money. Well Joel said to him, "I have to have a little money to keep the devil off." Well, George looked in his pocket. He had ten cents. [Joel] said, "Well, that'll do." And he cured for him. I think he helped him. I don't know what he's a-curin' for.

Johnny Arvin recalled that Ben Moats once said, "Curing was a good way to put meat on the table." Robert Simmons said that Ben Moats and other witch doctors fooled people for money, and he added that in that respect they are like medical doctors today (who charge people exorbitant amounts for dubious services).

It is thought that occasionally witches have their efforts backfire on them. Irvin Propst told me that a suspected witch in his neighborhood had such power that she could cast an evil spell directly "through a mountain" onto an unsuspecting victim on the other side. Once, however, when she worked magic on one of Irvin's acquaintances, it "backfired," and news spread that the witch got seriously ill.[9]

Occult belief goes beyond thought, oral tradition, and folklore to become actual practice when it becomes a physical presence in one's life. When it leads to taking extreme action, as in sacrificing a calf, it is not a curious superstition or folkloric remnant, it is an actual practice. If superstition includes a fear of the unknown, the next step taken is a result of that fear, taking it out of the imaginative and into the physical realm.

If one's ancestors experienced the wrath and tribulations of the infamous witch-hunts of Europe, and were caught up in a spiritual life that encompassed an intricate cosmology surrounding occult belief, family and cultural traditions would reflect these notions as reality. These traditions put a "real face" on situations, infusing them with reality, and lead to fears most of us can only imagine. In such cases, these beliefs will not quietly go away. In places where these beliefs have had a chance to ferment while being protected from scientific scrutiny, they become entrenched, or at least reside somewhere in the psyche where they can be accessed when needed.

The Bible's literal description of creation does not stand up to scientific scrutiny, but that does not stop large numbers of people from holding it as a sacred belief. We should not be surprised, then, when people take other prescientific occult, esoteric, or religious concepts seriously and depend on witch doctors to help them navigate life's journey. When experience and belief team up to form a part of one's identity, it is powerful. These people are connected to a natural procession of beliefs that were observed, retained, taught, and practiced through family, community, and religious tradition that honored an oral tradition. Their actions are simply a projection of their beliefs.

Among people who accept the presence of witches as a fact of life, there is hesitation in labeling it bad luck. Sometimes animals naturally die, but often they are believed to have been destroyed, surreptitiously, by an evil party out of spiteful revenge for some real or imagined offense. Social tension is responsible for this aspect of witchery, with its gossip-inspired oral transmission and the individual quest for social acceptance. Any incident is nothing more than a reaction to something else, or possibly to some cosmological occurrence. Often someone who is thought to be up to no good, or against whom a grudge is held, is blamed. People explain their use of magical methods as a way to take the situation in hand. Through a process of folk spirituality, they strive to alter the course of events. Witch doctors are working liaisons in the process.

Historically, religious Germans did not accept the concept of fate. They embraced a cosmology whereby everything has a purpose and bearing on the actions of something or somebody else, whether in the human or the extended natural environment. This distinguished them from their Scots-Irish, Calvinist neighbors, whose historic belief in predestination left little room for active participation in one's own destiny.

Witch Doctors

Among early German settlers, life experiences were determined through adherence to a cosmology in which cosmic powers predominated. Good triumphed, but only if they followed natural laws that tied everyday activity to a harmonic relationship with those powers. Measured response to evil actions of mysterious forces assured a prosperous life. Witch doctors were important participants in the process. All good and natural well-being was obtained through a course of action in harmony with the natural world, often through a mental battle with the perceived evil actions of others.

Trouble caused by witchery or the perceived spells and actions of others had to be challenged in this mind-set. At the calf-burning event, a witch doctor was determined to intercede. Charlie Moats probably burned the calf by following instructions about cures known through family tradition, as did his father Ben Moats, who most likely sacrificed calves in his time. This tradition is reminiscent of the sacrificial laws of the Judaic tradition and the imitative magical reasoning of occult doctrine. It stands to reason that Charlie would have inherited the family knowledge. Down through history, people in his station in life have been alternately honored, respected, feared, hated, and embattled.

The "wise men" or "magi" whose presence play a role in the Christian nativity and epiphany were no more than the witch doctors of their day. At that time, distinctions between good and evil were not made among the magi, who were thought to use superior intellects and godly knowledge in doing good against evil. These wise men used divination to recognize a supernatural occurrence evident in the heavens. There is no biblical questioning of their powers of extrasensory perception. Brauner says that magic was not viewed as a diabolical art until the fifteenth century.[10]

Johnny Arvin explains the occult curative powers of his great-grandfather, a witch doctor, by acknowledging that "he had some extra power someways," showing that the concept of a God-given gift made the transfer with ethnic Germans to the New World. Johnny recalled:

> They came from a long distance. Oak Flat, Brandywine, Smith Creek, a long distance (for his) cures he knew. . . . .
>
> He had a way, when the rats got bad, he had a cure for rats when they came around the house. What he did, now, he didn't do that so much through words, he'd kill a black snake and drag it around the house, clear around the house, and bury it under the eaves of the roof. And he'd point the head in the direction he wanted the rats to leave. And he did that, and a week or so after—he pointed it east, and ah, after that, down at Laban Harris Propst's, said that so many rats came down there that they nearly eat 'em up down there. I've been told that. But anyway they got rid of the rats that-a-way.[11]

Stanley Propst.

As a show of respect, old witch doctor Ben Moats, according to several neighborhood sources, saw to his father's needs even after his death. Robert Simmons, who was a pall-bearer at old Ben's funeral, told me that for a while after his father's death, Ben would take meat and leave it near the grave so his father (apparently coming out of the grave) would have something to eat. Ben noticed that the meat was being eaten and thus continued the practice for some while. Robert laid the blame on neighbors who knew of his actions and took advantage of the opportunity to secure some free provisions. They were careful to leave the remaining ham and bones in a state that obviously indicated they had been eaten so more would be forthcoming. People interpret "life after death" in various ways. In this thought process, the dead retain hunger and food should be provided, much in the way Egyptian pharaohs were provided for in their afterlife journey.

There are many, many stories around Thorn Creek about Ben Moats. He had such a reputation that even school children brought him into their schoolyard play. Johnny Arvin recited a rhyme they used:

A bushel of wheat,
A bushel of oats;
Whoever isn't It,
Call Old Ben Moats!

Johnny remembered that Ben Moats used to like to dance barefooted, and that he did an old-time dance step called the "inchin' hook." Forms of step dance to fiddle music were common in this German Appalachian neighborhood. I am reminded of ninety-three-year-old Tyson Propst, who sprang to his feet and danced in my presence when his brother, Stanley, started playing a fiddle tune that struck his fancy.

King Solomon, who according to the Bible was granted great wisdom, may have been deeply mired in the magical arts. He was a witch doctor of his day. Solomon's wisdom was seen as a blessed and sanctified talent. In places in the Western world, most notably in Germany, where it lingered, white or good magic was not only tolerated and recognized as a gift but also practiced by religious ministerial officials. Long after skepticism leading to disbelief was widespread in the Anglo/Celtic world and, indeed, in all of the Western world, occult belief found in rural Appalachian folk magic continued. The cunning folk, wizards, wise men (in biblical terms), and Merlin figures of much older Anglo/Celtic renown had counterparts (witch doctors) that were widely embraced by Germanic folk. This mind-set was brought to the Appalachian frontier in the eighteenth century by, but not limited to, religious clerics. This explains the lingering use of occult practices among the descendants of Germanic people of the Appalachian region.

Chapter 16

Exhumations, Tokens, and Water Witching

Then a spirit passed before my face;
The hair of my flesh stood up.
—Job 4:15

Aside from Ben Moats's father's peculiar exit from the grave due to postlife hunger, other accounts of bizarre neighborhood exits and exhumations based on occult belief were revealed to me in Pendleton County. Johnny Arvin remembered a local character, Ailey Propst, who exhumed his mother. The man explained that he had to do it because "he didn't think her head was a-layin' right." Johnny, however, claimed that everyone in the community knew he did it for a sinister reason, that is, to get a nail from her coffin. Johnny said that old people always told him that there are great magical powers in a coffin nail. He remembers that there were some words that should be said when using these nails for malevolent reasons. The nails have so much power, according to Johnny's tradition, that if one is driven into the ground in an apple orchard, it can kill a number of apple trees standing nearby.[1]

Randolph notes that coffin nails were recognized in the Ozarks as having occult power,[2] and in the Old World they were used to cure toothaches, among other maladies.[3] There are many objects and substances similar to coffin nails used in maleficent ways. In seventeenth-century European belief, toads were used in a concoction that could cause the complete destruction of crops in a field and destroy fruit in orchards. Such destruction was often blamed on witches using magical objects.

Dana Keplinger tells of a woman on Reeds Creek who was exhumed because she did not receive her death wish, a serious infraction of folk integrity. She had wished to be buried with her knitting needles. A death wish is extremely important in traditional belief. A corpse is restless if it is not so honored. As a lifelong knitter, the knitting needles were deemed important to this woman. After her death and burial, according to the story, her descendants could not sleep at night because of the sound of knitting needles clicking together. The family took action. They exhumed her body, put her knitting needles in her hands, and reburied her. "The clicking stopped."[4]

Like clicking knitting needles, large numbers of supernatural incidents are known in West Virginia as tokens, signs, or omens. Robert Simmons told of the terrible times that were had in the Thorn Creek community during the flu epidemic of 1918. Almost every family lost a member or members. Robert fondly remembered one old neighbor who would give them a loud hoot in the evenings when he was out doing his chores. Presently the daily greeting stopped, and they learned that he had come down with the flu. One evening, after a week or so, they heard his loud hoot salute them again and were happy to know he was getting back to normal. However, Robert said, his eyes welling up with tears, the hoot was just "a token"; they soon learned he had died about the time they heard his last call.

Phoeba Parsons said that a rooster crowed the night her baby died. They were up all night attending to the child, who had fallen and received a serious head injury. When the rooster crowed, they feared the worst, and directly the child died. They determined then and there to kill the rooster the next day, which Phoeba did. She had determined, through an unclear methodology, that the baby had a "bad growth behind its liver."[5]

Johnny Arvin said that when his young sister Rose passed away while lying in bed in what is now the living room of his house, a neighbor was on his way from home to sit up with her for the night.[6] It was about midnight, and when the neighbor was nearing the house, coming through the "steep fields," he had to stop because of hearing "the prettiest music he ever heard." It sounded like it was "coming from the sky." When he arrived at the house, he learned he had heard the music at the same instant that Rose had passed away.[7]

There seems to be a strong inclination to believe that the natural world in some way acknowledges the death of a person. Johnny Arvin remembered an incident in which somebody was practicing the Appalachian custom of sitting up with an old person who was near death. The man was relieved at 3:00 A.M. but was made to wait until a shower was over to start for home. After the shower, he started home, and all of a sudden the moon broke out and was shining "pretty." He could not find any dampness on the ground from the rain. He later found the person had died at that time and he thought it was a token.

Johnny Arvin recalled that a man in his neighborhood who made coffins had said he often heard sawing going on in his shop when somebody died. He would know then that there was a death in the neighborhood and that he would need to make a coffin.[8]

Just a few hollows over from Dry Run, where Johnny Arvin lives, on another branch of the Thorn, is the African American community of Moatstown. There are two distinct Moats clans in Pendleton County. There are the old German Moats, some of whose witch doctoring talents brought them local fame, and there are the "colored Moats," whose genealogy traces back to the German Moats but whose physical distinction and segregated location causes them to be regarded separately. Harmon Moats, a community leader in Moatstown, told me, "We go for black now, but we're German too."

People such as the "colored Moats" are often called *Black Dutch* (a mixture of black African and Caucasian German people). But this widely used term has many other definitions. For instance, the Melungeons of Appalachia have called themselves Black Dutch, and Gypsies, mulattos, and mixed-race Native Americans have borrowed the term. One plausible theory has it that the true Black Dutch are thought to be the "Schwarzer Deutsch" or "Black Germans" who are found in Germany, including in areas along the Danube and, especially, the Rhine River. These Black Dutch are thought (in this theory) to have descended from mercenary soldiers in Germany in the third and fourth centuries C.E. who were Tubu Africans from the central Sahara.[9]

The term has been borrowed by many to get around laws limiting the freedoms of people with African, Native American, or Gypsy blood, thus confusing the situation. Today, swarthy or dark-complexioned people of varied backgrounds are still often categorized by this misused term.

While the mixed-race people of Pendleton County have their own unofficial community, locally known as Moatstown, they are segregated in many ways. They still maintain their own church, and they have a choir that is sought after by the white congregations in the region. Most of the "colored Moats" easily have more European than African blood. Most everybody in Moatstown under the age of sixty has at least some German Moats ancestry.

Johnny Arvin seemed like the person to ask about the oral traditions of Pendleton's Moats family history. He told me that there was an early Scots-Irish settler in the neighborhood named McClure who had a black slave named Tom. Johnny (who always carefully records who passed such knowledge on to him) said that Tom had children by two different white Moats girls. These children then used their mother's Moats surname.[10]

Community hog butchering, Moatstown, Pendleton County, 2000.

Over the years, African Americans from small rural communities near Moorefield and in Pocahontas County have contributed the other surnames that exist in Moatstown, but most folks there are still of the Moats surname.[11] Johnny's oral history is supported by an unpublished genealogical study done by William Lindsay, who lists Susan and Mary Moats (white females) as having mulatto sons and daughters. The original German settler was Jacob Moats, who arrived in Pendleton County in 1771.[12]

I attended a hog killing and butchering with Harmon Moats on a cool Saturday morning in early November 2000 at Moatstown. There were about thirty-five people present and roughly fifteen of them were white. Four large hogs were butchered, and everything, even down to the brains, were distributed in an incredibly equitable atmosphere of ritual celebration, joking, storytelling, kidding with much sexual innuendo, and forecasting of the delights that the meat would bring through the cold winter.

The brown-skinned people of Moatstown[13] share a recognition of the occult just as do their white cousins, such as old witch doctors Ben and Charley. One day I was hanging out with Fred Moats, a man in his seventies, and somehow introduced the subject of witchcraft. Memories flooded his mind, and he immediately launched into stories that provided truth (to him) of the existence of witches.

Fred said that once he was working at hoeing corn for an old woman in the neighborhood. After dinner, she said she thought she heard a chicken. She went outside and there was a rooster under a barrel. The next day at dinner, she said she thought she heard a turkey. They looked and there was a turkey in the corner of the room. He quickly exclaimed, "She was a witch!"

Fred said that he and his mother had met a gypsy. The woman wanted to see his mother's baby. His mother would not let her. The gypsy said the baby would start crying and would not stop. When they got a quarter of a mile down the road, the baby started crying and cried all the way home.

In another tale, Fred said that an old man, a suspected witch, was putting a roof on a stable nearby. The man laid tarpaper down but did not nail it down. Someone came along and said it was not a very good job. The man said it would last as long as the rest of the building did. Then Fred said, "It did!" Fred offered these tales as proof of the supernatural, which to him is the same thing as witchery.

Johnny Arvin sees the power of the curers in his neighborhood as akin to the powers of water witches, common practitioners in many communities who still command respect for their talents. "Seems like some people have the power to do it and others couldn't do a thing," he noted.

Water witching (rhabdomancy) is very common in West Virginia. According to a study done about fifty years ago, at that time there were twenty-five thousand practicing water witches in this country. The actual practice of divining with a forked stick, as we know it, began in the late fifteenth or early sixteenth century in Germany. Martin Luther believed the practice violated the first commandment. Through the ages it has been roundly denounced as the devil's work and praised as a remarkable aid to a basic necessity of rural life—finding water. It is often categorized with such rural customs as planting by the signs.[14]

I have personally experimented enough with water witches to know that Johnny's assessment is correct, at least in my mind. There must be scientific reasons why some people have special powers to locate water through divining. We just have not determined what those scientific reasons are—or perhaps I am enough of a romantic to allow for belief in its efficacy. I agree with a quotation that sums up the situation: "There are more things in heaven and earth, Horatio, than are dreamt of in your philosophy."

I once blindfolded a water witch so there was no possibility he could see. I set a large bucket of water within a 360-degree circle around him, turned him around until he was so dizzy I had to support him until he got his balance back, and then let him turn in a circle to locate the water. He found the water every time, and I conducted this test about a half dozen times. In fact, when his divining rod got directly over the water, his arms would shake violently. When I tried to do this myself, I actually found the

Burt Thompson, water witch, Randolph County, West Virginia.

water the first time, but it was more guessing than feeling a specific draw on the rod, although I thought I felt something.

Another test I tried was to have a local Randolph County water witch find a course of water in an open field. At that exact spot, I clamped his rod to a supporting stand, where, without him touching the rod, it did not move on its own. I then had him walk close and reach out with one hand and touch the rod. It still did nothing. He then grasped the rod with two hands as I unclamped it from the stand. It dipped down again, indicating the watercourse.

Vogt and Golde reported one test with a water witch who had a brother without the power. He walked behind the powerless brother and held onto his ears. In doing so, the divining rod worked like normal in his brother's hands.[15]

After knowing and working with this local Randolph County witch for a while, I became comfortable enough with him to ask a personal question. This man did not cut his fingernails, and some, including one thumbnail, were about two inches in length, growing out in a long curve. Some things seem best not questioned at first, but I was dying to know about this. At last, one evening when I was passing near his home and stopped by to say hello, I decided the time was right. At a pause in our conversation, I said, "Burt, I've been curious as to why you have such long fingernails." I then paused anxiously, waiting for an answer to my question, thinking that perhaps it related to some unknown occult methodology involving secretive aspects of divining. Barely looking up, Burt said, "To scratch my ass." It seems things don't always appear to be what you think they are.

Chapter 17

Dairy Products

Then, without further circumvention,
Give metaphysics your attention.
There seek profoundly to attain
What does not fit the human brain.
—Goethe

Mary Cottrell told me that she once stayed with a neighborhood witch for a week and that the only thing the witch served for food that entire week was cornbread, sauerkraut, and beans, a fact she found very curious. Some sort of neighborhood relationship with a suspected witch was the norm where Mary lived, and Mary probably did not tell her host that she was suspected of witchery. Of all the neighborhood witchery that still exists in oral tradition I have documented, and in a historic sense, there is no larger body of lore than that which surrounds food, especially dairy products.

Still today, people do not fully understand the effects that bacteria, temperature, and environment have on milk, butter making, and cheese making. People knew that springhouses kept milk from "blinking," or turning sour, so there was at least some scientific understanding.

The term blink is commonly used in central West Virginia to indicate that milk has soured. A common expression is "The milk blinked." Originally, when milk would blink, it was considered to have been tampered with by witches. In people's minds, a witch could look at milk, blink her eye, and in an instant turn it sour. Thus when milk blinks, it sours. This is an Appalachian twist on the "evil eye" syndrome common in the folklore of various ethnic European people.

The butter-making process, which solidifies cream into butter, escapes understanding for many, myself included. Magic is sometimes used in butter's preparation. A common rhyme in Pendleton and Randolph Counties was used to encourage the butter-making process.[1] Johnny Arvin Dahmer's version is:

> Come butter come,
> Come butter come;
> St. Peter at the gate,
> Waiting for a johnny cake,[2]
> Come butter come.

It is probable that the words "come butter come" in this charm are repeated three times for magical power. While I have found this charm among people of German descent in West Virginia, it is probably from Gaelic tradition. In the *Carmina Gadelica: Hymns and Incantations*, there are two butter-making charms that include similar, though much longer, charm/ hymns. The three-page selection titled the "Charm of the Churn" includes the line "Come thou churn come" repeated many times. A similar incantation titled the "Charm of the Butter," includes the lines "Come ye rich lumps come!" This is repeated throughout.[3] These charms may have filled the role of a work song as in keeping rhythm with the dasher in the churn to make the work go faster, at the same time helping the process in a supernatural way.

In Pendleton County, if the cream was hexed and would not turn to butter, it was poured into a trough and whipped with a stick. Through imitative magic, this beating would be transferred to the witch who was causing the problems.[4]

Among the vast supernatural occurrences that were attributed to witchcraft in Germany and in the rest of Europe three and more centuries ago, as in West Virginia, there are constant references to dairy products. Often it was butter and cheese making that were affected. Briggs cites a German example in which a hot iron was put into some hexed milk, thinking this would effect a reversal of a spell, causing the witch severe pain.[5]

Johnny Arvin recalled a similar story about a friend who knew old witch doctor Ben Moats:

> He said that he'd never forget that time he [went] up there [with] Ben Moats. He lived at McDowell.
> He said, "The cows, when they got up there were bawling and carrying on." He said, "They never heard such a time." It was in the evening. Of course, Mr. Rexrode told him what, what he came for, about his cows giving bloody milk.[6]
> Well, he said, he said he could help that. And he told him what to do. He said, "A man will be coming there in a couple days. He'll

be coming to your place and he'll say"—what he'd like to know was who bewitched his cows? It was a Halterman was supposed to have bewitched his cows. He said, "He'll be coming in a couple days and he'll say he's awful hot, and he'll want to borrow something."

And sure enough, one day Mr. Rexrode was up there on the mountain a-workin' and a man come across the mountain and pulled his coat off and said, "I'm hot." He wanted to go to the house, said, "I want to borrow—get some cabbage plants of you." And he went to the house, and he did. And Ben told him after he did that, told him what to do after that man did that.

He said, "Take a hot iron and put in that milk and that'll stop that bloodyness in the cow's milk." And sure enough, he said some words, and it did help it. Now whether the hot iron did it or what—but he told him what to do.[7]

Here again the concept of a witch having to borrow something from a victim to gain some power over them to do evil is present. Further, the concept of reversing the spell here is exactly as has been found in Germany, indicating that these participants are simply practicing old Germanic superstition. Also, within this tale and others I collected in this neighborhood, the witch doctor, in this case Ben Moats, has the ability to divine and forecast the event. He predicted not only that the man would come but also that he would be hot when he arrived.

In 2003, I visited old fiddler Stanley Propst at his farm in Pendleton County. Stanley was boiling traps in an old metal barrel filled with water and spruce branches. He said there were coyotes in the neighborhood (a modern bane to sheep farmers) and he was going to try to trap them before they started getting his young lambs. Whether the "spruce" (the local term for hemlock) served any magical property or was simply used to hide human odor was unclear to me. Nearby, outside an outbuilding in Stanley's farmyard, there were a bunch of unusual rocks and stones that the family had picked up on the place over the past 250 years. Among the rocks were two about six inches in diameter, two inches thick, with what looked like natural holes all the way through them in the center. While I was looking over the curious collection, Stanley asked me if I knew what those rocks were used for. Genuinely ignorant, I said that I did not know. Stanley said that if a cow had bloody milk, they would milk it through the hole in the rock and into a pail, and that would cure the cow. This cure, a form of lithotherapy, exists within folk medicine. The thought process behind passing something through a seemingly unnatural passage serves to conquer and reverse illness and sickness, conditions that are seen as manifestations of evil.

A woodcut published in 1517 at Strasbourg in the work *Die Emeis*, credited to Johannes Geiler von Keisersperg, is captioned, "Witch Milking the Handle of an Axe." In March 2000, I conducted a videotaped interview with Sylvia O'Brien, née Cottrell, of Clay County. She made a big deal about an ax handle in connection with some milk that she felt sure had been witched and, in this case, stolen by a neighbor lady:

> There was a woman come from the head of Booger Hole to buy a hand axe handle. And she asked for a drink of water. She stood right there, and I had a tin cup then, and water buckets on the table. I just dipped her up a tin full of water and reached it to her and I think she drunk it dry. And she bought that handle. Jenes was there. She paid Jenes for this handle, and took that handle and walked off and never said another word to me, him, nor nobody.

Sylvia Cottrell O'Brien.

Later that day, after milking the cows she said,

> You couldn't make butter with this milk. You had to milk them cows—they'd pretty near go dry and they was suckin' young calves, but the milk was a-goin' some place else—witches!
>
> I het [sic][8] this stove so hot it was red all over and I put that milk in a iron kettle, set it on there, and it was red hot. And I poured—and I put a fifty-cent piece of money in the bottom of that kettle and it says, "In God We Trust." And I let it get as hot as I thought it could get, and I just upended that milk right there in that kettle and that milk just went all over this place, but it didn't burn me at all. I got plumb back out and just let it flop and pop till there wasn't a drop of nothing in this kettle on this stove. And that night the cows come in with milk in their sacks!
>
> The cows was [back to normal] a-givin' milk, and I had bought a bread pan down at a store, and I was to take butter and pay for that bread pan to bake in there with, and ah, she [the suspected witch] was sellin' her butter to the same store. And some way or another they wanted me to finish bringing butter to them after I paid for my pan. But now when that [milk poured on the wood cook stove] was done, the cows come back to givin' their milk. But now I quit sellin' butter! I was afraid to, for people was afraid of 'em. They absolutely, I believe, that they made children sick. You know they had the power, almost as much power as the Heavenly Father.[9]

Sylvia's narrative here is rife with folkloric suggestion. A remedy is known for butter when it will not churn. Usually a silver coin is put in the churn. The fact that the coin Sylvia used in her milk was marked "In God We Trust" on one side increased its power. Sylvia was careful to mention the fact that the "fifty-cent piece" she put into the kettle of milk was a silver coin, as silver is thought to have power over witches.[10]

The fact that Sylvia used a coin marked "In God We Trust" is indicative of the connection between religion and the occult in Appalachian folklore. Sylvia has no misgivings about mixing the two, in the same way that occult traditions and religion have been mixed since the spread of Christianity in the Old World. Sylvia is adamant about the existence of witches, that they are the antithesis of godly people. She pointed out to me that the biblical "Witch of Endor" confirms her belief that witches are real.

Sylvia's continual insistence that the ax handle was unusually important to this story made no sense to me at the time. After the interview, when I saw the sixteenth-century woodcut, her many suggestive uses of the ax handle made perfect sense. This magical practice shows up in Germany,

Witch milking an ax handle. From Die Emeis (Strasbourg, 1517).

England, and Scotland.[11] Émile Grillot de Givry praises the characteristics of the German woodcut in his classic work *Witchcraft, Magic and Alchemy*. He points out that not only are two astonished housewives looking on, but there is a rather bony cow (*poor* or *sorry* cow in Appalachian dialect) in the scene. While the witch works at her ax handle, her cauldron boils away as well. This early-sixteenth-century scene is played out in numerous West Virginia accounts. We do not know if in Germany the witch had to obtain the handle from the intended victim, but Appalachian accounts, as with Sylvia's, suggest this.

The supernatural aspects of axes go back to belief in the sky god Thor. In northern Europe, archeology shows that prehistoric stone axes were kept to ward off storms and fire.[12]

Grillot de Givry notes that in Germany, when a witch wanted to deal a heavy blow to a neighboring milk maid or farm wife, she commonly dried up the milk of her cows. Such is the case in many occurrences in West Virginia. Bill Fay of Pocahontas County was thought to cure spells of witchcraft. When confronted by the realization that it was a witch who caused his cow's problems, he reacted as Sylvia did to get rid of her milk problems. He took some of the milk, put it in a kettle, and boiled it until there was nothing left.[13]

In the old Dahmer cure book, a cure for cows who went dry included the following process: "Milk the cow on the bottom of the pail. Take the pail to a sheltered place so nobody comes to it. Take a knife, make an X through the milk and stab three times through the milk. Keep the pail with the milk. Do the same the following day." Somehow, the bewitched milk is thought to represent the witch herself, so various things done to it, through a process of imitative magic, harm the witch.

Booger Hole, a place near Sylvia O'Brien's Clay County home on Deadfall Mountain, automatically suggests the supernatural. *Haints* and *booger* tales, along with tokens and signs from this place, are endless.[14] Fiddler Wilson Douglas told dozens of stories about this neighborhood. A history detailing murders and supernatural occurrences there is widely known.[15] The fact that Sylvia's antagonist came from Booger Hole, in Sylvia's mind, was further proof of her sinister nature.

Also playing into these magical events is letting a witch borrow or get something from you when they are bewitching you, as in obtaining the ax handle and drink of water. Mary Cottrell believed that after doctoring a person for witchery, you should not let that person have anything, even a drink of water from your house, for nine days to effect the cure. Her sister, Dovie, admonished that one should not give a witch anything out of the house after doctoring someone. She bemoaned the fact that after she recently doctored a bewitched baby, when someone came in the house, even just to get a drink of water, she had to doctor the baby again or "it don't do no good."

Propst gravestone, old Propst church.

In Sylvia's story above, the fact that she let the witch have a drink of water, in her mind, helped enable the witch to work her magic. Both the ax handle and the drink of water suggest supernatural events that double the witch's advantage.

In Kentucky, Leonard Roberts found people who believed that getting something from a person's house enabled them to lord power over that person. Most often the thing obtained was a drink of water.[16] A Pendleton County man told me that once, when he got sick, a member of his family went to Brandywine to consult a witch doctor to effect a cure. Apparently the witch doctor did not need to be in the presence of the patient; at the time the witch doctor carried out his cure, the patient, still at home, threw a fit. The witch doctor told the family that someone would show up at the house wanting a drink of water and they should not oblige. Someone came and asked for the water, but a family member took the bucket of drinking water and threw it out on the ground to foil them. The suspected witch left, apparently disgruntled and unfulfilled.

An old man from Williams River in Webster County, Zeph Christian, told me that old Nan Hammons could go behind a door and "get milk out of a dish towel." In West Virginia, very often dish towels and axes are involved in milk-stealing witchery. In Kentucky, a woman who "didn't own a cow" could take her churn and a dish towel behind the door and produce butter.[17] So this place, "behind the door," seems to be a magical spot as well, or perhaps it just indicates that the magical ceremony must be performed in secret. In Pennsylvania German country, this practice is known, and in one example the four corners of the dish towel are draped over something to symbolically represent the cow's four teats, from which the milk is magically extracted.[18]

Oleta Poste Singleton, from an old German family (Poste) in Braxton County, described an instance involving an ax, a dish towel, milk, and witchery in her neighborhood. Some boys visited at the house of an old woman believed to be involved in witchery. While preparing supper, the woman's granddaughter told her that they did not have any milk for supper:

> At that time she was about 100 years old, but she lived to be 114 before she died. She lived then in with her granddaughter most of the time. Her [great] grand children would go across to visit a neighbor across the hill by the name of Groves. The two boy's names were Everett and Earl, and the Groves' boys was Arch and Brooks. So they had been going over and staying a lot with Arch and Brooks, so they kept begging Arch and Brooks to go over and stay over there, but they

were afraid because of these spooky things they kept hearing, you know. But they finally decided to go.

Arch was watching. He was the oldest and he was watching to see anything that was the least bit odd that he . . . if it didn't suit him he was going home. So Ethel came in, the granddaughter Ethel, and she said, "Granny, we don't have no milk for supper."

And she said, "Mm-hmm."

So directly she come back and said, "Granny, we need that milk now."

"Mm-hmm," she said. She gets up and walks out and as she goes by the stove, she takes a dishrag from the top of the stove, throws it over her shoulder. There was a hand axe sittin' by the door, a one-bitted axe, and she picked that up. And she also gets a bucket that holds about ten quarts. And she goes out around the log cabin to the dark side on the backside, and she puts that dishcloth across the end of the log. And with a good hefty swing, she puts that axe into that dishcloth. And after that she twisted the dish cloth and set the bucket down under it, squatted down, put her knees down on the ground so she was comfortable, sit there, and Arch Groves was watchin' her. He had followed her. He said she milked the ten quart bucket of milk out of the log and picked it up and went in the house.[19]

After witnessing the magical milk incident, Arch got word to his brother back in the house that things were not normal around there. Needless to say they did not spend the night—or even stay for supper.

This narrative closely resembles the scene depicted in the old woodcut. Somehow, in this old belief, it is dish rags and axes that are used to effect the stealth. Dish rags often show up in other magical ways. Like axes, they have been used in folk belief for occult curing purposes.

Mary Cottrell described another milk-stealing scene: "Dad worked way up Rich Mountain there. And he said there's a woman [there who] cooked. And they never had no cow but she always had milk! There's cracks in the floor and he looked down and she was milking a towel, [and] she's gettin' milk. She was a witch!"[20]

Johnny Dahmer knows of the same witchery practice. He described an event that took place just over the hill from his house involving Annanias Pitsenbarger and a neighbor woman. He took me to the remains of an old log house in the neighborhood. According to Johnny, numerous witch tales emanated from this place, a neighborhood center for supernatural occurrences: "One day [Annanias] come by there and she was a-sittin' there and she was a-milking a towel, like she was milking a cow, and she had a

Dahmer farm, Dry Run, Pendleton County.

bucket full of milk! Out of that towel! So see that made Mr. Pitsenbarger more than ever believe in this witch business."[21]

An incident of milk stealing was documented in Indiana among Germans: A witch put a different pin in the dish towel for each cow from which she stole milk, and she named the cow as she did it.[22]

Dovie described the bloody milk affliction of cows and the cure her mother used. (Cows can get blood in their milk from mastitis, and this is often seen as the result of witchery):

> Mom had a cow over there. Now we went out and milked her
> that morning . . . suckled her calf, and milked her, and dribbed out
> what the calf didn't take. Mom always dribbed the last milk out and
> put it in her cream jar, she called it. That was the rich part of your
> milk. Me and Mom went out . . . like we'd go out this morning, suckle
> the calves, milk the cows. The cows would go on off to eat. That eve-
> ning we'd go to milk and the one cow . . . you didn't get milk, you
> got blood.
>
> Well I said, "Mom, the Devil's on her." I said, "Her milk ain't
> worth a whoop." I said, "Her calf'll starve." So Mom made her calf go
> over in a pen and we let her cow . . . that had the bloody milk . . . we
> let her calf go over and finish the other cows.
>
> Mom said, "I'll fix her." Said, "Come on, I'll fix her." She said,
> "Milk out what she's got, on the ground." She said, "Here's my strip
> cup. Milk me out some in it."

Dairy Products

I said, "What are we going to do. Can't sell the cow like this."

She said, "No." She said, "Come on, let's go to the house." She went in the house and there's a verse in the Bible where you can write a ticket. She wrote that ticket, put it, put it in that milk, and beat it up.

"Now," she said, "Dove, go out and get me a handful of good dry chips." I went out and got her a water bucket full of chips, you know, where Dad split wood . . . little shivers. [I] brought it in. She put [the milk and chips] in the cook stove. I'll bet you she poured a quart of coal oil in it. [She] set it on fire and poured that in, and [said] the three highest names. It wasn't an hour till [a woman] come up and she was just madder than the devil. She just cut a heck of a shine.

Mom said, "you done me dirty." She said, "You get the hell down the road and stay down the road and don't come back." Well, she left.

I said, "Mom, old Speck will have bloody milk again this evening."

"No," she said. "Ain't." She said, "I'm gonna write a ticket and tie it in the end of her tail in the hair." Well, she went and wrote a ticket and went out in the field and tied the ticket in the cow's . . . that long hair [end of the tail]. She parted that hair and tied it right up here where the cow'd switch her tail, [so] she wouldn't throw the ticket away.

Nine o'clock that night here come [a man], that was [a man's] daddy, and Mom was going to shoot him. She said, "I put up with [a man's] devil, now you're the next thing to it." She said, "Now, you motor or I'm going to pull the trigger." Now, he went and he didn't come back. That ended them a-devilin'.

The Bible will speak of the devil. Well, if there was witches back then, why ain't they here? The devil has to have his work a-goin if he has to put it on his own family. If you're a witch, you have to keep that a-goin' if you have to put it on your wife or your kids. You have to keep it a-goin'.[23]

Chapter 18

Spells, Charms, and Confrontations

The human brain is not an organ of thinking but an organ
of survival, like claw and fangs. It is made in such a way as
to make us accept as truth that which is only advantage.
—*Albert Szent-Gyorgyi*

Sylvia Cottrell O'Brien believed that witches could "absolutely make children sick." Numerous accounts of witchery's victims involve sick, defenseless children. Dovie told me she once took drastic curative action against a witch because of a grandchild who would not stop crying. She was convinced the child was under a spell.

Similarly, Robert Simmons recalled a time when a baby was sick in his neighborhood. Everyone thought it was bewitched, so they called on Ben Moats. Ben did some curing for the baby, but when he left, he told the family that someone would be coming there to get some beet seed from them. Under no circumstance were they to give the man beet seed. Robert notes that it was not in the right season for planting, so the family thought Moats's prediction was odd. The problem was that not everyone in this big farm family was told what to expect. A man showed up a few days later and asked an unknowing family member for some beet seed. It was given to him, and Robert noted that just after that, the baby died. He said that everyone was sure it died from "being bewitched."[1] Again, as is common in Appalachian folk magic, if a witch gets something from your house, he or she can work their magic and lord their power over you.

According to a Raleigh County minister, an instance of suspected witchery that took place recently in southern West Virginia caused four children to become sick, resulting in convulsions. A witch doctor was consulted, and among other curative efforts, he cast a silver bullet to shoot the

Robert Simmons in his workshop.

suspected witches in effigy. However, the effigies could not be hit with the bullet. This, they deduced, was because the witch had made a pact with the devil. Some methods, such as those above, were employed to cause this witch to come to the door and ask for water. Still, the spell could not be broken and another witch doctor was consulted. This second witch doctor claimed to need nine days to effect a cure. Finally, a medical doctor attended to the children and they were cured, though many still believed in an occult cause of their trouble.[2]

Certain motifs turn up over and over again in these accounts. The numbers three and nine, silver used to repel, a witch showing up at the door requesting a drink of water, axes and dish towels procuring milk, and so on are all common.

Oleta Poste Singleton was a charming ninety-plus years old when I met her. She related several accounts of witchery in her hollow. Less than five feet tall, a devoted Christian, she has a no-nonsense approach to life. She did not condemn or approve the subjects or their actions in the stories but related them for what they were, at face value. Indeed, the stories she told are well known and believed by many in the community, including the families of the suspects.

Oleta told me several stories about the old witch she observed as a child. Among the powers of this old woman, the one who lived to be 114 years old, was her magical way of obtaining food and money:

> The main person in this community that did these strange things . . . that they called spirits that she would call up, and things like that, her name was Eunie Conrad.[3] This old lady, Eunie Conrad, that lived across the hill, she does have people living in here but they all know these stories anyway. She did this magic work. Witchery, they called it. She had a certain stone in the fireplace that she would remove and lay on her hearthstone. Then she would go through her magic, and she wouldn't go to bed that night, she would stay up, and the next morning there would be ample amount of corn meal on that clean stone for to make hot cakes for the family for their breakfast. And if people would happen in, she would ask the children, "When you fellows wake up be sure that I know it before anybody comes in." She didn't want anybody to catch her corn meal on the stones and give away her secret—how she got her corn bread.
>
> Aunt Eunie's husband had been an officer, a minor officer, in the Civil War. He got . . . he lost his life in the war, and some people helped her apply for a pension. And it was seven dollars and she had eleven children. And she got seven dollars and, of course, after everybody grew older she still got the seven dollars. And she would run close on money. The seven dollars wouldn't go through the whole month. So she had this magic way of getting her money. It was similar to the way she got her food—that corn meal. She would take this little stone from the fireplace, above the fireplace, and she would lay it in another place on her hearth. It was another stone in another place. It had another category. It was her money stone. So then she would do her magic over that and then she would go off and sit real quietly in the corner. And the next morning when they would get up there would be money for them to go buy the things that they needed, whatever it was.
>
> The storekeepers and everything knew that she only got seven dollars a month and she'd spend forty and fifty. So they were very curious, so they watched to see what went on, and someone caught her putting the stone, and of course she would lose her magic when she was caught doing her magic.[4]

This is a widely held theory: One loses one's ability to do magic if it is done in a nonsecretive way. It is similar to the widely held belief that if people capable of doing some kinds of occult curing tell their method to someone of the same sex, they will lose their power to accomplish the curing.

Oleta described both positive and negative activities carried out by this suspected witch. She concluded that Eunie was "useful in one way and very destructive in another, if she took a notion to be."[5]

A belief similar to the one Oleta described, in which a rock from a chimney has magical power, was found in recent times among Germans in Rockingham County, Virginia,[6] and in the eighteenth-century among German Brethren with ties to the Ephrata, Pennsylvania, community.

The observance of familiars has become entangled in the shape-shifting beliefs. Most often, in Appalachian folktales, it is black cats that are the new-formed shapes of witches who are up to no good.[7] Mary Cottrell told me, speaking of a local witch and her witch sister, "She had a black cat she'd send across the hill to her other sister."[8] She somehow felt that these witches could communicate through this cat, or, perhaps, the woman (witch) became the cat herself.

A more common Appalachian tale has the (usually black) cat getting injured in some way and the person it personifies is revealed later. The well-known Appalachian Jack tale, "Sop Doll," is a prime example.[9] Here is a tale of this type as told by Phyllis Marks of Gilmer County:

> My mother also told a story about the young man who wanted to leave home. And his mother didn't want him to. He said he was going to anyway, so he built him a cabin out in the woods. He had it pretty well finished, but he was going to make a chubby hole [sic] up in the top of the loft, and he hadn't put a door there yet. He was stirring up the fire one night and he just had the feeling that something was look-ing at him. He looked up and there set a big black cat ready to jump on him, and he threw the poker and hit it. It jumped down on the ground and screamed like a woman. The next morning he heard his mother had been out in the night and broke her hip![10]

The transformation of witches into animals, called *shape shifting* or, more formally, *lycanthropy*, is still a part of regional traditional beliefs. Once, while shooting a film in Haiti, a Haitian who was a devout Christian told me he believed that the voodoo men of the neighborhood could turn people into pigs if they caught them abroad on certain nights and at certain times. The belief that animals can represent persons in some demonic way is widely held in many cultures. In fact, it is hard to find any traditional culture that does not have a witchcraft tradition, and almost all of them have a tradi-tion of lycanthropy.

Familiars are demons in animal form that accompany witches. Belief in their existence stems from sources as old as ancient Babylonian and Sumerian demonology.[11] While often confused today, the concept of familiars is different from the shape shifting or lycanthropy that was common in old European belief.

Johnny Arvin spoke of some neighbors who were convinced that a cow was bewitched. They told him they knew it was because they saw black cats "riding her." This term, "riding her (or him)," is used here again to denote the fact that witches were affecting a victim. The term witch-riding was widely known in Europe, and in the north of England, hag-ridden was a term similarly used.[12] In the southern Appalachians, horses are thought to have been witch-ridden or hag-ridden, causing them harm.[13] This belief goes back to medieval times, when horses found in the morning in a sweat were thought to have been ridden by witches through the night on their journey to the Sabbat.

It seems witches have two very different personality manifestations in West Virginia. On the one hand, they are the supernatural beings of European history in instances in which the stories about them have reached genuine folktale status. On the other, they are known, practical people who work their evil magic on the sly in league with Satan.

Johnny Arvin recalled a man who lived in an old house on his place. The man said that every night, while he was sleeping, a witch would somehow get in his house, come upstairs, and pull the covers off of him and put them under the bed. He would try to keep a light on in the room, but every night something would blow it out. One time this old man caught the witch by the hand as it was doing its nightly deed. Alas, he could not hold it, and the witch got away. Afterward he said, "It had a small hand."[14]

An old term in West Virginia is flyting, or getting rid of witches by seriously scolding them.[15] Johnny Arvin's old neighbor said that "the best way to get rid of a witch was to cuss 'em." While the word cussing (cursing), the same as flyting, is widely used in a loose way today, even on the airwaves, its meaning was more significant and negative among the older generations. Old Woody Simmons once told me that a man "cussed me 'til a fly wouldn't light on me."

The contemporary witch, the one most often cited in this book, is very much a natural human being and lives a carnal life. She is usually an older woman (less often, a man) in the community. She often has rough physical features, but does not present any clear-cut image to folks, and is often a composite of two versions: the old acquaintance/neighbor and the supernatural being. Whatever composite she/he is, they are thought to have the power to accomplish supernatural acts.[16]

Bill Dahmer and his cousin Johnny Arvin both said that their old neighbor, Annanias Pitsenbarger, was down in bed one time for two weeks. Bill's father went to see how he was doing. When he inquired about Annanias's health, Annanais said, "Them damned old witches are ridin' me."[17] According to Johnny, it was some old women down the road who were suspected of riding him, meaning they had gained power over him, or had ridden him in the night.

After stewing over Annanias's situation, Bill called for Ben Moats to come. Johnny said that Ben Moats was thought to be able to "knock witches." *Knock* is another verb that is used to indicate power over witches. Ben looked him over and "pitied him," according to Johnny. Annanias asked if he could help him. He then rubbed his hands over him, "said some words," and then instructed him:

> "Annanias, sit up in bed!" And he sat up in bed. He said, "Annanias, put your shoes on." And he set up and put his shoes on. After a while he said, "Annanias Pitsenbarger, go out to the horse stable and feed the horses." And he got up and walked clear out to that horse stable, from the house, out there, and fed the horses and come back, and he seemed to be all right then![18]

There is no doubt in Johnny Arvin's mind that Annanias was cured. He reasons that Annanias had so much faith in Ben Moats that it cured him. As proof, Johnny Arvin says, "Daddy told the story—he was accurate on that."[19] Johnny also noted that Annanias probably paid him a little something for curing, including the laying on of hands ("rubbed his hands over him").

In this particular cure, it seemed that Ben Moats cured Annanias with a practice similar to one in the old Dahmer family cure book. A similar example is found within one of the old cures for "Evil People." The cure is directed toward "Beelzebub." He is instructed to leave the bed, leave the house, and leave the stable:

> I forbid you in my bed.
> I forbid you in my house and stable.
> I forbid you in the name of the Holy Trinity my blood, flesh, my body and soul. I forbid you all nail holes in my house and stable until you have shaken all the mountains, crossed all the rivers, counted all the leaves on the trees, counted all the stars in the heavens until the

blessed day comes when the Mother of God gives birth to her second son.

Aspects of this charm or "word magic" may be found in the riddling tradition and in the Jack tales, where Jack is challenged to overcome impossible odds in order to achieve some gain. When Johnny Arvin relayed stories in which a witch doctor was invoking such a cure, he often would say he "mumbled some words."

Annanias Pitsenbarger's son Alben was a fiddle player, and the Blizzard boys played string music in the neighborhood as well. It is a well-known old belief that fiddlers make pacts with the devil in order to obtain their talent. Players of old-time fiddle music commonly kept (and still keep) rattlesnake rattles in their fiddles, perhaps unconsciously associating a symbol of the devil with the instrument. The devil appears as a serpent in Genesis, and he is more modernly portrayed playing a fiddle. The conservative religious belief is that fiddle playing is sinful. The instrument has been called the devil's box, the devil's riding horse, and similar terms.

A common belief is that a fiddler has to make a pact with the devil in order to be a good player. Country artist Charley Daniels popularized the devil-fiddler relationship (again) in "The Devil Went Down to Georgia," the hit country number. Phyllis Marks says that she always heard that fiddlers had to "sell their soul to the devil" to be able to play. It is common for the pact to be made at a crossroad or, sometimes, "forks in the road." This is not exclusive to Appalachian folklore; the belief shows up today in many Western cultures.[20] But while the crossroads belief is of European origin, putting objects such as rattles inside fiddles is of West African origin. There, special ceremonies were conducted to give new musical instruments their power. Magical objects were put inside of these instruments to assist them. Older black blues men commonly put rattles inside their guitars, and they surely put them in fiddles when that was a folk instrument among African Americans.[21] I suppose African gourd banjos, with their enclosed bodies, would have contained magical objects as well.

Chapter 19

Magical Places and Substances

The old crossroad now is waiting,
Which one are you going to take?
—Charlie Monroe

Writing in 1608, Francesco Maria Guazzo tells of a man who, in the late sixteenth century, was unable to consummate his marriage because a supernatural force, thought to be Venus, came between him and his new wife. He was instructed to "go at such an hour of the night to the crossroad where four ways meet, and stand there in silent thought." He did this, and following an ordeal, he eventually cut a deal with the evil one to gain access to his new wife. Soon after, he paid the supreme price, after mutilating himself in despair.[1]

One crossroad theory has it that all of the ancient religious sites of Europe, from monolithic stone circles to places currently occupied by cathedrals (having replaced older pagan structures at those sites) are situated over major crossings of underground water courses. Further, it is suggested that all of the ancient Roman roads extant in Britain are over major watercourses. The theory is that animals have an ability to travel paths that follow underground watercourses (there is some evidence of this). Early on, humans took up these animal paths for their own use. In the Roman era, roads eventually replaced these footpaths, and modern roads have replaced the old Roman roads.

In prehistory, the places where these paths (and the underground watercourses below them) crossed or came together were considered sacred. They became places of pagan worship, and now, at many of these locations, Christian cathedrals replaced the old pagan sites.[2]

The magical significance of crossroads, or forks, where a road splits, are why magical pacts were commonly thought to be made at these spots—they were special places worthy of solemn activities. Further evidence of crossroads as magical spaces comes from the Latin word *trivium*, literally, "place where three roads meet." Of interest to the crossroad theory is that the related word *trivius* means "a temple at a spot where three roads meet."

Chimneys are also magical places in popular witch lore. In old European traditions, it is where witches were thought to enter and leave the house to go to their Sabbats.[3] Of course, Santa Claus always entered by way of the chimney as well.[4] In West Virginia, a cut stone made to cap a chimney and still let smoke out is called a *witch's hat*.

Like the crossroad and chimney, thresholds too are very much interactive spaces when it comes to magical belief. The *threshold* word originates from its position as an entrance to the threshing floor, where grain was removed from the chaff. Thresh "holds" were slightly raised doorways intended to hold the threshed grain within. Folklore pertaining to thresholds may, in some cases, relate to that usage. Various occult motifs include sprinkling water from foot-washing ceremonies on the threshold to keep out witches. We know that even modern brides should be carried over the threshold, perhaps to foil a witch's designs on the couple. Doors, in effect, are thresholds. A common way to ward off the devil, or bring good luck, is to place a horseshoe, open side up, over a door.[5] Special substances were buried under thresholds, and such symbols as the cross were affixed overhead so that a witch would not enter.[6] In Ireland, thousands of spirits are thought to congregate at the threshold at night.[7] In West Virginia, several of my interviewees thought it common to lay a broom across the doorway, because a witch will not cross over it.

A Pendleton County cure for a baby who is "doing poorly" involves a threshold. One should strip the baby, hold it up by one foot, and use a length of yarn to measure it. The string is then put over the threshold and a curative salve is applied to the baby.[8] Systems of measuring and then doing something with the string are found wherever Pennsylvania German occult traditions have spread.[9]

If we think of thresholds simply as doorways or doors, much folklore applies to and is ascribed to this particular place. In western Germany, it is a custom to chalk the initials of the three magi, Caspar, Melchior and Balthasar, on the outside of the door on January 6 (Twelfth Night or Epiphany). In West Virginia, Phyllis Marks recalled the custom of throwing cabbage in people's "doorways" on New Year's Day for luck. In the Ozarks, pawpaw pegs were put in doorsills (thresholds) to keep evil away.[10]

It makes me wonder if those species of wood, such as pawpaw, presumed to have magical properties were used in olden times for the thresholds themselves. In German mythology, some woods, such as ash, are believed to have distinct magical properties. An ancient belief that I have found is still current in West Virginia: Poisonous snakes will not cross over ash wood.[11] Pliny the Elder, writing almost two thousand years ago in his *Natural History*, made this very claim about ash wood. Serpents are linked to evil through association with the devil, who in turn is thought to direct the evils of witches, and ash wood provides superiority over this evil. Phyllis Marks recalled that when women took their babies to the field where they were hoeing corn, they would take strips of ash bark and lay them around the quilts on which the babies laid to keep the snakes away.[12]

Aside from pawpaw and ash, other species of wood have magical properties, including fruit tree wood, oak, cherry, hazel, peach, willow, and cedar. Many more have curative properties. Most Appalachian grave-yards traditionally have a yew, hemlock, or cedar tree within, because these "evergreens" symbolize everlasting life. West Virginia water witches (diviners) favor using a peach or willow limb for their forked stick to make their divinations. Superstitions also come into play; for instance, it is bad luck to burn apple wood.

Traditional knowledge of various species of trees leads to sayings such as "Ash wood green or ash wood dry, a king can warm his slippers by." Ash has the unique quality of burning equally well whether green or dry.

Other tree species that old-timers have mentioned traditional uses for include sumac (with its corky center), which makes good sap spiles to use in the maple sugaring process; river birch, which makes the best ox yokes because it wears smooth and does not splinter; chestnut, which makes long-lasting fence rails; and white oak, which makes singletrees, doubletrees, and whiskey barrels. Hickory is best for smoking meat, dogwood or apple wood is best for making shuttles, and locust and cedar make the best fence posts. Hickory makes the best chair rungs, and hickory and ash make the best ax handles. Sassafras makes the best rake handles and boat oars. Black gum makes the best post mauls. Basswood is the best for carving and whittling, and walnut and "sugar" (sugar maple) make the best gunstocks. White oak splits make the best baskets. Hickory inner bark makes the best chair seating, but white oak "splits" work as well. Old-timers (and modern luthiers) harvested "yew pines" (red spruce), which grew on West Virginia's highest mountains, for making fiddle tops because it has great resonance. When it was plentiful, it was even used for log houses and barns near where it grew and could be transported, because it also has great weathering properties.

For some reason, old chestnut wood makes the best fire for molasses making, probably because it burns at a reasonable, and thus controllable, temperature. The making of sorghum molasses is still a common rural practice in the central-southwest part of West Virginia. Because the word *molasses* ends with an *s*, "they" (molasses) are regarded as plural. Used this way, people say of molasses, "They are good." Once an old-timer told me he was "raised on cornbread, molasses, and heartburn." Similarly, because the word *license* ends with an *s* sound, in Appalachian dialect, "they" are needed for driving.

Kent Lilly described an incident in his neighborhood that required a particular kind of wood to be used in a cure.

> These old timers had a terrible time with witches. I can remember old man George Meadows had a cow down there that got sick. And ah, they split her tail and put salt and pepper in it, and that didn't pep her up. . . . They called it the hollow tail that they had. Their tail would just hang limp like hangin' a mop across a clothes line, and the only time there'd be any movement there is when the wind would blow it along or something like that. So a, he got out his almanac and got to reading and called Doctor Pettycoat, he was a moon doctor, and talked to him about it. He told him what to do for the cow. And a, so they bored a hole in a log in the barn and filled it full of sulfur. And then they drove a white hickory peg in there. Now, and when that peg rotted off and spilt that sulfur out there it would cause this curse to die and go away.[13]

Kent specifies here that "white hickory" is used for the peg. That is because the plug rotting off is essential in the occult cure described above. It is common folk knowledge that hickory, though a strong hardwood, easily rots when exposed to the weather. The more common method to cure this condition called *woofin' the tail* is widely known in West Virginia but is not considered occult in nature. It is believed that when salt and pepper are used it brings the cow out of its enervated slump.

Springs are often deemed magical places or have occult importance. Clamper Spring in the Valley was used to effect a cure for guns that were bewitched. Some flax fiber was put on a stick, wetted in this particular spring, then pushed through the barrel—removing the gun's curse.[14] The superstitious practice of tossing money into springs, fountains, and wells for good luck is still widely practiced. At the Town Center shopping mall in Charleston, West Virginia, there is generally an enormous number of coins in the depths of a large multistoried fountain at the central point of the building. There are even quarters among the pennies, nickels, and dimes, all sacrificed for good luck. Paradoxically, "well wishing" was a way of cursing people at one time,[15] whereas, more modernly, "wishing wells" are considered places of hope and luck. This comes from their association with springs as magical places.

Historically, springs are considered restorative places where you can regain your health through the curative properties of the water. Many mineral springs in eastern West Virginia and western Virginia were developed as healing places, through both drinking and bathing in the spring's mineral waters. This is still a popular activity in much of Europe, just as the "baths" were for the Romans.

Development of these healing springs were western Virginia's first incursion into the tourism industry. The old Germans in the Shenandoah Valley frequented springs, often using Orkney Springs for the purpose. Circuit-riding Brethren preacher John Kline moved there so that his sickly wife might regain her health.[16]

Aside from thresholds, chimneys, and springs, numerous cures involve other magical spaces. Another place that turns up in various forms of folklore is the place where water drips from the eaves of the roof of a house. If the eaves drip on "Old Christmas,"[17] it predicts a good fruit year.[18] The eaves are commonly brought into play regarding the removal of warts: "I'll tell you how they tell me to take them [warts] off. Go to some of your people who's got a dirty dishrag, when they wash the dishes. [They] said, take that dishrag and wipe it over every wart you got, take it out where the water drips off the house and bury that rag and when it rots, the warts will leave."[19]

Corn kernels are rubbed on warts and then fed to a chicken to assist in the warts' removal. Warts may be "sold" (gotten rid of) for a small amount of money, even a penny, another case where a small sacrifice is beneficial.

In the Ozarks, people have put pictures of victims under the eaves where rainwater drips on them. Serious consequences are then in store for the unfortunate subject.[20] Imitative magic is at play, as water makes the photograph, and thus the victim, disintegrate.

Phoeba Parsons described the dishrag method as a way to remove warts. She also said that she herself never had warts because she never handled those "hoppin' toads," confirming an old folk belief that handling these creatures causes warts. Several people, including Phoeba, told me that if you step on a hoppin' toad, your cow will give bloody milk. These instances and others, mentioned above, whereby toads lay eggs themselves or influence chickens to lay more eggs, tie toads to many aspects of witchcraft and magical belief. In Pennsylvania, cases in which dozens of toads were put on a sick person to bring relief from an ailment are documented.[21]

An old neighbor in Webster County told me that a local doctor told her to visit a certain woman named Armentrout on Thomas Mountain who was better at removing warts with magic than he was with today's medicine. The Armentrout couple drew suspicion on many magical and witchery fronts. The husband grew his hair long before long hair came in style, and he wore a long overcoat all year long. His wife was considered to be a curer, but, harkening back to the ancient fertility/granny woman paradigm, in modern time she is considered to be a witch. Another neighbor, when telling me about the Armentrout woman, said, "Old lady Armentrout sold her soul to the devil."

Johnny Arvin recalled a curse put on a gun that involved putting blood, which is often associated with magic and witchery, in the end of the barrel. In late medieval times, it was thought that witches abused the power of blood by including it in their potions. Some think that early Germanic tales and beliefs involving blood-sucking women were also forerunners of the more modern European concept of witches.[22]

Chapter 20

The Pact

Use any sheet, it is the same;
And with a drop of blood you sign your name.
—Goethe

The German approach to language, the law, and, to a large extent, religion was subsumed within greater American society and culture over time. Folklore, however, born of Old World experiences, has held its own through time within the distinct Appalachian cosmology and belief system.

The concept of people going to a crossroad or fork in the road to meet with the devil and sell him their soul or make a pact signed with blood comes from the Old World. In the area that is present-day Germany, lay sorcerers put bread and wax figures at crossroads as offerings to deities.[1] The Greek goddess Hecate, who is thought to have represented a fertility cult in the Middle Ages, was worshiped at crossroads. She was considered a moon goddess as well as a "goddess of the crossroad."[2]

During the height of presumed witchcraft activity on the Continent, it was thought that a satanic pact was made by witches in order to attain desired skills and maleficent powers. This notion, still apparent today in Appalachian folklore, may be tied to Germanic beginnings. Tradition allows for writing or signing the pact in blood. A ritual kiss of the devil's backside and other bizarre ceremonial activities were invented during confessions at the time of the Inquisition.

In the 1790s, the Brethren press at Ephrata issued a pamphlet containing the story of a man who sold his soul to the devil.[3] Many of these old German-language tales that are now significant to Appalachian folklore found their way with Pennsylvania German pioneers to the Virginia frontier, both as published works and (more commonly) in oral tradition.

Dovie described a pact that may be made with the devil at a spring. She ascribed the knowledge of how to do this to the "Black Bible" or the "Black

Book," an ancient text that is often credited to the pen of King Solomon.[4] In it, the pact, which is the foundation of much witchery and magical lore reported through the centuries, is described. Dovie claimed to have stolen a look at a Black Bible that belonged to a cousin. She said, "I've seen 'em, but I never got to see what was in 'em."

When asked how the pact works, she said:

> Now say you're going to be a witch. Okay, now I don't know where you get 'em, but they call 'em the little Black Bible. Take that little Bible and you go to a spring where it's a-running from the sun . . . not towards the sun, away from the sun. Now, this one in here is running away from the sun. And that one up yonder in the Godwin holler is running direct toward the sun.
>
> Take that little Black Bible and go to that stream, strip off, and wash in there—take a bath in that water—and tell God you're as free from him as the water on your body. And you turn out to be—you go according to the Black Bible, the witch Bible. I had a first cousin that had one of 'em. And I'll a-tell you, I wish you could read one of 'em. It explains in there what to do and when to do.[5]

In another old Appalachian ritual of this type, candidates hide a small amount of dirt in a secret place. Unlike the use of water for the initiation, here the evil one is invoked by pronouncing, "I will be as clear of Jesus Christ as this dish of dirt."[6] Clearly, these processes of becoming a witch are believed to be an antireligious act through disowning any reverence for God.

Dovie's disgust of this process, obvious in her tone of voice, stemmed from her peek at a Black Bible. The process she described was similar to the process described in the *Key of Solomon*, which remains in print as a magical text, still popular with contemporary new age groups and magic practitioners, who bristle at the suggestion it has to do with witchcraft. While Grillot de Givry traces this book directly to the twelfth century, he points out that a text is mentioned and ascribed to Solomon in the *Writings of Josephus*, the early history of the Jewish people that was completed in the first century C.E. Another book of occult methodology known to exist in West Virginia and of historic association with Germans is called *The Seventh Book of Moses*.[7]

Dovie's note, that the naturally flowing water used in the ritual has to have a particular orientation regarding the sun, touches on mystical spiritual belief. Followers of Emanuel Swedenborg, who formed another early Pennsylvania German sect, put much emphasis on the sun as being the representation of God. Dovie's example may come from even older pagan sun worship beliefs, which pervade European witchcraft traditions.

In *The Key*, the instructions to become a sorcerer are directed at candidates who are resolved to gain Solomon's knowledge. The ritual is directed at God, putting it in the category of white magic:

> The Disciples then, being well and thoroughly instructed, and fortified with a wise and understanding heart, the Master shall take exorcised water [as in Dovie's explanation of water running away from the sun], and he shall enter with his disciples into a secret place [Dovie's obscure mountain spring] purified and clean, where he must strip them entirely naked; after this, let him pour exorcised water upon their heads, which he should cause to flow from the crown of their head unto the sole of their feet, so as to bathe them entirely therewith; and while bathing them thus, he should say:—be ye regenerate, cleansed and purified, in the Name of the Ineffable, Great, and Eternal God, from all your iniquities, and may the virtue of the Most High descend upon you and abide with you always, so that ye may have the power and strength to accomplish the desires of your heart. Amen.[8]

This seems no more than a baptismal ritual whereby higher powers are appeased for some earthly gain, also a clear implication in Dovie's account. In Dovie's account, the oral tradition varied in that the practitioner had to make a verbal denouncement of God. In *The Key of Solomon*, the candidate goes through this ritual cleansing of the body and soul in order to achieve station in the magical arts as a sorcerer. Sorcerers and witches have been considered one and the same throughout the ages. The debate as to whether sorcery is all bad or if only its negative elements are bad is the same debate as that over white and black magic.

Wolfgang Behringer says that magical powers, including these kinds of white magic, were "proudly paraded in the popular culture of Central Europe in the sixteenth century."[9] Ozment's study of "private life" in early modern Germany concurs; he notes numerous overt practices involving talismans, amulets, and the adherence to astrological principles as everyday fare. These traditions of positive magic not only reached the New World in the eighteenth century, as with Johnny Arvin's great-great grandfather but also are still in evidence today in Appalachian folklore.

Early Germans on the frontier were familiar with *The Key of Solomon*. Bastian Keller, who was connected to the occult through freemasonry and its secretive provisions, was known to have brought the book to the early western Virginia settlements.[10]

The witch's sacrilegious baptism is described as the method by which witches gained their power and demonic station in life in various places throughout Europe.[11] Dovie expounded on this subject:

If you want to be a witch you'll have to get with one—another witch—and find out where you can get your Bible and the rules and regulations. One makes you tell another, but just like you and me a-talkin', we wouldn't know nothing about it. We couldn't get it, 'cause we're not a witch. The witches keeps in contact with one another. And they ain't gonna let you know what they're doing, either. You can talk to one of 'em and he won't talk with you right.

You can pretty near tell he's a witch by the way he talks and the way he acts. I can tell 'em just as quick as I see 'em by the way they talk, the way they walk, the way they go. I can tell 'em, and we've got a few around here. And they're all over. You don't know how many is a-servin' the devil. There's more servin' the devil than there are servin' the Lord. And where are they a-goin' when they die? The old devil's goin' to have a heck of a pile a-burnin', ain't he? He'll have a big fire![12]

To Dovie, the mysteries of witchcraft and its sources are as confusing as the mysteries of what she regards a similar but more modern problem: "The witches is the only ones that knows where them books is. Just like the drugs. . . . It just goes like—the witchery is like the drugs today!"

While Dovie appears gripped by paranoia, the whole drug culture, commonly presented on the front page of local newspapers, is baffling and bewildering to many older people who did not closely witness or experience substance use or abuse, other than moonshine, in their lives. It is common for a person in Dovie's station to seek an explanation for misfortune. In her cosmic world, everything is connected, and she feels a need to act to oppose her foes and project victimization back on the enemies, in her case, neighbors and distant relatives she perceives as witches.

If, through a pact, the devil is granted your soul in exchange for some talent, gift, or magical power, it is thought that he then receives some gift of the body in return. This could be a fingernail or even a withered finger. While not physically removed from the subject's body, it belongs to Satan, as may be evidenced by its withered condition. Incidents of this nature show up in fifteenth-century witchcraft trials.[13] Sometimes just a piece of one's garment was used as a token of homage for the devil.[14] This may be the root of the strong belief that if someone gets physical possession of something belonging to you or even a drink of water from your house, he/she has power over you.

The sacrificial motif,[15] as in the case of Doctor Faustus[16] and the even older legend of Theophilus,[17] describes the arrangement by which one's soul is sold to the devil. The motif easily made its journey to the New World within several European cultures, but the practice was unknown in Great Britain.[18] It was a belief strongly held by the Germans who pioneered the old western Virginia frontier.

The early establishment of German presses in America, in both Pennsylvania and Virginia, played no small part in settlers' retention of German occult belief. This occurred while German identity faded and a regional identity continued its inevitable march to prominence. Tradition is resilient, and the devil-pact motifs that Germans brought to western Virginia spread through both early printed media and oral tradition. The latter was especially important as time went on and rural areas became nonliterate pioneering societies.

One West Virginia pact tale of this type, collected by Ruth Ann Musick, comes from Jackson County. In it, a man casually says he will sell his soul for some advantage, in this case money. Satan magically appears and forces the man into the pact. The man is to receive all the money he wants in exchange for his consent, unless he gets too greedy. Of course, he eventually does get too greedy, and soon after he endures a painful death and eternal torment.[19]

The pact is similar to that Dovie noted, but Dovie's is different in that the devil does not make an appearance in person to make a proposal or a request for a signed document. It entails a ritual baptism and requires an oath at a magical spot. While different from the pacts described above, these types of pacts are central to the initiation process within the classical definition of folklore surrounding witchcraft.[20] In Dovie's mind, it is all the "devil's work."

Chapter 21

Witch Balls, Conjuring, and Divination

The greatest discovery of my generation is that human beings can alter their lives by altering their attitudes of mind.
—William James

Witch balls and/or hairballs are an unusual but fairly widely known supernatural phenomenon in the Appalachians. There are two very different classifications of a witch ball. The first kind, also called a *hairball*, is believed to be sent to people supernaturally as a curse. The second is made of glass and is commonly used for divination. Dovie described an experience with a hairball:

> Well now, I was at a woman's house one time, and she kept a-hollerin', "There's a ball of hair goin' through the house, a ball of hair goin' through the house."
>
> Well, I said, "Aunt Mary," I said, "what for ball of hair is it?"
>
> Well, she said, "You just set still and you'll see it go through the house." Well, she was settin' over there and I was settin' over here, and right now, a ball of hair went through—between us!"[1]

Old Anthony Swiger laughed about a neighbor who reported that his cow was bewitched because the cow was rolling over and acting strange. When he asked the man if there were any yellow jacket's "nestes"[2] around there, the man said, "No, it was a witch. I heard the witch balls hit the cow."[3] Witches are thought to be able to aim hairballs at cows and kill them. Apparently, the hairballs are often invisible.

This same man who heard the witch balls hit the cow was of an old Brethren German family in Randolph County. He was accused of making hairballs himself out of horse and human hair, according to a neighbor. She told me he would try to hit people with these hairballs, and if he did, you were in big trouble because they would bring misfortune on the victim. At one point, after the man had threatened to curse some children, the father of the youngsters shot a hole in his high-crowned hat. The trouble ended.

Johnny Dahmer regards a hairball as being the same as a *witch bullet*, a rare term. He described it as a bullet made out of hair. His neighbor described a local man who claimed to have been shot by a witch bullet and would often show people the mark it left on his leg. Robert Simmons and the man's nephew both remembered seeing the place on the man's leg. This same man described a shape-shifted witch, in the form of a squirrel, whose "hair was turned the wrong way and could not be shot."[4]

Johnny's insight into the tradition of hair making up the bulk of a witch ball or bullet is confirmed in descriptions from Missouri. Randolph notes witch balls described as being the size of a marble made of black horse hair, and another one made of black hair and beeswax that was rolled up into a hard pellet. The belief is that a hairball (or witch bullet) could be thrown or shot at a person by a witch. This hairball (or bullet) would be found on the body of anyone killed by this method.[5] The terminology here can be confusing, but the term *witch ball* has two meanings. A *hairball* relates to only one of those meanings. Hairballs are sometimes called witch balls, and are also called witch bullets, and represent a curse. This concept has been around for centuries. Waite reports a case from 1598 in which a child is believed to have been bewitched and possessed by demons. Her parents' fervent prayers exorcised the demons, described as "fist sized balls" that danced about the fire before vanishing.[6] Of course, cats and even cows cough up physical hairballs. Whether it is these entities that are considered witch balls (in the minds of believers) or similar manmade objects is unclear.

The second type of witch ball is actually a glass ball, and it is an entirely different entity. They are not a curse at all but are used (some say profitably) as a way of gauging the future. Both Western and Eastern cultures employ some version of a reflective surface for augury. Crystal balls are rare, although they were produced commercially in Oberstein, Germany, for occult usage.[7] Folk practitioners in much of the Western world used leaded glass balls that are blown into shape instead of being solid crystal.[8]

The Greeks and Romans used crystal balls for a form of divination called *scrying*. It is explained "scientifically" (within the occult belief) thus: Points of light from a reflective surface overcome the optic nerve, and the eyes cease to see out. The brain then observes normally inaccessible information as it "sees in." Many different reflective surfaces have been used in this way.

Witch balls are described as multicolored glass spheres, usually green or blue, in occult reference books.[9] Some of the ones I have seen have the multicolored carnival glass effect, and others are tinted in one color only. These were described as witch balls and were purchased at farm sales in eastern West Virginia and in the Valley. Johnny Arvin's old neighbors, the Pitsenbargers, used one that is still in the neighborhood. Johnny Arvin remembered that Gilly excused himself to consult one before making important decisions.

A physical inspection of a witch ball shows that it is used in the same occult way a mirror is used, but it allows for a wider variety of divination. This form of clairvoyance may be found in the Old Testament. In Genesis 44:5, Joseph uses a cup in this way, showing an occult or magical side to his person, and he is castigated for it: "Is not this it in which my lord drinketh, and whereby he indeed divineth? Ye have done evil in so doing" (KJV).

Joseph was probably looking down into liquid in the cup, as in the way people learned or divined who bewitched them by looking at a mirror or other reflective surface. Tyson Propst told me of the curious but widely known practice of looking in a reflective surface, in this case a rain barrel, to discover the identity of the person who is bewitching you. Tyson said that doing this so inflamed a local man that he threatened to kill the person whose face was revealed to him upon learning (or seeing) the originator of the bewitchment.[10] I have collected similar instances of this practice in Randolph County.[11]

The concept of divination with witch balls or other devices did not end in biblical times. Undeterred by the biblical verse cited above, the original mystical German Brethren, led by Johannes Kelpius, and some of the Dunker members who ended up on the Virginia frontier, gained a living by telling fortunes and "casting horoscopes."[12] Again, the practice of occult methodologies was not problematic to religious practitioners of the time, evidence of which can still be found among their descendants.

Germanic people have long held to these beliefs. A German manuscript from 1658 includes a divination invocation very similar to cures used by witch doctors in Pendleton County. The "three highest names" are invoked, along with the name of the person who desires to determine answers to certain questions. George Frederick Kunz notes that this ritual is unusual in that it has religious overtones and in fact a priest wrote the manuscript. He notes a disposition of German clergy to engage in "white magic,"[13] and that affected Appalachian folklore. While white magic is loathed by today's clergy, some practicing Christians in West Virginia of German ancestry still retain the magical traditions.

A man from Braxton County once told me about another form of divination, that of "writing spiders." By looking at ways in which a spider spins its web, certain aspects of life could be divined. Sometimes the letters of a significant word might be apparent within the structure of the web. The ancient Romans also practiced a form of augury associated with spiders. Pliny said their webs were "tokens of divination,"[14] and he is most likely an early disseminator of the belief.

Fortune telling was practiced in Johnny Arvin's Pendleton County neighborhood. One woman, described by Johnny Arvin as being a "dirty woman," had an old former slave with whom she would "go a-journeying," as Johnny put it. Her journeys were taken to make money through telling fortunes. Another local woman gained recognition through practicing necromancy (talking with the dead).[15]

I asked Johnny why the "journeying" woman was considered dirty. He said that her general appearance was dirty, causing one local man to claim that the woman's husband married "a damned old witch." In the tradition, old and dirty or ugly women easily get accused of witchery, while perhaps young, clean, and pretty women do not. Patriarchal values and traditions encompass the varied levels of distinction.

Johnny Arvin said this old woman would store apples under the house in the fall and the chickens would roost on them. This did not deter her from cooking them up for food. He said that one time an old hog had died of unknown cause on Mitchell Mountain and was not discovered until it was old enough that the "flies had blowed it."[16] This woman set to work cutting off the hams and picking the flyblows off of it while saying, "The Lord killed it, it must be good!" She would do the same at home with dead chickens, breaking standard mores and rules of cleanliness, conduct, and common sense.

Johnny said that one time this woman was "stirring" at an apple butter making, where the butter was being made outside in a big copper kettle. A cat happened to venture in too close, whereupon she pulled the stirrer out of the kettle, swatted the cat across the rump with it, then put it right back in and stirred the apple butter. Johnny noted that she was so dirty her husband eventually left her, and she finished out her years living with the old former slave, who today is buried in a nearby field.[17]

This woman represents the stereotypical witch, the hag or beggar, common in various folktales and lore. It is a stereotype that goes back in old Germanic folklore to the "wild woman," who shows up in an eleventh-century German charter. She was dirty, lived like an animal in the woods, and was thought to have magical powers. She could, for instance, materialize or disappear at any time.[18]

While older, ugly, and/or dirty women are commonly connected with female witchery in the popular mind-set, two important masculine symbols of Appalachian culture, guns and dogs, are often the subjects of witchcraft. Johnny Arvin recalled instances of conjuring. Once, when Louis Propst and Annanias Pitsenbarger were going to Franklin, hunting along the way, their dogs struck off after a deer. There was a place called the "pump hole" (deep water hole) in the river, where deer would go to get away from the dogs. Annanias noted that the dogs were "headed for the pump hole":

> Louis said, "No they won't." He then went and mumbled some words!
>
> Soon after, the dogs came over the mountain on the backtrack, a-howlin! He stopped the dogs! People could stop dogs through their magical power. Annanias was a little afraid of Louis [after that].[19]

Johnny retold this story with careful attention to detail—the facts of the case, the people involved, his own amazement at the witchery—every manner of detail down to the local place names where the incident happened.

How, then, did a story that is a very close parallel come down to us from Kentucky? Roberts collected a version of this story there. In it, a man heard dogs running after a deer and followed them, knowing that they were headed for a "big waterhole" on a creek called Leatherwood, where deer would go to get free from dogs. As he approached the spot, he was amazed to see the dogs suddenly turn about face. Someone had "witched the dogs and turned them on their backtracks." He then encountered a local man in the act of imposing the spell and realized he was a witch.[20]

These two tales tell us much about the power of motifs that travel widely within traditional belief systems. Unfortunately, Roberts gave fictitious names for the people involved; their real names could have given some indication of their ethnic origin. In the West Virginia incident, the German names involved, Pitsenbarger and Propst, belong to families that go back to eighteenth-century settlers from Germany. Roberts did give one surname for a local witch in his study area. That name, Coontz, is a German name that has been anglicized from Kuhns.

Johnny Arvin told me of another incident, on Ned's Mountain, where dogs were witched so powerfully that they stopped and returned on the backtrack. In a somewhat similar West Virginia event, the Hammons family told a tale whereby a witch, hunting deer, magically caused the animal to turn around and backtrack so he could kill it. This amazed a neighbor, who determined that witchery was at play. Maggie Hammons Parker spoke of a man, a witch, who claimed he could witch people so hard he could "pop their eyeballs out."[21]

Among the numerous tales of witchery that Sylvia Cottrell O'Brien told are a stack that she wrote down and gave to me when I visited her. One involves a dog that was "witched" to the point where it could no longer hunt. I have left Sylvia's spelling and punctuation intact:

> This was in hunting time. Men and boys to go hunting for anaml pelts to sell. They used dogs to hunt them with. I seen this happen when I was 15 or 16 years of age. Daddy had renters at that time. Teen age boys. There Daddy had a good hunting dog. They would take this dog and go hunting at nite.
>
> Won day 2 men come to there door and wanted to bie this dog. These boys Daddy dident want to sell the Dog away from his boys. He talked to these two men told them money was scarce and hard to combie. The boys would need shoes to wear to school. Thes too men, well grown men, left this renter house.
>
> This Dog never was knowin to hunt again if he was led into the wood. If he got looce he would start barkin and howling. And runin till he got back home. This Dog was takin care of for severel years he never hunted any more.
>
> How did all this evel sistim get in our country. There is witches * hiprets [hypocrites?] * charmers * that can do most any thing they wanto. It's still here today.

Implicit in Sylvia's story is that the dog was witched. Before she died, Sylvia went to great lengths to document her many occult and supernatural tales about events she witnessed. After I had interviewed and filmed her several times, she wrote out several dozen tales of this type for me, which I treasure. She died soon afterward, at the end of 2001.

Other occult tales among some German people in Pendleton County show great respect for a plant known as *master root*. Some men would carry it in their hunting coats to stop spells from affecting their dogs.[22] When I questioned Johnny Arvin about master root, he remembered it. Then, after he consulted with his sisters, he told me they determined that it is a plant listed as masterwort in some taxonomy books. Much of the thinking here has to do with the term *master*. When something is master over something else, it has a supernatural power to control it. So witch masters are, in effect, witch doctors. They have power over witches. Master root seems akin to the

Folk painting in a farm house near Moyers, Pendleton County.

root known as *high john the conqueror*, well-known to African American root doctors. Phoeba Parsons of Calhoun County used a plant called *rattlesnake master* for snakebite, only she called it "rattlesnake masterfield."

Much witchery belief involves hunting and guns, subjects that were important to the well-being of early settlers. Johnny Arvin noted that in his great-great grandfather's old cure book, there was information about how to "stay a shot," that is, keep a gun from firing through invoking a magic spell. Here is the English translation from Johnny Arvin's great-great-grandfather's German manuscript: "To Stay a Shot. Shot stand still in the name of God. Give neither fire nor flames. As sure as the beloved mother of God has remained a pure virgin (Rock of Gibraltar) +++ while dissolving it say: God, his joy and glory!"

The reference to "Rock of Gibraltar" is unclear, but it appears to mean a magical substance of importance that may be dissolved.

There are other documented instances in West Virginia's Hammons family in which guns were bewitched, causing them to not shoot straight. In one case, when a deer was shot at, the deer raised and flew through the air and the shot was harmless. A series of occult actions were taken to remove the spell on the gun.[23] A rare occult manuscript from colonial South Carolina includes a cure for a gun that is "speld."[24]

Maggie Hammons recalled one instance in which an old witch doctor, Bill Fay, took the witchery off a gun belonging to a family member. The cure involved placing two pubic hairs, crossed, over the gun muzzle and shooting at the first prey seen.[25] Also in Pocahontas County, Burl Hammons remembered a story about selling your soul to the devil and using a gun in the process. A ritual was followed: Nine mornings in a row you went to a mountaintop and shot at the sun ball when it appeared. After this, you found a drop of blood on your gun barrel, the devil appeared, and you sold your soul.[26]

Chapter 22

Magical Imprints

Magic is the best theology,
For in it true faith is grounded and found.
—Jacob Boehme

Through her method of doctoring, Dovie Lambert is a conduit for an ancient form of binding spell that precedes Christianity and was known to Plato. Old spells of this type that have been unearthed are mostly inscribed on paper-thin lead or lead-silver alloy tablets. It may be that organic materials such as parchment paper or skins on which these types of spells were written did not last long enough for archeologists to discover one to two thousand years later.

Dovie's occult tradition is important because it brings a thought process, a belief system, into a tangible form. Her many uses of the ticket—putting it over a door, tying it in a cow's tail, pinning it on a baby, burning it, poking it full of holes, chopping it all to pieces—preclude its longevity. There are a few oak trees around that could attest to her methodologies, just as there are fruit trees and barns that could confirm other auger-boring stories. Indeed, archaeology all across Europe confirms similar actions and behaviors since pre-Christian times.[1]

I found material evidence of serious occult practice not far from Johnny Arvin's farm. Many area residents speak of the "witch war" that went on among local residents who were very caught up in occult practices, including spells and counterspells. The two antagonists in the war openly accepted the occult as a real and dangerous presence in their lives. One neighbor complained that one of these people burned so much sulfur in their practice of witchcraft, or counterwitchcraft, that it smelled even when just passing the house, which was about forty yards from the road.[2]

Witch doctor Charlie Moats of Brushy Fork would visit these sulfur-burning witches to be cured of his own ailments. Another area resident who visited a later occupant of the house "where the witch wars went on" said:

> The house still had sulfur—where they had burned sulfur. . . .
> The kitchen walls and the ceiling were blacked up with sulfur. There
> was brooms over the door. There was something else hanging over
> the door, I can't remember what that one was. They had the little
> square symbols for protection over every opening, every window,
> every door of the house, to keep out curses, or bad people, or
> whatever.[3]

Acting on this tip, I investigated in the neighborhood by contacting the current owners of this abandoned house and barn. This led to an inspection of the premises, where I found signs of very curious activity.

I was told that these witches would curse and countercurse each other. A relative who lived down the road said that they would accuse each other of witchery and that any bad luck they suffered they blamed on the other. Dana Keplinger remembered that one would make the other's cow go dry. Then one would make the other's spring go dry. One would make the other's crop fail. It was spell and counterspell "until they cursed each other out."

The witch war did not end before getting openly violent. Johnny Arvin said that guns were fired, and the growing seriousness of the situation led a local resident to call in "the law." The deputy sheriff, Johnny said, came and talked to neighbors, including Johnny's father, asking what they should do about it. Johnny's father told them that the two witches were basically good people and would probably work things out themselves. Apparently, no arrests were made, but the presence of the law, according to Johnny, "quieted things down."

The current owner of the house, a resident of the rural area where the witch war took place, mentioned to me that he observed a strange symbol in the barn that is located a few hundred yards from the house. He explained that he had installed a window in the barn, as it was extremely dark in there, and when he did, the new light allowed him to notice a piece of heavy paper tacked on a beam over a manger. He agreed to take me there to see it.

When we got there I was quite taken by the scene. In researching annals of occult history, I had read about a well-studied symbol often called a *sator* or *rotas-sator* square. It has been used for occult purpose for over two thousand years. While I knew that this symbol was known to Johnny Arvin Dahmer's great-great grandfather and that, in fact, it appeared in his book

Barn interior showing occult symbols on paper tacked to the beam.

of magical incantations and cures, I doubted I could find one. I questioned Johnny Arvin about the possible existence of these symbols in the neighborhood, but he did not think any existed. Yet here one was.

The square, shown here, uses five words:

R O T A S
O P E R A
T E N E T
A R E P O
S A T O R

This square was placed directly over a manger that was used by cattle. In the German powwow book *Long Lost Friend*, printed in English in Pennsylvania in 1856 and credited to John George Hohman, the following cure is given for use regarding cattle:

> To be given cattle against witchcraft.
> This [the square] must be written on paper and the cattle made
> to swallow it in their feed.

The square was also thought to protect one's house from burning down (if kept in the house), and it is/was used to prevent miscarriages.[4] Upon asking the owner if I could inspect the house, he agreed. Once inside, I found the rotas-sator square written on one-inch-square papers glued over every window. The owner was surprised at the discovery.

Rotas sator square in a farm house.

This magical symbol has a long history with mystical groups, especially Pennsylvania Germans. At the Ephrata community, special rituals involving the rotas sator square were carried out to protect their large frame buildings from fire. Some marvel that these buildings, dating from the eighteenth century, have survived at all, given that they are framed wooden structures with log chimneys.[5] They also performed a fire-protection ritual that had to be done on friday between 11:00 and 12:00 at night during a waning moon.[6]

Upon questioning Johnny about the man, a neighbor now deceased who had written and used this symbol in this barn, he told me that yes, this old neighbor was known to take bus trips to Pennsylvania. In his younger days, he would leave to visit an old uncle who had moved there from Pendleton County. Johnny thought this relative was involved with witchcraft before he left and most likely continued the practice in Pennsylvania. This could explain how this particular cure made its way to this neighborhood, affecting this farmer. But because no one in this community has ever heard of the term powwow, the old local source, Johnny's great-great grandfather, seems a more likely origin for the use of this symbol. Within the Dahmer cure book, the square is used against arthritis, to prevent lightening, and to cure the bite of a mad or rabid dog.

According to Johnny Arvin and Eva Simmons, there were several families they could name in the community who "had a book," (meaning a cure book) and were, in Eva's opinion, witches. She believed that Johnny's great grandfather was a witch, declaring so in Johnny's presence. Johnny responded that yes, his great grandfather possessed that old cure book, but that was a common thing in that early generation. Both Johnny and Eva acknowledged that a local preacher had declared that a cure book in the possess-

Log chimney, Pendleton County, built 1920.

ion of one local family was "the work of the devil."[7]

Johnny did not know, previous to me telling him, of the use of the rotas-sator square in his neighborhood. He was familiar with the symbol and its magical properties, having seen it in the old cure book, and he had even made note of it in his notebooks that he has kept since he was a boy.

The rotas sator symbol is thought to descend from the Mithraic religion. Historian Walter O. Moeller argues this in his treatise *The Mithraic Origin and Meanings of the Rotas-Sator Square*. He claims that the square contains the Mithraic triad, that the anagrams it contains have theological import, that it is fundamentally a number-square, that the symbols represented are Mithraic and, in short, that the square is a product of the syncretic paganism of the Roman Empire.[8]

Ralph Merrifield, in *The Archaeology of Ritual and Magic*, supplies several translations of its meaning as a Christian symbol, but he reports that it has been found in places where Christianity did not exist. He details discoveries of the square in Portugal and in Germanic regions that date to at least a century before Christianity was known in those places.[9] While scholars may continue to argue its origin, archeology tells us that it shows up in many places among the hundreds of sites where the Romans practiced the Mithraic religion. In fact, it was recently found on a wall at Pompeii.

The roots of the Mithraic religion are also disputed. While most sources claim it to be of ancient Persian birth, David Ulansey makes a strong case for it being a Roman phenomenon, linked to their astrology. The main Mithraic icon is of Perseus slaying a bull, and Ulansey proves that this represents the end of the age of Taurus in the astrological world of ancient Rome. Mithras was seen as a God who controlled the cosmos, actually having the power to slay Taurus, the bull, to end its reign.[10] Many aspects of the religion are shrouded in mystery; for instance, practitioners carried out their rituals in underground worship caverns.

It seems current scholarly thought places the origin of the rotas-sator square in pre-Christian times, at a place dominated by Roman rule, when and where Romans were practicing the Mithraic religion. We may never understand the journey the square took from a house wall in Pompeii to a Lutheran minister in Germany and then to a barn in Pendleton County. For over two thousand years, this symbol, a palindrome, with its captivating arrangement of letters and their possible meaning, has clearly influenced the efforts of folks who placed it in their tool chests of protective amulets for use against unseen dangers.

The barn that contained the rotas-sator square also had a number square consisting of nine numbers. Any way the numbers are added, horizontally, vertically, or diagonally, their sum is eighteen:

5	10	3
4	6	8
9	2	7

Numerology, as borrowed from Jewish Cabalists, was prominent in the writings and teachings of the Old World German Pietists. Their spiritual descendants were among the first German families and settlers in Pennsylvania, and those settlers' children ventured west and south with many who made it to the Appalachian frontier. They were responsible for the thinking that provided motives for installing these magical imprints in barns and houses and cure books in the Potomac Highlands of West Virginia.

The barn-beam amulet I saw also contained the word *abracadabra*, written in two different triangular forms. This word is thought to be a combination of three Chaldean words for the Trinity.[11] These, too, are thousands of years old when used in the triangular form. I had only seen and heard the word used as a way of mocking magicians or magic in general. But I quickly determined that its use in this secluded barn was not some form of light entertainment. Here, various symbols were used in the true sense of the term *hex sign* (witch sign). While scholars continue to argue the occult/non-occult context of hex signs as barn symbols,[12] here in this barn and nearby house in Pendleton County, ancient symbols were used, without question, for apotropaic purposes. They literally were consciously placed for the protection of these buildings and the surrounding property against witchcraft.

While most Old World references to sator square symbols show up in archaeological digs, a farmer used these squares in Pendleton County in the twentieth century in an occult context. While the source of the square is unknown, it was clearly used for occult purpose here and most likely was in oral tradition. It traces to a traditional source and practice, one that has a long and direct link to the past. Another magical number square, whose sum of fifteen, similar to a *saturn square*, is known by Johnny through the old Dahmer family occult manuscript:

4	3	8
9	5	1
2	7	6

Whether these squares were talismans or amulets, they served their owners in important ways. Having arrived with the region's early German settlers, the symbols offered comfort to people who needed comfort when simply "getting by" was a challenging daily occupation. The many unknowns of the natural, spiritual, and cosmological world in which they lived could be confronted through actions learned from and practiced by their ancestors and delivered to them through an unbroken chain of tradition. Rather than learning these practices through the popular new age movement, as do modern neopagans, these folks "came by 'em honest."

Chapter 23

Revels and Belsnickles

> Then great spirits, looking lowly,
> Rush to help those whom they can;
> Whether wicked, whether holy,
> They would heal the wretched man.
> —Goethe

It has been proposed that the cold and dark northern European winters held such authority over human existence that, in prehistory, people sought to give assistance to powers that could influence the change to longer, lighter, and warmer days. Early European folkways that reflect that historical activity are still found in West Virginia. The midwinter period received great attention and was assigned great importance, and the period from November to March was filled with ritualistic activity.

Traditions center on the light and dark aspect of the calendar year. It is known from megalithic stone circles that in prehistory, people calculated the decrease and increase of sunlight and marked the arrival of the winter solstice, which turned the tide of darkness to light. Anthropologists such as James Frazier (*The Golden Bough*) have carried the paradigm far in relating almost all of the origins of Western religion, folklore, and other ritual human activity to magical and fertility thought processes centered on this concept.

Frazier's work prompted a spurious social movement through books such as *The Witch Cult in Western Europe* (1929), by Margaret Murray. Scholars today discredit Murray's work, but its wide dissemination inspired the neo-pagan movement that began in the mid-twentieth century and has carried on into the twenty-first.[1] Bookstores harbor sections with hundreds of new age titles proposing modern activity with direct connections to historic pagan activity. As author Ronald Hutton[2] asserts, few or none stand up to scholarly scrutiny. But with published approval given to ritualistic behavior and magical methodologies, the practitioners are here to stay, and they believe that their actions assist nature's processes in ways that have lingered since prehistory. This is not surprising, because West Virginia tradition bearers believe that negative, satanic forces of evil still lurk in the countryside. It becomes clear that both groups, traditional and modern, are drawing from their own psyches. People in all strata of society believe in the literal accuracy of supernatural biblical stories and mythological folk tales. No one group holds distinct ownership of belief in metaphysical activity.

Pennsylvania's first settlers of any number were Swedes and Finns, who were about a thousand strong when the English claimed the Delaware River territory in 1664. Being Lutherans, they intermingled with, and no doubt influenced, German Lutherans, who began arriving in the 1690s. A description of how these early Pennsylvanians observed Christmas includes numerous rituals to drive away evil spirits.[3] As English, Welsh, Scots-Irish, and German immigrants added their beliefs to the mix, variations of the practices emerged. Since pagan times, this time of year (the solstice) has presented the opportunity to dislodge the old and start anew within a province of good luck and hopeful tidings. Now associated with Christmas, these rituals reveal our not-so-distant heathen past.

European masked or "mumming" practices allude to the death sacrifice, curative reactivation, and rebirth of the spirit that form the basis of these seasonal activities. They range in time of year from late October to early November (All Souls' Day, Day of the Dead,[4] and Halloween—the Celtic Samhain) to the winter solstice (Saturnalia, Christmas) and on into spring (Fastnacht, Mardi Gras, Carnival, Lent, Easter). All have an element of ritual disorder.

Most Americans have participated in Halloween masquerading or trick-or-treating. In my own earliest childhood memories in Pennsylvania, this was only done after dark and included the tradition of going from house to house in costume. This is a common example of community-sanctioned begging—in my case, for apples and candy. We were made to visit long enough for neighbors to attempt to guess our identities. It was called *begging*, and we were *beggars*. Variations on begging exist from place to place, but today it remains a national activity, despite some Christian attempts to bring about its demise. "Mischief night" preceded the actual day of Halloween.

The word *mumming* comes from a word meaning "masking" (as in a disguise). It is currently used by scholars to describe all of the various forms of masquerading and ritual practices that occur from Halloween through Lent. Halpert classifies four different categories of mumming activities: the "Informal Visit," a "Visit with a Formal Performance," "Informal Outdoor Behavior," and "Formal Outdoor Movement."[5]

Philadelphia is famous for its Mummers Day Parade, an organized community expression of a midwinter ritual (the fourth category). The present Pennsylvania custom exhibits some of the common "Lord of Misrule" and Saturnalian reversal traditions of Europe. Parade participants are masked, cross-dressing is practiced, black face was common until recently, and other manners of oppositeness are acted out.[6]

Originally, mumming traditions were sporadic and spontaneous. But as various groups of ethnic people arrived and brought similar midwinter traditions, mumming evolved from the third to the fourth classification. A New Year's song of masquerading beggars in Philadelphia is ascribed to the English and Scots-Irish *guisers*,[7] a word that comes from *disguise*. It includes a request for charity and contains a New Year's blessing. Early forms of the ritual celebration of mumming traveled southwest with the tide and landed in places such as Lewisburg, West Virginia. By that time, mumming had acquired a new name: *shanghai* (see below).

At the center of the fall-to-spring ritual period, at the midwinter solstice, the British mummer's play tradition is said to deal with the very delicate time of death and the rebirth of life and light. This is personified and acted out in comic form with what is said to be deep archetypal purpose. The plays feature the death and resurrection of the central figure in the play, who is revived by "the doctor." This mock-death folk drama is lost in America; however, it was documented in the Appalachians in association with what is called *Old Christmas*. Mumming traditions were strong in Northern Ireland.[8] The Scots-Irish no doubt brought them to the New World.

The play may not have the deep links to our prehistory that many claim. Hutton notes that there is no evidence that the play existed before 1738. He says it spread through chapbooks that popularized the play in the eighteenth century.[9] So while the play may be a relatively recent invention, perhaps it provided a way to ritualize an ancient thought process. Henry Glassie says of the mummers play he studied in northern Ireland, its "meaning lies unavailable to scrutiny in the deep unconscious." He adds, "Traditions are maintained largely for unconscious—known but unarticulated—reasons."[10] This accurately describes West Virginia rituals such as belsnickling, shooting, and shanghai.

We can assume that the midwinter folk rituals in West Virginia arrived with the various European ethnic groups who solidified the various Old World forms into New World practices. An examination of the terminology shows that the words *shooters, mummers, belsnicklers, guisers, fantasticals,*[11] *Fastnacht observers,* and *shanghais* once described more clearly defined activities and character traits in their Old World forms but have since melded into the aggregate forms found in the Appalachian countryside. Regardless of their origins, they are used to describe the ritual actions of people largely of German and Scots-Irish descent.

Mummers and guisers are terms associated with Anglo/Celtic origin. However, numerous versions of the mummers play were also collected in Germany.[12] So terminology here is not a good indicator of origin. In an early Pennsylvania account, mummers, also called shooters, went from house to house performing music in exchange for food and drink. The various traditions there eventually joined and evolved into the formal Mummers Day Parade.[13] This event and its many cousins were first practiced in eastern Pennsylvania, but eventually the practice covered a wide swath of geography that stretched from Philadelphia west to the Appalachian range then down the Appalachian valleys and into old Virginia, western Virginia, Kentucky, Tennessee, North Carolina, and beyond.

In Don Yoder's conclusive afterword to Alfred L. Shoemaker's *Christmas in Pennsylvania*,[14] he effectively summarizes and evaluates numerous European American midwinter rituals. He explains their medieval commonality and purpose and traces their recent documentation and contexts in the New World. He places particular emphasis on the various incarnations of northern European characters, especially the German *belsnickle*.

To people in the Potomac Highlands, *belsnickling* is the action of going from house to house in masquerade, with residents guessing the belsnicklers' identities (the third category of mumming activity). Sometimes treats were offered to the belsnicklers, and sometimes the belsnicklers offered treats to the household. The custom is strong in living memory among older people in areas of eastern West Virginia, and the practice itself persists. During a holiday visit with Johnny Arvin Dahmer just after New Year's Day 2002, he told me that a small troupe of belsnicklers had visited his farm house the previous week. I heard of a few other such instances of belsnickling activity in that area as well, including a report from the Brandywine area. Belsnickling is still practiced in Grant County. Somehow, against great odds, this custom has found a way to continue into the twenty-first century in West Virginia.

Belsnickling and similar activities, as group practices, have obscure beginnings, but they may well go back to the old Teutonic concept of the wild hunt. In Scandinavian and German versions of this myth, a huntsman with dogs, accompanied by spirits, hunts the wild woman. In some versions, the huntsman, a lost soul, leads a band of wild spirits to overrun farms at Christmas time (the winter solstice).[15] If masking in the modern era represents the "wild spirits," and they sometimes rambunctiously act that way, it fits the pattern of belsnickling in West Virginia.

Belsnickles in 2001. Photo by Johnny Arvin Dahmer.

Belsnickles in the Bland Hills, Pendleton County. Date and photographer unknown.

Belsnickles, Pendleton County. Date and photographer unknown. Courtesy Robert C. Whetsell.

    The name for the practice takes its cue from the belsnickle, a Germanic midwinter elf who had a dark side to his being. The word anglicizes the German term *Pelz Nicholas*—*pelz* meaning "fur" or "pelt," and *nicholas* as in St. Nicholas, combining to mean St. Nicholas in fur.[16] The "Nicholas cult," as scholars term it, draws upon ancient legend to personify Santa Claus, originally St. Nicholas, who became the jolly old elf with whom many of us were familiarized as children. But while this benevolent figure makes his rounds in lower-, middle- and upper-class America, his older and somewhat darker cousin, the belsnickle, still surfaces in West Virginia.

    Robert Simmons said that he and friends dressed in masquerade in his younger days. As belsnickles, they would roam the countryside, stopping at farm houses. If the belsnicklers were invited in, the occupants of the house would try to guess the names of those in disguise.

    Robert told me that they carried switches with them. If children were present, they would throw candy onto the floor, and if the children reached for the candy, the belsnicklers would switch their fingers.[17] This same custom is documented in Lancaster and Easton, Pennsylvania, in the nineteenth century,[18] in western Maryland,[19] in the Valley until World War II,[20] and in Germany. In Germany, perhaps overstating his general theory, Frazier relates the overall custom to a process of ritually securing the fertility of the crops.[21]

Looking into the Pendleton County tradition in years past, I found several mentions of the practice in Pendleton newspapers in the early twentieth century. A twentieth-century sampling:

South Branch Review, Friday, January 11, 1901: "W. Hammer and son were out belsnickling" (it goes on to say they were scolded for being late—after New Year's Day).

South Branch Review, December 25, 1908: "Minnie Harper, an expert in the belsnickling business of the Bland Hills."

South Branch Review, January 8, 1909: "Belsnickles have been more plentiful than hen's teeth the past two weeks" (a confusing reversal of the usual "scarce as hen's teeth" analogy).

A positive report in the Pendleton Times, January 9, 1920: "Christmas was good, not a person drunk. The boys and girls have been having a great time belsnickling during the holidays, fooling people. A man with a short leg [even fooled others]."

A disdainful report in the Pendleton Times, January 5, 1923: "The weird voice of the belsnicklers is again abroad in the land, this is a splendid way to spread both mud and diseases."

And a positive report seven days later in the Pendleton Times, January 12, 1923: "Snicklers this year were nice peaceable crowds."

Pendleton Times, January 6, 1928: "[Circleville] Belsnickling has been the order of the night for a couple of weeks."

"Not many belsnicklers during the Holidays [in Teterton]."

Pendleton Times, January 13, 1928: "[Dahmer] Belsnicklers were numerous and lively, more so than usual. 28 visited the home of the writer." (The writer here is Johnny Arvin's father.)

Pendleton Times, January 4, 1935: "[Valley News] Masquerading with the young folks is making a big hit as usual at this time of year. We hope they enjoy it as much as we do having them call."

"Belsnicklers were not as numerous this year as before due to some people not letting them into their homes [in the Cave News section]."

Pendleton Times, January 6, 1949: "Christmas programs, league meetings, caroling and bellsnickling [sic] have been the order of the day for the past week or more."

The 1935 Pendleton Times above, in the Cave News section, a section south of Franklin, makes a telling statement. It appears that incidences of belsnickling were down that year because people were not letting belsnicklers into their homes. Today, this is the reason given by most people for the demise of belsnickling in the countryside.

This fear of belsnicklers coincided with the advent of easier access to state and national news, which began with widespread radio broadcasts at about this time. West Virginia, and especially rural Pendleton County, is among areas with the lowest reported crime rate in the nation, but when national news arrived, detailing hideous crimes, it changed the way people related to crime. Now crime was not some phenomenon that took place many mountain ridges away. It was in their living rooms and was thus projected into their world view. In people's minds, it became a risk to open their doors to people whose masquerade concealed their identity. While I can find no report of an incident in which anyone was actually mistreated or misled by belsnicklers, the possibility was presented and accepted.

This is not to say that belsnicklers were not troublemakers at times, living up to the tradition of drunkenness and rowdiness inherent in the midwinter revels through the centuries. Jocie Armentrout of Harman in Randolph County remembered this sort of belsnickler. But the revelers, though rowdy, were known people, as they had to live within walking distance of the homes they were visiting:

> Nearly all the young people, they'd gather up gangs and they'd dress up in all kinds of silly costumes. Whatever they had to put on, you know, and hide their faces and then go visit the neighbors.
>
> You know how young people are, carrying on all the time. Nothing special, but they'd get into trouble sometimes. They'd get kicked out. I know my Dad kicked them out once. They'd put off some kind of firecracker inside the house, and he got mad and run 'em off. They'd do all kinds of silly stunts. They'd hide their faces and have you guess who they were and all that.[22]

Belsnickling is a ritual tradition so strong that you can not find an older Pendleton Countian who did not participate in, or is at least well acquainted with, the practice. Belsnickles were once dark characters, as Robert Simmons remembered, who carried switches and caused children to be warned, "Be good or the belsnickle will get you." The transfer of this once solitary character, the foreboding belsnickle, to a group mentality and group activity (belsnickling), as in the informal visit, is generally attributed to the influence of mumming traditions in Pennsylvania. The process of going from house to house in masquerade, sometimes begging, eases a primeval urge to act out in a ritualistic way during the darkest period of the year. These rituals are observed among people of European inheritance.[23]

Nineteenth-century pronunciations of and variations on *belsnickle* compiled by Wentz include *Mr. Bellschniggle*, *Belsh-nichel*, or *Bell-schnickel*. Still, in

West Virginia, people have not solidified a common pronunciation for the character, indicating that he is still a folk figure with much variation, even in terminology, and has not been typeset through popular media and become a commonly known and pronounced entity like Santa Claus. In Pendleton County, the figure is the belsnickle. The eyes of my old Hardy County friend, Hoy Saville, lit up when I asked if he knew about belsnickling. "Oh yes," he said. "We used to belschniggle every year."

Many scholars, including Elmer Smith, who researched and chronicled midwinter traditions in the Shenandoah Valley, claim that Anglo/Celtic mumming traditions accepted the belsnickle figure (or vice-versa). What emerged is the tradition whereby people went from house to house, around the time of the winter solstice, in disguise, sometimes begging for food and drink, but in all cases with a mischievous bent.[24]

Many people remember a lot of hooting and yelling during the night-time belsnickling that went on in the Pendleton countryside. One woman I spoke with remembered that the belsnickles would say, "Want to see a pretty man tonight?" as they approached a house. Most changed their voices and even swapped costumes to change identity between houses after telephones were in place and farm families could warn neighbors about belsnickles headed their way.[25]

I have not discovered any particular music associated with the belsnickling tradition, but belsnicklers did sing upon visiting homes in Pendleton County.[26] Throughout the region, belsnickles hooted and hollered, some-times in falsetto.[27]

In Germany, the belsnickle was likely to be a solitary figure. Sometimes he was a figure known or related to Zwarte Piet (Black Pete). He traveled with St. Nicholas[28] but terrified children as he did in eastern Pennsylvania, and still does occasionally in the Appalachians. There may be a connection between the belsnickle and Knecht Ruprecht (Rupert the Servant), who showed up as an eighteenth-century German midwinter figure whose dress seems a burlesque on the dress of gentlemen.[29]

Upon being asked about belsnickling, a Hardy County source told me that yes, she remembered when everyone went Kris Kringling. Kriss Kringle is yet another figure/term associated with the Nicholas cult. Fearing that Christmas was taking on far too much of a secular tone in its celebration, church leaders in Germany decided to introduce the Christkindle (Christ child) as the giver of presents at his nativity commemoration. In very short order in this country, however, Christkindle became Kriss Kringle, a Santa Claus–like figure who sported all the dress and tomfoolery of the Santas and belsnickles he personified.

Our modern Christmas owes much of its form to nineteenth-century works of literature. Wentz allows that our tradition is the accomplishment of three men: Washington Irving, Clement Z. Moore, and an anonymous Pennsylvanian who wrote *Kriss Kringle's Christmas Tree* in 1845.[30] By this time, Kriss Kringle was an entrenched Santa Claus figure.

The folk concept of Christmas within the realm of German Americans, and probably up until the 1845 publication, was geared toward children. The Christkindle brought them presents, but if they were bad, the belsnickle would get them. A Pennsylvania tradition had it that children would set a basket outside the door containing hay for the donkey on which the Christkindle rode. In the morning, it would contain presents left by this Christ child figure.[31]

By the mid-nineteenth century, Kriss Kringle had entirely replaced the Christ child figure in name and purpose. In West Virginia he also took on some of the dark presence of the belsnickle, to the extent that Hardy County youth, in masquerade, roamed about in the night, hooted and howled, knocked on doors, and scared little children, all the while terming what they were doing *Kriss Kringling*.[32]

In Greenbrier County, West Virginia, another midwinter event, the Shanghai Parade, occurs on New Year's Day. *Shanghai*, as a verb, similar to the practice of belsnickling, existed as an unorganized folk ritual in the heavily Germanic areas of eastern West Virginia and was documented in the Valley in the nineteenth century.[33]

The shanghai tradition once included music played on violins, flutes, horns, and drums in the Valley. There is even a fiddle tune called "Shanghai" that is known in West Virginia and may be connected to the shanghai ritual. Today, this activity unfolds as the Shanghai Parade in Lewisburg— Halpert's fourth category of mumming activity. At Lewisburg, people also cross-dress and put on exotic, mostly homemade costumes. Reversal is a theme, and they generally whoop it up in the spirit of old midwinter revelry. As with the Philadelphia mummers, at least some are encouraged by strong drink and a party spirit. No one in Lewisburg knows much about the origins of the parade, although some have put forth weak theories. Like the Mummers Day Parade, the event stems from a folk tradition, an archetypal ritual that pervades the mind-set of these Appalachians just as it did those living in eastern Pennsylvania. The older form that I was able to document in Pendleton County, strongly tied to the tradition of ritual visiting, had given way, in Lewisburg, to a public parade.

Swedish, Finnish, German, English, and Scots-Irish immigrants to Pennsylvania influenced the evolution of the mumming event based on the various traditions of their homelands. Two hundred years later, among practitioners in Lewisburg, none know where it comes from, when it started, or why they do it. An examination of the old Pennsylvania practices, however, provide clues. In all cases, these are boisterous attempts at revelry in the spirit of old Saturnalia events.

Only my oldest (in their eighties to nineties) informants in Pendleton County remember shanghai. These people say that it is much like belsnickling, except it was practiced in daytime and always done on horseback.[34] These same descriptions are documented in the Valley, where the practice has also died out.[35] In Pennsylvania, similar practitioners were called *fantasticals*. All of the people I questioned about shanghai traditions in West Virginia include the qualification that it had to be done on horseback. As horses went out of favor as transportation, so did this ritual activity.

The word *shanghai* itself is still a mystery. A December 16, 1992, article in Lewisburg's *Valley Ranger* reports that in the early 1930s, H. B. Graybill of Lewisburg set out to research the name and the practice. Alas, those he interviewed, even at that early date, had no idea from whence they came.

A photograph has come to light in Pennsylvania showing belsnicklers in masquerade with a few on horseback.[36] Another in the Shenandoah Valley, dated 1910, shows shanghais on horseback.[37] In all cases, masquerade, sanctioned begging, ritualized visiting, and general revelry were the common factors of the shanghai practices I have collected in West Virginia.

The traditional time of year for these practices is in dispute. My old sources have told me that shanghai was done in the week before Christmas and in the daytime, which distinguished it from belsnickling. Most who remember the shanghai tradition say that belsnickling was done after Christmas, up until New Year's or later, and was always done at night.

The question remains whether the shanghai tradition is German or Anglo/Celtic, or both. The possibility of a Scots-Irish origin has been considered in the Valley.[38] I have considered that the word *shanghai* might derive from the Gaelic *sean* (old) and *aghaidh* (face), making the term *sean-aghaidh* (eventually anglicized as *Shanghai*). This could relate it to the masking (old face) tradition. But the overwhelming German population in places where this rural folk observance is still remembered indicates otherwise.

Midwinter revelry as practiced by common folk throughout the Western world to affect good fortune is barely alive, save for some academic interest. It remains in only a few out-of-the-way places and in the subconscious mind of participants. The drive to reexperience and influence the ancient tug of war between the cold, dark, and negative aspects of winter and the good, light, fertile, and growing aspects of spring/summer still form an archetypal force that will not be denied—for instance, at Lewisburg. Some scholars have looked directly at the psychological aspects of the practices in their modern usage and meaning as a way of explaining their continued existence.

A widely held folk belief in the Appalachians is that on Christmas Eve, at midnight, the animals in the barn will all bow down and speak. This was known and documented in the German Palatinate, the area from which many early Appalachians came. The belief's message is that the natural world acknowledges Christ's nativity, and in the Appalachians, this was often tied to the concept of Old Christmas. The British Old Christmas tradition used the same motif, of animals and plants somehow acknowledging the virgin birth, to prove the Julian calendar date of Christmas as the true date. The Old Christmas belief was that Christ's birth occurred eleven days after December 25.

Some who participate in mumming events call themselves *shooters*. *Shooting*, another midwinter ritual with roots in Germany, to some may simply mean taking a shotgun out of doors and shooting up in the air on New Year's Eve at midnight (as my brothers and I did growing up). But *shooting* as a ritual practice had meaning and bearing on the fortune of local residents in West Virginia.[39]

New Year's shooting has a long history in eastern West Virginia, having been introduced by German settlers. Shooting traditions at both New Year's and Christmas have been collected in many areas of the country where German people settled.[40] The tradition was common in West Virginia, in the Valley, and it continues in Cherryville, a small town in Western North Carolina. This North Carolina event is three hundred miles or so down the Appalachian range from where the German settlements of which I speak took hold. Among Germans in Pennsylvania, a song was sometimes sung after the shooting ritual.[41]

In the past, I believe the shooting tradition would have marked the end of the belsnickling season.[42] Masquerade was not a part of the shooting ritual. In all three states where there is evidence, a long blessing was recited as part of the ritual by the "captain," interrupted (in West Virginia) at intervals by the firing of guns. Some believed it was a dangerous practice because a lot of drinking went on. In all cases it fulfills a basic objective of ritual visiting, that is, to bring good luck or fortune to the farmstead or household for the upcoming year.

In the late fifteenth century in Germanic Alsace, a tradition of momeries or Fastnacht was practiced.[43] *Fastnacht* translates to "fast night," or the night before fasting begins for Lent. The pre-Christian thinking was that through sacrifice (fasting), the rebirth of nature could be assisted. The word *Lent* comes from words meaning "length," or "lengthen," as in the lengthening of the days. It is a ritual fast/sacrifice to assist the onset of spring, tied to the moon's position, reinterpreted as a Christian observance.

In Randolph County, the Swiss/German Helvetia community observes Fastnacht prior to the beginning of Lent. It happened that in Helvetia some of the original families were Catholic, and now their pre-Lenten observance is celebrated by all in a nonreligious way.[44] At Helvetia, an effigy of old man winter is burned on a bonfire (from a non-Catholic Swiss winterfest tradition) at the conclusion of the dance that is held to commemorate the fast night, directly dramatizing the purpose of the ritual.[45]

A Tyrolean tradition, occurring on the last Thursday of Lent, was named *Senseless Thursday*, during which belsnickle-like figures with whips and brooms ran about creating havoc, according to Frazier to ensure a good flax crop.[46]

Fastnacht in Helvetia is a time to rid the house of animal products before the Lenten fast. It is also seen as a time to kick up one's heels and celebrate in a ritualistic way. In Helvetia, this celebration takes the form of a dance in the community hall. Tables are laden with doughnuts, crullers, and hosenblats (all traditionally cooked in deep fat) brought by local residents. Many of the residents are in costume and masks, sometimes particularly hideous ones. People now travel considerable distances to take part in the revelry. While a likely excuse to party for some, many also feel the celebrations is somehow connected to something more meaningful than just another weekend bash. The event there has existed since the late 1850s, when the residents' Swiss ancestors came. They came with their *mookas*, their term for superstitions, traditions, and curious habits, intact.[47]

Fastnacht traditions continue in Randolph County, West Virginia, but are also known in neighboring Pendleton. To remove animal products from the house, Pendleton residents, as with those in Helvetia, maintained the tradition of eating foods fried in fat at Fastnacht.

Religious groups originally organized their religious practices around the liturgical year. Catholics, Lutherans, Reformed (now Church of Christ), and Moravians, but also Episcopalians (generally the English), observed Christmas in early times and were more apt to participate in midwinter reveling. The Scots-Irish Presbyterians, the Methodists, and the Baptists, along with the Mennonites and Brethren (Anabaptists), did not.[48] This makes the evidence for a German Lutheran provenance for fall, midwinter, and spring traditions stronger. Lutherans are sometimes referred to as the *Gay Dutch* because they were not reserved about having traditional fun.

To conclude, perhaps I make too much of ethnic origins in trying to pin down the European roots of these seasonal observances. Mumming traditions in America in general, and in the Appalachians of West Virginia in particular, clearly have many sources. There is a movement among folklorists to simply label all of these fall-to-spring activities *mumming*."[49] Folklorists working in both German and Scottish communities in Newfoundland found similar but separate practices of mumming and belsnickling there.[50]

I believe that all of these practices stem from ancient midwinter observances that originally were efforts to assist nature in the death/rebirth process. Various versions of the same observance came from all European countries, especially those in the northern regions, where weather was more of a factor. Perhaps grouping them as simply European mumming traditions is enough, as all Europeans practiced, evolved, and named their versions of the same observances. In the United States, the existence of the various seasonal rituals is the result of three hundred or so years of stirring the pot.

Many aspects of the ritual visiting by neighbors during holiday season were aimed at bringing good fortune to the visited. New Year's shooters had a poetic blessing that I found in both Hardy and Pendleton Counties. This blessing was formally recited in front of farm houses beginning at midnight on New Year's Eve. Johnny Arvin Dahmer furnished the following one. His old copy is in his father's elaborate script and was recited by his father as the "captain" of a band of shooters. The blessing includes his (sometimes confusing) wording and spelling throughout:

> Awake, awake my neighbor dear,
> And to my wish prolonging year,
> The new year now is at the door;
> The old one's past and comes no more.
>
> I wish to you a happy year,
> That you from bad luck may be clear;
> You and your families and all the rest
> May with content be ever blest.
>
> That health and plenty may abound
> With you and all the rest around,
> That you may be free and able
> To feed the hungry at your table.
>
> Your barn may well with grain be filled,
> Your fields and meadows handsome flocked;
> Your cribs may well with corn be flowing
> And the thirsty may not be known.

But mind beside that blessed hand,
Is that which takes at your command;
All that we have can be destroyed
In which are minds are most employed.

By day, by night, at home, abroad
Still we are guarded by our God
By his uncreased bounteous led
By his uncreased closet fed.

Then far beyond that mortal shore,
We'll meet with those that's gone before
Then to think we'll gain the day
To load and shoot the good old way.
(one shot)
Though he may his power employ,
For to exist, for to destroy;
Yet never we'll gain the day
To load and shoot the good old way.
(all shoot)
Any wish now to make an end
For too much time I cannot spend
Shall I salute your wish again
Or would you be opposed to shame

Either pudding, sausage, cider bounce or brandy
Or any such a thing which is handy
The noise should sound throughout the air
This is the day I do declare

And you I will incline
This shall be an ending wish of mine. (volley)[51]

Afterword

People need explanations for that which is unexplainable. They use a keen awareness of signs, omens, or tokens and ascribe to a traditional belief system that accepts these concepts. Belief in spirits (spiritualism) is still a necessary aspect of world religions today, and of course it is sanctioned by the clergy. As eighth-century Germanic tribes converted to Christianity, and on through the ages, older pagan beliefs and myths became stored in the archetypal mind-set, where they remained, ready for use when needed to explain the unexplainable. Adherence to these forms of folk spirituality does not give ground easily, as evidenced throughout this book.

Modern reactions to occult concepts vary. Johnny Arvin is not harsh on local practitioners, be they religious or not, and especially on old-time relatives and people who used the old cure books. He admitted, "It seems like they were getting their religion and witches kind of mixed—kind of together—mixing it." Johnny's neighbor, who was present and listened to Johnny say that, made this keen observation: "You can still be pretty smart, but if you've been conditioned a certain way from little up, it stays with you, you know. What happens when you're young, has a lot of bearing on you later in life."[1]

Johnny agreed, and both men possess a surprisingly sophisticated understanding of culture, tradition, and human nature. They are not quick to judge people who have used folk spirituality to cope with life's trials and fears. They do not readily dismiss as heresy concepts and emotions real people have in dealing with the so-called otherworld and its forces of evil.

I have determined that people believe what they want to believe regardless of circumstance, often because of tradition, a need for hope, or the need to fill a void they cannot fill through normal religious or professional intervention. Preexisting motif easily overrides historical accuracy within folk tradition. This is engaging, unless you are a historian. But then, as someone once said, "What is history but a fable agreed upon."

Folk spirituality is imaginative and fascinating, and it tells us much about those who perpetuate it. Myth, religion, legend, magic, superstition, and ritual behavior serve to provide the realm in which people's extreme hopes and fears may exist, thus explaining why people hold to and act on the values found in this material.

Fetching narratives attract listeners who then promote and affirm the subject matter by passing it on. Occult and magical reasoning provides information known only to a few, thus creating wonderment and curiosity. As the cycle continues, it influences traditional belief through periods of time. The best conduits instinctively and intuitively master the narrative process and gain respect for themselves. Lesser examples, be they stories, songs, jokes, or sayings, fall by the wayside. The values expressed in traditional folklore stand a test of time, and they find their way into and guide standards of community behavior. The process establishes transmission and communication of a subject matter that is attractive as secretive information but may also be humorous, nostalgic, or provide a sense of security.

Occult belief and action as identified within folk curing and the more unusual practices of folk spirituality I have described above, do not now, and have never, defined life in Appalachia. But as curious and abstract as it is, it still persists. The belief system and the practice of the occult, outside of the new age movement, is categorized as antiquated or prescientific by modern standards. Yet a few retain occult methodologies and pass them to younger generations, who adhere to the tenets of the belief. They respect those from whom they learned these practices, and that counts for a lot in itself. As Dovie told me, "They all done it!"

The rise of modern science has affected magical and occult belief in all regions, and what was once common practice increasingly has been relegated to memory. In West Virginia, those who actively practice these traditional beliefs reside in their own little out-of-the-way space, and their beliefs can exist without threatening the greater status quo. Whereas the German clergy both practiced and spread forms of folk spirituality on the eighteenth- and early-nineteenth-century frontier, the clergy of today will have nothing to do with religio-magical practices. Still, folk practitioners invoke the Trinity in their incantations and cures, confirming the religious nature of German occult methodologies. In so doing, they verify the Bible as a sacred text in ways that transcend normal religious practice. The Bible is still used in magical ways by people who find no objection to directing its power to their personal needs within their own folk belief, however distanced from established church doctrine.

During the Civil War, the Union army commonly brought telegraph wires forward with them as they advanced and maintained new positions. As they fortified themselves at their Cheat Mountain camp in Randolph County, West Virginia, they soon laid wire to this forward position. A local backwoods settler, Mathias White, observed this action with great interest. When messages began flowing instantaneously, he determined that what transpired was witchcraft.[2] Here is an early instance of technology existing (to the observer) as occult practice.

Advanced science is the new magic. The cunning folk or magi of old are the scientific specialists of today. For many, prediction of a solar eclipse or the exact timing of some other heavenly event is a magical thing. We have come to a station in the development of human existence where we may not be able to understand the scientific explanation of how a lunar landing occurs or a nuclear reactor works. So we have to depend on and have faith in someone who says that there is, in fact, an explanation for that which we do not comprehend. It literally takes a team of specialists to conceive of and set into motion the many scientific principles at play. So this "coven of adepts" brings about Mars landings, clones animals, and creates unexplainable contrivances and magical objects, but most of us are not able to explain how.

If religion is man's explanation of the universe, and if truth is a goal of human endeavor, religion will have to change to concur with established scientific facts. However, formal religion is not a clay model to be shaped and reshaped to conform to emerging truth, although it grudgingly does that over time. It is a set of timeless laws that are said to be the same yesterday, today, and tomorrow.

Practitioners of folk spirituality, however, have a much more liberal approach, one based on tradition. Classical mythologies (early religions) were relegated to mythical status for adhering precisely to a path of unbending interpretation. Enlightened people accept that religious faith and scientific theory are separate entities, and this allows them to participate in both.

I wonder about those early pious Germans who helped settle the old frontier. They left Europe's religious tradition, with its great formality, learned theological scholarship, advancing civilization, arts, industry, and architecture, for a simple log cabin in the midst of the Appalachian wilderness. They chose a clearer path to an idealistic setting, one that was free from many diversions. They also depended on folk spirituality to cope with life's mysteries.

The Germanic people, who in part established Appalachian culture, had a wide acceptance of occult and magical theories and a participatory relationship to that process of understanding. What makes some of the people described in this book special is the fact that they have not lost faith. They have not found reason to reject traditional processes with which to engage life's trials and tribulations.

A nineteenth-century Swiss/German in Randolph County had the following carved over his door: *Zeit und Raum is alles* ("Time and Space is everything"). This backwoods philosopher was right. Time and space is indeed everything, but the relationship of time to space varies greatly. For some, mostly older folks, what distinguishes the Appalachian back country (happily, in my opinion) is the space it provides for beliefs that are not generally in synch with modern times. Here, some rich folkloric traditions, what I've called folk spirituality, support imaginative concepts that have helped generations deal with everyday life, offering peace of mind and presenting clear-cut choices as an alternative to the complex psychological ramifications of modern living.

Down through the ages the wondrous flights of imagination of people who have related these varied concepts and metaphysical elements of belief have found a way to survive, or "keep a-goin'" as Dovie would say. In truth, these fictions connect people in a cosmic way to the world around them because they are a virtual reality. In other words, these supernatural notions and concepts exist only in human minds and don't have a physical presence. Indeed, much occult belief exists because people believe what they want to believe. Among those I quote here, extreme conceptions have passed in a nonliterate way from one's thinking to another's over a long period and are accepted as reality. Today, many hundreds of books, academic conferences, web sites, advanced courses of study, back-country gossip, and constant public fascination surround this primary subject matter. The subject matter itself is wholly invented, constrained, and transferred in mental space, even as it has transcended continents and oceans. This process further proves the human mind to be the most astounding feature of the universe.

Notes

Introduction

1. Cecil Sharp in John C. Campbell, *The Southern Highlander and His Homeland* (1921; reprint, Lexington: Univ. Press of Kentucky, 1969), 70.
2. Henry Glassie, *Pattern in the Material Folk Culture of the Eastern United States* (Philadelphia: Univ. of Pennsylvania Press, 1968), 79.
3. See John L. Heatwole, *Shenandoah Voices: Folklore, Legends, and Traditions of the Valley* (Berryville, Va.: Rockbridge, 1995); Scott Hamilton Suter, *Shenandoah Valley Folklife* (Jackson: Univ. Press of Mississippi, 1999); and Klaus Wust, *The Virginia Germans* (Charlottesville: Univ. Press of Virginia, 1969).
4. Known as "scrapple" in some areas and available in some local restaurants.
5. Dried apples boiled in a meat broth with dumplings.
6. "There Was a Jolly Butcher Man," as sung by Phyllis Marks of Gilmer County.
7. See David Hackett Fischer, *Albion's Seed: Four British Folkways in America* (Oxford: Oxford Univ. Press, 1989), 731.
8. Pendleton County Commission, *Pendleton County West Virginia Past and Present* (Franklin, W.Va., 1991), 63.
9. Irvin Propst speaks a German dialect and descends from pre-1750 German settlers.
10. The German influence on Appalachian material culture is first credited in Allen H. Eaton's *Handicrafts of the Southern Highlands* (1937; reprint, New York: Dover Publications, 1973) and Glassie's later work, *Pattern in the Material Folk Culture.*
11. The German migration (begun in 1683) was mirrored by the Scots-Irish experience (begun in 1711).
12. Elmer L. Smith, John G. Stewart, and M. Ellsworth Kyger, *The Pennsylvania Germans of the Shenandoah Valley,* Pennsylvania German Folklore Society, vol. 26 (Allentown, Pa.: Schlechter Printing, 1964), xiii.
13. A second wave of Germans came to America in the nineteenth century. Their influence affected eastern and midwestern urban areas the most. See Russell A. Kazal, *Becoming Old Stock: The Paradox of German-American Identity* (Princeton, N.J.: Princeton Univ. Press, 2004).
14. The Blue Ridge Institute and Museum at Ferrum College, the Augusta Collection of Folk Culture at Davis and Elkins College, and the Museum of Appalachia in Norris, Tennessee, contribute evidence.
15. See the introduction to Kazal, *Becoming Old Stock,* for a discussion of the high German percentages of the national figures. John B. Rehder, *Appalachian*

Folkways (Baltimore: Johns Hopkins Univ. Press, 2004), leaves Pendleton County out of his interpretation of "hearth areas."

16. Rehder, *Appalachian Folkways*, describes how cultures assimilate or acculturate, but this leaves out the Appalachian paradigm in which ethnic cultures combine to form a new regional identity.

17. See Kazal, *Becoming Old Stock.*

Chapter 1

1. Montague Summers, *The History of Witchcraft and Demonology* (Seacaucus, N.J.: Castle Books, 1992), 24.

2. Alan C. Kors and Edward Peters, *Witchcraft in Europe, 1100–1700: A Documentary History* (Philadelphia: Univ. of Pennsylvania Press, 1972), 253–59.

3. Herrmann Schuricht, *History of the German Element in Virginia*, 2 vols. in 1 (1898–1900; reprint, Baltimore: Genealogical Publishing, 1977), 60.

4. The Reformed Church, of Swiss origin, recognized Huldreich Zwingli and John Calvin as spiritual leaders and attracted followers in Germany, Holland, and France.

5. In 1683, Franz Daniel Pastorius led thirteen families to America and founded Germantown. He was a writer, he protested slavery, and he organized the country's first fair. Originally a Pietist, he later became a Quaker. See Gerald Wilk, *Americans from Germany* (New York: German Information Center, 1976), 39–40, and Louis D. Winkler, "Pennsylvania German Astronomy and Astrology Conjunctions of 1683, 1694, and 1743," *Pennsylvania Folklife* (Autumn 1975): 32.

Chapter 2

1. George W. Cleek, *Early Western Augusta Pioneers* (Staunton, Va.: Published by the author, 1957), 9.

2. Jon Butler, *Awash in a Sea of Faith: Christianizing the American People* (Cambridge: Harvard Univ. Press, 1990), 175. See also Sally Schwartz, "Religious Pluralism in Colonial Pennsylvania," in *Appalachian Frontiers: Settlement, Society, and Development in the Preindustrial Era*, ed. Robert D. Mitchell (Lexington: Univ. Press of Kentucky, 1991), 52–68.

3. John Alexander Williams, *Appalachia: A History* (Chapel Hill: Univ. of North Carolina Press, 2002), 31—34.

4. Harrison Williams, *Legends of Loudon* (Richmond: Garrett and Massie,1938), 46.

5. Smith, Stewart, and Kyger, *Pennsylvania Germans*, 59.

6. James T. Lemon, quoted in Roger W. Fromm, "The Migration and Settlement of Pennsylvania Germans in Maryland, Virginia and North Carolina and Their Effects on the Landscape," *Pennsylvania Folklife* 37, no. 1 (Autumn 1987): 34.

7. Glassie's maps of folk cultural regions, in *Pattern in the Material Folk Culture*, bear this out.

8. Corliss F. Randolph, ed., *Seventh Day Baptists in Europe and America* (Plainfield, N.J.: American Sabbath Tract Society, 1910), 2:1119.

9. Long was born in 1678. Witch accusations lasted until the 1730s in Europe. See Ian Bostridge, "Witchcraft Repealed," in *Witchcraft in Early Modern Europe: Studies in Culture and Belief*, ed. Jonathan Barry, Marianne Hester, and Gareth Roberts (Cambridge: Cambridge Univ. Press, 1996), 333. Witchcraft was a topic of almost daily discourse among the yeoman class. Smith, Stewart, and Kyger, *Pennsylvania Germans*, 25. See also Kors and Peters, *Witchcraft in Europe*.

10. Emmert F. Bittinger, *Allegheny Passage: Churches and Families, West Marva District, Church of the Brethren, 1752–1990* (Camden, Maine: Penobscot Press, 1990), provides hundreds of family names of Brethren who settled in this area.

11. Klaus Wust, *The Saint-Adventurers of the Virginia Frontier: Southern Outposts of Ephrata* (Edinburgh, Va.: Shenandoah History, 1977), 15.

12. Ibid., 11.

13. Jeff Bach, *Voices of the Turtledoves: The Sacred World of Ephrata* (University Park: Pennsylvania State Univ. Press, 2003), 89–90.

14. Wust, *Saint-Adventurers*, 56–57.

15. The route taken by eighteenth-century pioneer Germans who arrived in Pendleton County.

16. A. S. Bosworth, *A History of Randolph County, West Virginia from Its Earliest Exploration and Settlement to the Present Time* (1916; reprint, Parsons, W.Va.: McClain, 1975), 18.

17. Wust, *Saint-Adventurers*.

18. Daniel Boone used this route into Kentucky beginning in 1767.

19. See Shane interviews in the Draper Manuscripts (State Historical Society of Wisconsin, Madison) as reported in Dale Payne, *Frontier Memories as Taken from the Shane Interviews of Rev. John Dabney Shane of the Draper Manuscripts* (N.p.: Published by the author, 2002).

20. See Maldwyn A. Jones, "The Scotch-Irish in British America," in *Strangers within the Realm: Cultural Margins of the First British Empire*, ed. Bernard Bailyn and Philip D. Morgan (Chapel Hill: Univ. of North Carolina Press, 1991), 300.

21. Samuel Kercheval, *A History of the Valley of Virginia*, 2d ed. (1833; reprint, Woodstock, Va., 1850), 136–37.

22. Leander Petzoldt, "German Tradition," in *Medieval Folklore: A Guide to Myths, Legends, Tales, Beliefs, and Customs*, ed. Carl Lindahl, John McNamara, and John Lindow (New York: Oxford Univ. Press, 2002), 176.

23. See H. A. Ratterman, *Kentucky's German Pioneers*, trans. and ed. by Don Heinrich Tolzmann (Bowie, Md.: Heritage Books, 2001).

Chapter 3

1. Wust, *Saint-Adventurers*, 77.
2. See Randolph, *Seventh Day Baptists in Europe and America* 2:1127.
3. Bach, *Voices of the Turtledoves*, 124–31, 135, 189.
4. This was reported by Sachse and thus is questioned by Bach (*Voices of the Turtledoves*, 178).
5. Cleek, *Early Western Augusta Pioneers*, 10, states that virtually all Appalachian German surnames can be found in I. Daniel Rupp's *Collection of Upwards of Thirty Thousand Names of German, Swiss, Dutch, French and Other Immigrants in Pennsylvania from 1727 to 1776* (1856).
6. Oren F. Morton, *A History of Pendleton County, West Virginia* (1910; reprint, Harrisonburg, Va.: C. J. Carrier Company, 1995), 159–62.
7. See John A. Hostetler, "Folk Healing and Sympathy Healing among the Amish," in *American Folk Medicine: A Symposium*, ed. Wayland Hand (Berkeley: Univ. of California Press, 1976), 253.

Chapter 4

1. Richard E. Wentz, ed., *Pennsylvania Dutch: Folk Spirituality* (New York: Paulist Press, 1993), 33.
2. Variations include "Dunkards," "Tunkers," and so on.
3. Donald B. Kraybill and Carl Desportes Bowman, *On the Backroad to Heaven: Old Order Hutterites, Mennonites, Amish, and Brethren* (Baltimore: Johns Hopkins Univ. Press, 2001), 7.
4. Ibid., 138.
5. Wust, *Virginia Germans*, 129.
6. The water used in foot-washing services has been used for protection against witchery. See Stith Thompson, *Motif-Index of Folk Literature: A Classification of Narrative Elements in Folktales, Ballads, Myths, Fables, Mediaeval Romances, Exempla, Fabliaux, Jest-Books, and Local Legends*, 6 vols. (Bloomington: Indiana Univ. Press, 1955–58), G272.13.
7. Wust, *Virginia Germans*, 45–46.
8. These spelling variations exist within the same family. "Hinkle" is the common modern spelling.
9. I make this assertion having scanned family genealogies published for Hardy, Pendleton, and Grant Counties.
10. See L. Allen Smith, *A Catalogue of Pre-revival Appalachian Dulcimers* (Columbia: Univ. of Missouri Press, 1983), 108–10. Smith's important work on Appalachian dulcimers credits Lewis N. Hinkle with making some early influential Appalachian dulcimers. Ralph Lee Smith, *The Story of the Dulcimer* (Cosby, Tenn.: Crying Creek, 1986), provides more primary documentation. See Gerald Milnes, *Play of a Fiddle: Traditional Music, Dance, and Folklore in West Virginia*

(Lexington: Univ. Press of Kentucky, 1999), 133–54, for other examples of the German connections to the Appalachian dulcimer.

11. Wust, *Virginia Germans*, 132, 140.

12. Ibid., 182.

13. Smith, Stewart, and Kyger, *Pennsylvania Germans*, 94. This sect was connected to George de Benneville, an eccentric who claimed he could visit the realms of the departed spirits. Moon worship is noted in fifteenth-century England, where practitioners were formally accused within the legal system (Keith Thomas, *Religion and the Decline of Magic: Studies in Popular Belief in Sixteenth and Seventeenth-Century England* [New York: Charles Scribner's Sons, 1971], 384), but it was tolerated among Pennsylvania Germans.

14. Bach, *Voices of the Turtledoves*, 12, 17.

15. Wust, *Virginia Germans*, 18.

16. Wentz, *Pennsylvania Dutch*, 85.

17. Reported in Wentz, *Pennsylvania Dutch*, 99–100.

18. Wust, *Saint-Adventurers*, 71.

19. James H. Lehman, *The Old Brethren* (Elgin, Ill.: Brethren Press, 1976), 84.

20. Wust, *Virginia Germans*, 62–63.

21. John L. Brooke, *The Refiner's Fire: The Making of Mormon Cosmology, 1644–1844* (Cambridge: Cambridge Univ. Press, 1996), 25.

22. See Peter Elmer, "Saints or Sorcerers," in *Witchcraft in Early Modern Europe*, ed. Barry, Hester, and Roberts, 145–81.

23. See Elder John Sparks, *The Roots of Appalachian Christianity: The Life and Legacy of Elder Shubal Stearns* (Lexington: Univ. Press of Kentucky 2001), for the beginnings of Appalachian Christianity, including preaching style and worship traditions.

24. For a cogent discussion of Appalachian religion and Calvinist thought regarding predestination through time, see Loyal Jones, *Faith and Meaning in the Southern Uplands* (Urbana: Univ. of Illinois Press, 1999).

25. Jon Butler, "Magic, Astrology, and the Early American Religious Heritage, 1600–1760," in *Witches of the Atlantic World: A Historical Reader and Primary Sourcebook*, ed. Elaine G. Breslaw (New York: New York Univ. Press, 2000), 524.

26. Ruth Little, *Sticks and Stones: Three Centuries of North Carolina Grave Markers* (Chapel Hill: Univ. of North Carolina Press, 1998), ties the use of celestial symbols to Scots-Irish gravestone motifs.

27. It has been pointed out that May would be in the sign of the bull.

28. From an old Dahmer family hand-written manuscript, reported by John Stewart and Elmer Smith in a Madison College sociology bulletin.

29. Butler, "Magic, Astrology," 519.

30. Kors and Peters, *Witchcraft in Europe*, 25–27.

31. Jeffrey Burton Russell, *Witchcraft in the Middle Ages* (Ithaca, N.Y.: Univ. of Cornell Press, 1972), 17.

32. Brooke, *Refiner's Fire*, 5.

33. Bach, *Voices of the Turtledoves*, 172–73.

34. E. G. Alderfer, *The Ephrata Commune: An Early American Counterculture* (Pittsburgh: Univ. of Pittsburgh Press, 1985), 131, 148.

35. Reported in Wentz, *Pennsylvania Dutch*, 26.

36. Brooke, *Refiner's Fire*, 8–10.

37. While some few Pennsylvania groups entertained Rosicrucian principles, the mystics at Ephrata, according to the best scholarship, were not as involved as previously thought.

38. A. Russell Slagle, "The Schlegel Family and the Rosicrucian Movement," *Pennsylvania Folklife* 25, no. 3 (Spring 1976): 32–38.

39. Robert Simmons, interview, Pendleton County, Apr. 5, 1997. The Gospel of St. John is known to have been carried to ward off dangers and mishaps. See Thomas, *Religion and the Decline of Magic*, 31.

40. Benjamin Funk, *Life of John Kline: 1797–1864* (Broadway, Va.: Brethren Press, 1900), 213, 382.

41. Thomas Rutter, a confidant of William Penn, protested bondage through a pamphlet in 1694, causing a split among Quakers. Rutter established iron making in Pennsylvania and influenced Conrad Beissel's group at Germantown.

42. Walter L. Eye, "A Compilation of Simmons Descendants of Pendleton County, West Virginia," unpublished MS, 1988.

Chapter 5

1. Wentz, *Pennsylvania Dutch*, 10-11, and Louis D. Winkler, "Pennsylvania German Astronomy and Astrology IX, Johann Friederich Schmidt," *Pennsylvania Folklife* 24, no. 3 (Spring 1975): 45-46.

2. Louis D. Winkler, "Pennsylvania German Astronomy and Astrology III, Comets and Meteors," *Pennsylvania Folklife* (Autumn 1972), 36–37. Some modern historians dispute some of Sachse's findings, but in this area he is considered reliable.

3. Louis D. Winkler, "Pennsylvania German Astronomy and Astrology XII: Conjunctions of 1683, 1694, and 1743," *Pennsylvania Folklife* 25, no. 1 (Fall 1976): 39–43.

4. Bach, *Voices of the Turtledoves*, 174–75.

5. See Louis D. Winkler, "Pennsylvania German Astronomy and Astrology XI, Contemporary Almanacs," *Pennsylvania Folklife* 24, no. 4 (Summer 1975), for a comparison of numerous German almanacs.

6. Louis D. Winkler, "Pennsylvania German Astronomy and Astrology," *Pennsylvania Folklife* 28, no. 2 (Winter 1978–79): 22.

7. See Butler, "Magic, Astrology," 519. Owen Davies, *Witchcraft, Magic and Culture, 1736–1951* (Manchester: Manchester Univ. Press, 1999), 66, notes that in early-nineteenth-century England, publishers of almanacs were prosecuted for public deception.

8. Keith A. Cerniglia, "The American Almanac and the Astrology Factor," http://www.earlyamerica.com/2003_spring/almanac.htm
9. Phebe Earle Gibbons, *Pennsylvania Dutch and Other Essays* (1872; reprint, with an introduction by Don Yoder, Mechanicsburg, Pa: Stackpole Books, 2001), 271.
10. Wayland Hand, "German American Folklore," *Journal of American Folklore* 60, no. 238 (1947): 368.
11. Otis Rose, interview with author, videotape, Braxton County, July 21, 1995.
12. Clyde Case, interview with author, Braxton County, Mar. 21, 1995.
13. Thelma Smith and Sharon Walker, interview with Kent Walker, Davis and Elkins College student, Webster County, April 11, 2005.
14. Case interview; Israel Welch, interview with author, Mineral County, June 30, 1995; Hoy Saville, interview with author, Hardy County, June 29, 1995; Phoeba Parsons, interview with author, Jan. 19, 1995; Rose interview.
15. From Edwin Miller Fogel's *Beliefs and Superstitions of the Pennsylvania Germans* (1915), reported by Louis D. Winkler, "Pennsylvania German Astronomy and Astrology XII: Health and the Heavens," *Pennsylvania Folklife* 26, no. 1(Fall 1976): 43.
16. Catfish Gray, interview with author, Mason County, Apr. 24, 1996.
17. Wentz, *Pennsylvania Dutch*, 299.
18. Case interview.

Chapter 6

1. Wust, *Saint-Adventurers*, 82–101. Only one copy of the original tract survives, reprinted in Wust, *Saint-Adventurers*. Also see Smith, Stewart, and Kyger, *Pennsylvania Germans*, 97–98.
2. Alf Aberg, *The People of New Sweden: Our Colony on the Delaware River, 1638–1655* (Stockholm: Bokförlaget Natur och Kultur, 1988), 142. The people of New Sweden were of both Swedish and Finnish ethnicity.
3. Robert Nelson, *Finnish Magic: A Nation of Wizards, a World of Spirits* (St. Paul, Minn.: Llewellyn Publications, 1999), 20–21.
4. Christopher Ward, *The Dutch and Swedes on the Delaware, 1609–1664* (Philadelphia: Univ. of Pennsylvania Press, 1930), 103.
5. Irvin Propst, interview, Pendleton County, July 21, 2000.
6. Translated by Elmer Smith and John Stewart from a Dahmer family manuscript. The reference to "n.n." indicates the first and last names of the patient.
7. Don Yoder, "Hohman and Romanus: Origins and Diffusion of the Pennsylvania German Powwow Manual," in *American Folk Medicine: A Symposium*, ed. Hand, 235.
8. The standard text for this approach is *Long Lost Friend*, first published in English in Pennsylvania by John George Hohman in 1856.
9. Vance Randolph, *Ozark Magic and Folklore* (1947; reprint, New York: Dover, 1964), 265. Power doctors are noted by Elizabeth Brandon, "Folk Medicine in French Louisiana," in *American Folk Medicine*, ed. Hand, 215–34.

10. Leonard W. Roberts, *Up Cutshin and Down Greasy: Folkways of a Kentucky Mountain Family* (1959; reprint, Lexington: Univ. Press of Kentucky, 1988), 88–99.

11. Mac E. Barrick, *German-American Folklore* (Little Rock, Ark.: August House, 1987), 173. Suter, *Shenandoah Valley Folklife*, 63, says it came from the Algonquins.

12. Bruce Jackson, "The Other Kind of Doctor," in *American Folk Medicine*, ed. Hand, 269.

13. Kent Lilly, interview with author, Nov. 11, 1997.

14. See Wolfgang Behringer, "Witchcraft Studies in Austria, Germany and Switzerland," in *Witchcraft in Early Modern Europe*, ed. Barry, Hester, and Roberts, 64.

15. Carlo Ginzburg, *The Night Battles: Witchcraft and Agrarian Cults in the Sixteenth and Seventeenth Centuries* (Baltimore: John Hopkins Univ. Press, 1992).

16. For an anthropological assessment of this form, see I. M. Lewis, *Religion in Context: Cults and Charisma* (Cambridge: Cambridge Univ. Press, 1986).

17. J. Hampden Porter, "Notes on the Folk-Lore of the Mountain Whites of the Alleghenies," *Journal of American Folklore* 7, no. 25 (Apr.–Jun. 1894): 107.

18. Ronald Hutton, in *The Triumph of the Moon: A History of Modern Witchcraft* (Oxford: Oxford Univ. Press, 1999), presents overwhelming evidence to this effect.

19. George W. Hudler, *Magical Mushrooms, Mischievous Molds* (Princeton, N.J.: Princeton Univ. Press, 1998), 74–77.

20. Andrew Nikiforuk, *The Fourth Horseman: A Short History of Epidemics, Plagues, Famines, and Other Scourges* (New York: M. Evans, 1991), 119.

21. Hudler, *Magical Mushrooms, Mischievous Molds*, 69–81.

22. William A. Imboden Jr., "Plant Hypnotics," in *American Folk Medicine*, ed. Hand, 159–67.

23. See Milnes, *Play of a Fiddle*, 63–65.

24. Robert D. Mitchell, *Appalachian Frontiers: Settlement, Society, and Development in the Preindustrial Era* (Lexington: Univ. Press of Kentucky, 1991), 12.

25. Butler, *Awash in a Sea of Faith*, 87.

26. William E. Monter, *Witchcraft in France and Switzerland: The Borderlands during the Reformation* (Ithaca, N.Y.: Cornell Univ. Press, 1976), 31, quoting from Nikolas Paulus, *Hexenwahn und Hexenprozess, vornehmlich im 16, Jahrhundert* (Freiburg: Herder, 1910).

27. Reported in Davies, *Witchcraft, Magic and Culture*, 12–14.

28. Cleek, *Early Western Augusta Pioneers*.

Chapter 7

1. A. G. Roeber, "The Origin of Whatever Is Not English among Us: The Dutch- Speaking and German-Speaking Peoples of Colonial British America," in *Strangers within the Realm*, ed. Bailyn and Morgan, 268.

2. Quoted in Alderfer, *The Ephrata Commune*, 115.

3. Suter, *Shenandoah Valley Folklife*, 28.

4. In 1810, John Wyeth published *Leichter Unterricht in der Vokal Musik*, written by Pennsylvanian Joseph Doll, for German singers. It was a mixture of traditional German hymns and New England (Anglo) favorites. Camp-meeting or Great Awakening spirituals, along with secular tunes and even popular fiddle tunes, supported the religious messages of the poetry. *Shape-Note Singing in the Shenandoah Valley: An Address Delivered to the Singer's Glen Music and Heritage Festival, Aug. 16, 1997, on the Sesquicentennial of Music Printing at Singers Glen, Virginia.*

5. Shape notation was invented by John Connelly in Philadelphia about 1790. It was introduced with the book *The Easy Instructor*, published in 1802 in Pennsylvania. By 1815, Funk was publishing hymnals in the Valley. See George Pullen Jackson, *White Spirituals in the Southern Uplands* (Hatboro, Pa.: Folklore Associates, 1964), 13–15, and John Bealle, *Public Worship, Private Faith: Sacred Harp and American Folksong* (Athens: Univ. of Georgia Press, 1997).

6. Wust, *Saint-Adventurers*, 41.

7. See Drew Beisswenger, *Fiddling Way Out Yonder: The Life and Music of Melvin Wine* (Jackson: Univ. of Mississippi Press, 2002), 13.

8. This method of holding the fiddle was not limited to Germany and is more tied to time period than place or ethnic origin.

9. Luther Bergdall, "The Morgan Dasher Family: Ten Generations in America, 1737–1984" (Moss Beach, Calif.: n.p., 1984).

10. Richard Raichelson, "The Social Context of Musical Instruments within the Pennsylvania German Culture," *Pennsylvania Folklife* 25, no. 1 (Autumn 1975): 43.

11. Milnes, *Play of a Fiddle*, 135.

12. Little, *Sticks and Stones*, 23.

13. The tulip reached its zenith as the "holy lily" in Germany, indicating religious affiliation. The flower had come to Europe from Asia Minor in the sixteenth century. Henry J. Kauffman, *Pennsylvania Dutch Folk Art* (1946; reprint, New York: Dover, 1964), 13.

14. Wentz, *Pennsylvania Dutch*, 19.

15. Ibid., 70.

16. Wust, *Virginia Germans*, 180.

17. Steven Ozment, *Flesh and Spirit: Private Life in Early Modern Germany* (New York: Viking Press, 1999), 95.

18. Wust, *Virginia Germans*, 181.

19. H. E. Comstock, *The Pottery of the Shenandoah Valley Region* (Winston-Salem, N.C.: Museum of Early Southern Decorative Arts, 1994), 12–14.

20. Elmer L. Smith, *Pottery: A Utilitarian Folk Craft* (Lebanon, Pa.: Applied Arts, 1972), 14, makes this assertion.

21. *Helvetia: The Swiss of West Virginia*, prod. Gerald Milnes, VHS, color, 60 min., AHV-93, Augusta Heritage Center, Elkins, W.Va., 1993.

22. Johnny Arvin Dahmer, interview with author, Pendleton County, videotape, Dec. 5, 2000.

23. Sylvia O'Brien, interview with author, Clay County, videotape, Mar. 13, 2000.
24. Dana Keplinger, interview with author, Pendleton County, videotape, July 21, 2000.
25. Rachel Nash Law and Cynthia W. Taylor, *Appalachian White Oak Basketmaking: Handing Down the Basket* (Knoxville: Univ. of Tennessee Press, 1991), 11.
26. Ibid., 203.
27. *Twisted Laurel: Folk Art, Folklore and Music from the West Virginia Woods*, produced by Gerald Milnes, VHS, color, 30 min., AHV-99, Augusta Heritage Center, Elkins W.Va., 1999. Tyson taught his techniques to an apprentice through the West Virginia Folk Art Apprenticeship Program.
28. See Yoder, "Hohman and Romanus"; Henry Glassie, "Folk Art," in *Folklore and Folklife: An Introduction*, ed. Richard M. Dorson (Chicago: Univ. of Chicago Press, 1972), 274; and Don Yoder and Thomas E. Graves, *Hex Signs: Pennsylvania Dutch Barn Symbols and Their Meaning* (Mechanicsburg, Pa.: Stackpole Books, 2000).

Chapter 8

1. Johnny Arvin Dahmer, interview with author, Pendleton County, Jan. 8, 1998.
2. Dahmer interview, Dec. 5, 2000.
3. Johnny Arvin Dahmer, interview with author, Pendleton County, Nov. 22, 1997.
4. Johnny Arvin Dahmer and Dennis Mitchell, interview with author, Pendleton County, Feb. 11, 2001.
5. Dahmer interview, Nov. 22, 1997.
6. An occult manuscript of similar cures has survived in South Carolina, but little is known of its origin. See Butler, "Magic, Astrology," 520.
7. This is an old occult text that was widely published in Europe. Elmer L. Smith and John Stewart discuss the properties of the Dahmer manuscript in "An Occult Remedy Manuscript from Pendleton County, West Virginia," *Madison College Studies and Research Bulletin* 22, no. 2 (1964): 77–85.
8. Yoder, "Hohman and Romanus," shows that Hohman's *Pow-Wows* draws many of its cures and remedies from the German *Romanusbuchlein*, published in 1788.
9. Wust, *Virginia Germans*, 182.
10. Wust, *Saint-Adventurers*, 62.
11. Petzoldt, "German Tradition," 176.
12. Johnny Arvin Dahmer and Eva Simmons, interview with author, Pendleton County, Aug. 12, 1998.
13. Robert Simmons interview.
14. Dahmer and Mitchell interview.
15. Dahmer interview, Dec. 5, 2000.

Chapter 9

1. Walter L. Eye, "A Compilation of the Descendants of Abraham Pitsenbarger," unpublished MS, 1990.
2. Robert Simmons interview, Apr. 5, 1997.
3. See George Korson, *Black Rock: Mining Folklore of the Pennsylvania Dutch* (Baltimore: John Hopkins Press, 1960), 157.
4. This mill sold for one dollar at the sale after the siblings had all died and Mable went to a "home."
5. Many believe the Swedes and Finns had the most influence on log cabins in America, having arrived in 1638 and introduced log construction to the Delaware Valley. See John Morgan, *The Log House in East Tennessee* (Knoxville: Univ. of Tennessee Press, 1990), 8–9.
6. See Rob Propst, field recording by Nick Royal, Augusta Collection, Booth Library, Davis and Elkins College, for an example of fiddling by a member of this family.
7. A West Virginia expression still used by some old-timers, meaning "gone to ruin" or "gone to rack and ruin."
8. Charles E. Martin, *Hollybush: Folk Housing and Social Change in an Appalachian Community* (Knoxville: Univ. of Tennessee Press, 1984), 17, argues that "pole houses" with weight-pole roofs were temporary shelters for the one or two years it took to construct a decent hewn-log house. These West Virginia examples challenge that history.

Chapter 10

1. A situation in which an animal's (or human's) extremity withers.
2. Don Yoder, "Folk Medicine," in *Folklore and Folklife: An Introduction*, ed. Richard M. Dorson (Chicago: Univ. of Chicago Press, 1972), 192.
3. Beatriz Barba de Piña Chan, "Spells," in *Hidden Truths: Magic, Alchemy, and the Occult*, ed. Lawrence E. Sullivan (New York: Macmillan, 1989), 217–23.
4. See David Sutton, *One's Own Hearth Is Like Gold: A History of Helvetia, West Virginia* (New York: Peter Lang, 1990), 19.
5. An unusual Scots-Irish dialectic word meaning "thick curdled milk."
6. Jeffrey Russell, *A History of Witchcraft: Sorcerers, Heretics, and Pagans* (London: Thames and Hudson, 1980), 42.
7. Wentz, *Pennsylvania Dutch*, 12–13.
8. Dovie Lambert, interview with author, Randolph County, videotape, Feb. 19, 1998.
9. Collected by Wentz, *Pennsylvania Dutch*, 303.
10. Lambert interview, Feb. 19, 1998.
11. So called by anthropologist I. M. Lewis. Lewis, *Religion in Context*, x.
12. Rosemary Ellen Guiley, *The Encyclopedia of Witches and Witchcraft* (New York: Facts on File Books, 1989), 10.

13. Told to me by a Swiss descendant near Helvetia, Randolph County.
14. Ozment, *Flesh and Spirit*, 92, 110.
15. Theodor H. Gaster, "Amulets and Talismans," in *Hidden Truths*, ed. Sullivan, 145–50.
16. Mary Cottrell, interview with author, Randolph County, June 30, 2000.
17. Charles H. Talbot, "Folk Medicine and History," in *American Folk Medicine*, ed. Hand, 7–10.
18. Reported in Barrick, *German-American Folklore*, 179.
19. Davies, *Witchcraft, Magic and Culture*, 128.
20. Lambert interview, Feb. 19, 1998.
21. Johnny Arvin Dahmer, interview with author, Pendleton County, Aug. 11, 1998; Bill Dahmer, interview with author, Pendleton County, May 17, 2000.
22. Cottrell interview. See Thompson, *Motif-Index of Folk Literature*, G269.17.
23. Stanley Propst and Tyson Propst, interview, Pendleton County, Dec. 4, 1997.
24. I have collected this term for this procedure in many areas of the state.
25. Lilly interview.
26. David J. Hufford, "Contemporary Folk Medicine," in *Other Healers: Unorthodox Medicine in America*, ed. Norman Gevitz (Baltimore: John Hopkins Univ. Press, 1988), 231.
27. Cornelius Weygandt, "The Red Hills," in *Pennsylvania Dutch*, ed. Wentz, 110.
28. John G. Gager, *Curse Tablets and Binding Spells from the Ancient World* (New York: Oxford Univ. Press, 1992), 18.
29. Ralph Merrifield, *The Archaeology of Ritual and Magic* (New York: New Amsterdam, 1988), 155.
30. Ibid., 12.
31. C. J. S. Thompson, *The Hand of Destiny: Folklore and Superstition for Everyday Life* (New York: Bell Publishing, 1989), 217.
32. Lewis, *Religion in Context*, 46.
33. Gager, *Curse Tablets and Binding Spells*, 6.
34. Heatwole, *Shenandoah Voices*, 53.

Chapter 11

1. Dahmer and Simmons interview.
2. See Hal Rammel, *Nowhere in America: The Big Rock Candy Mountain and Other Comic Utopias* (Urbana: Univ. of Illinois Press, 1990).
3. Porter, "Notes on the Folk-Lore," 116.
4. Smith, Stewart, and Kyger, *Pennsylvania Germans*, 138.
5. Robin Briggs, *Witches and Neighbors: The Social and Cultural Context of European Witchcraft* (New York: Penguin Books, 1996), 30.
6. Émile Grillot de Givry, *Witchcraft, Magic and Alchemy* (New York: Bonanza Books, n.d.), 136.
7. Phyllis Marks, interview with author, Apr. 20, 1995; Hazel Stover, interview with author, Oct. 2, 1995; Elouise Mann, interview with author, Dec. 1,

1995. Aarne-Thompson tale type 285. Considered a Pennsylvania German tale by Wentz in *Pennsylvania Dutch*, 305–6. Collected by the Brothers Grimm.

8. Marks interview; William May, interview with author, May 24, 1995.

9. Summers, *History of Witchcraft and Demonology*, 158.

10. Guiley, *Encyclopedia of Witches and Witchcraft*, 341. Russell, *Witchcraft in the Middle Ages*, 251.

11. Cottrell interview. This is a motif that occurs widely. Randolph notes that ducks were killed after their owner refused to sell them to a witch. Randolph, *Ozark Magic and Folklore*, 271.

12. Dahmer and Simmons interview.

Chapter 12

1. Roeber, "Origin of Whatever Is Not English," 270.

2. Heatwole, *Shenandoah Voices*, 50.

3. Parsons interview.

4. Emogene introduced me to the difference between "red" and "white" sassafras.

5. This is edited from Emogene Nichols, interview with author, Sept. 21, 1990.

6. Ibid.

7. Recorded in Smith, Stewart, and Kyger, *Pennsylvania Germans*, 129.

8. Cottrell interview.

9. Smith, Stewart, and Kyger, *Pennsylvania Germans*, 133–34.

10. Described in a Madison College bulletin by John Stewart and Elmer L. Smith.

11. See Alan Dundes, *Life Is Like a Chicken Coop Ladder: A Study of German National Character through Folklore* (Detroit: Wayne State Univ. Press, 1989).

12. Waneta Brown and Jack Mayse, interview with author, Braxton County, May 4, 1988

13. Carmen R. Rexrode, "Take Moonshine According to Age: Healing in Pendleton County, West Virginia 1900–1940," senior thesis, Harvard Univ., 1982, 58.

14. Ibid., 56.

15. From Raleigh County.

16. Rexrode, "Take Moonshine According to Age," 57.

17. Cottrell interview.

18. Korson, *Black Rock*, 285–87.

19. See Don Yoder, *Groundhog Day* (Mechanicsburg, Pa.: Stackpole Books, 2003), 41–54.

20. Brown and Mayse interview.

21. Rexrode, "Take Moonshine According to Age," 80.

22. James George Frazer, *The Golden Bough* (1922; reprint, New York: Macmillan, 1950), 12–55.

23. Dahmer manuscript.

24. Ibid.

25. Welch interview; Anthony Swiger, interview with author, Randolph County, June 29, 1995.

26. Rose interview.

27. Lambert interview, Feb. 19, 1998.

28. Smith, Stewart, and Kyger, *Pennsylvania Germans*, 159.

29. May interview.

30. Barrick, *German-American Folklore*, 174.

31. Virginia Folklore Collection, "Valley Folklore" (Madison College pamphlet), no. 8, 1966, Madison College Library, Harrisonburg, Va.

32. Brown and Mayse interview.

33. An English translation was made by Smith and Stewart.

34. *The Egyptian Secrets* or *The Book of Secrets*, credited to Albertus, is thought to be a naïve compilation by one of his students.

35. Hohman's book was published in German in 1820 (English translation, 1856), according to Yoder, "Hohman and Romanus," 235–36.

36. Earl F. Robacker, *Arts of the Pennsylvania Dutch* (New York: Castle Books, 1965), 213.

37. Ioan Petru Culianu, "Magic in Medieval and Renaissance Europe," in *Hidden Truths*, ed. Sullivan, 111–12.

38. See Smith, Stewart, and Kyger, *Pennsylvania German*, 162; Alan Dundes, *Interpreting Folklore* (Bloomington: Indiana Univ. Press, 1980), 134–59.

39. Victor C. Dieffenbach, "Powwowing among the Pennsylvania Germans," *Pennsylvania Folklife* 25, no. 2 (Winter 1975–76): 31.

40. Smith, Stewart, and Kyger, *Pennsylvania Germans*, 136.

41. Barrick, *German-American Folklore*, 174–75.

42. Smith, Stewart, and Kyger, *Pennsylvania Germans*, 158.

Chapter 13

1. Ginzburg, *Night Battles*, xx.

2. Russell, *Witchcraft in the Middle Ages*, 25.

3. Kors and Peters, *Witchcraft in Europe*, 48–49.

4. For another West Virginia example, see S. P. Bayard, "Witchcraft Magic and Spirits on the Border of Pennsylvania and West Virginia," *Journal of American Folklore* 51, no. 199 (Jan.–Mar. 1938), 49.

5. Davies, *Witchcraft, Magic and Culture*, 195.

6. Catharina Raudvere, "Nightmare," in *Medieval Folklore*, ed. Lindahl, McNamara, and Lindow, 292.

7. Charles Zika, "Images of Circe and Discourses of Witchcraft, 1480–1580," *Zeitenblicke*, online journal, July 2002, http://www.zeitenblicke.de/2002/01/zika/zika.html.

8. I have heard these two methods in Braxton County.

9. Roeber, "Origin of Whatever Is Not English," 270.

10. Russell, *Witchcraft in the Middle Ages*, 15.

11. Dorothy D. Lee, "Greek Personal Anecdotes of the Supernatural," *Journal of American Folklore* 64, no. 253 (1951): 309.

12. Ginzburg, *Night Battles*, 1–8.
13. Dahmer interview, Aug. 11, 1998.
14. See Allison P. Coudert, "The Myth of the Improved Status of Protestant Women," in *Witches of the Atlantic World*, ed. Breslaw, 309–21.
15. Briggs, *Witches and Neighbors*, 77–78, 279.
16. Dana Keplinger in *Signs, Cures and Witchery: Appalachian Cosmology and Belief*, prod. Gerald Milnes, VHS, color, 60 min., Augusta Heritage Center, Elkins, W.Va., 2001.
17. Behringer, "Witchcraft Studies in Austria, Germany and Switzerland," 78.

Chapter 14

1. Culianu, "Magic in Medieval and Renaissance Europe."
2. See *Fiddles, Snakes and Dog Days: Old-Time Music and Lore in West Virginia*, prod. Gerald Milnes, VHS, color, 60 min., Augusta Heritage Center, Elkins, W.Va., 1997, for numerous examples of snakes "charming" people.
3. Charlotte H. Deskins, "New Moon, True Moon: Love Lore from McDowell County," *Goldenseal Magazine* 12, no. 1 (1986): 62. Used with permission.
4. Julio Caro Baroja, "Magic and Religion in the Classical World," in *Witchcraft and Sorcery*, ed. Max Marwick (Middlesex, England: Penguin Books, 1970), 67–75.
5. Samuel X. Radbill, "The Role of Animals in Infant Feeding," in *American Folk Medicine*, ed. Hand, 28–29.
6. Russell, *Witchcraft in the Middle Ages*, 38.
7. Discussed in Behringer, "Witchcraft Studies in Austria, Germany and Switzerland," 87.
8. Dahmer interview, Aug. 11, 1998.
9. See Jones, *Faith and Meaning*, 74–96, and Dieffenbach, "Powwowing among the Pennsylvania Germans," 40.
10. See Behringer, "Witchcraft Studies in Austria, Germany and Switzerland." Cecil Sharp in Campbell, *Southern Highlander*, 70.
11. Ginzburg, *Night Battles*, 6.
12. Probably the last maypole that was used in the region was at Helvetia, West Virginia, Randolph County, where Swiss settlers brought the tradition and practiced it up until the 1950s.
13. Collected by Vance Randolph and reported in *Folklore in America: Tales, Songs, Superstitions, Proverbs, Riddles, Games, Folk Drama and Folk Festival*, ed. Tristram P. Coffin and Hennig Cohen (New York: Doubleday, 1966), 137–39.
14. Dieffenbach, "Powwowing among the Pennsylvania Germans," 41.
15. Ginzburg, *Night Battles*, 7.
16. Ozment, *Flesh and Spirit*, 36.
17. Briggs, *Witches and Neighbors*, 83.
18. Rossell Hope Robbins, *The Encyclopedia of Witchcraft and Demonology* (New York: Crown Publishers, Inc., 1959), 305–7.
19. Dahmer interview, Pendleton County, Aug. 12, 1998.

20. Dahmer and Mitchell interview.
21. Lambert interview, Randolph County, Feb. 19, 1998.
22. Ibid.
23. Cottrell interview.
24. Keplinger interview.
25. Deskins, "New Moon, True Moon," 64.
26. Jackson, "Other Kind of Doctor," 260.
27. Thompson, *Motif-Index of Folk Literature*, G272.7.2.

Chapter 15

1. Dahmer interview, Aug. 12, 1998.
2. Marks interview, and Glen Smith, interview with author, Feb. 15, 1995.
3. See Thompson, *Motif-Index of Folk Literature*, D1786 (magic power at crossroad).
4. Wallace Notestein, *A History of Witchcraft in England from 1558 to 1718* (New York: Thomas Y. Crowell, 1968), 94–97.
5. Dahmer interview, Jan. 8, 1998, Dec. 5, 2000, and Dec. 11, 2001.
6. Collected by Dwight Diller in Carl Fleischhauer and Alan Jabbour, eds., *The Hammons Family: A Study of a West Virginia Family's Traditions* (Washington, D.C.: Library of Congress, 1973), 9–10. This event took place on the Williams River in the mid- to late nineteenth century.
7. Dahmer interview, Dec. 5, 2000.
8. See Briggs, *Witches and Neighbors*, 171.
9. Irvin Propst interview.
10. Sigrid Brauner, *Fearless Wives and Frightened Shrews: The Construction of the Witch in Early Modern Germany* (Amherst: Univ. of Massachusetts Press, 1995), 6.
11. Dahmer interview, Aug. 11, 1998.

Chapter 16

1. Dahmer interview, Dec. 5, 2000.
2. Randolph, *Ozark Magic and Folklore*, 298.
3. Iona Opie and Moira Tatem, eds., *A Dictionary of Superstitions* (Oxford: Oxford Univ. Press, 1989), 92.
4. Keplinger interview, July 21, 2000.
5. Parsons interview, Jan. 18, 1995.
6. See Thompson, *Motif-Index of Folk Literature*, E563, D1827.1ff (magically heard noise). "Sitting up" with a person who nears death is an important community activity.
7. Ibid., A661.0.2.
8. Dahmer interview, Nov. 22, 1997.
9. Mike Nassau, "Black Dutch," article promoting the Tubu African theory, http://www.geocities.com/mikenassau/BlackDutch.htm
10. Dahmer interview, Nov. 22, 1997.
11. Ibid.

12. Morton, *History of Pendleton County*, 169.
13. Moatstown is not a post office, just a locally named and recognized place.
14. Evon Z. Vogt and Peggy Golde, "Some Aspects of the Folklore of Water Witching in the United States," *Journal of American Folklore* 71, no. 282 (Oct.–Dec. 1958): 519–31.
15. Ibid., 527.

Chapter 17

1. Thompson, *Motif-Index of Folk Literature*, D1573.
2. A johnny cake is thought to be a "journey cake," a cake made for a taking on a journey.
3. Alexander Carmichael, *Carmina Gadelica: Hymns and Incantations* (Hudson, N.Y.: Lindisfarne Press, 1994), 165, 351.
4. Smith, Stewart, and Kyger, *Pennsylvania Germans*, 147–48.
5. Briggs, *Witches and Neighbors*, 90.
6. See Thompson, *Motif-Index of Folk Literature*, M471.1.
7. Dahmer interview, Aug. 11, 1998.
8. Sylvia uses "het" instead of "heated" for the past tense of "heat."
9. O'Brien interview, Mar. 13, 2000.
10. Ibid. For a similar cure, see also Ronald L. Baker, *Hoosier Folk Legends* (Bloomington: Indiana Univ. Press, 1982), 108.
11. Thompson, *Motif-Index of Folk Literature*, D2083.3.1.
12. Hilda Ellis Davidson, "Supernatural Weapons," in *Medieval Folklore*, ed. Lindahl, McNamara, and Lindow, 396.
13. Collected by Dwight Diller from Burl Hammons and Maggie Hammons Parker.
14. For more discussion about Booger Hole, see Milnes, *Play of a Fiddle*, 28–29.
15. See ibid., 28–29.
16. Roberts, *Up Cutshin and Down Greasy*, 90.
17. Ibid., 94.
18. Dieffenbach, "Powwowing among the Pennsylvania Germans," 37.
19. Oleta Post Singleton in *Signs, Cures and Witchery*, prod. Milnes.
20. Cottrell interview.
21. Dahmer interview, Aug. 11, 1998.
22. Barrick, *German-American Folklore*, 111.
23. Lambert interview, Feb. 19, 1998.

Chapter 18

1. Robert Simmons, interview with author, July 8, 1998.
2. Reported as a "recent" occurrence in Eleonore Schamschula, *A Pioneer of American Folklore: Karl Knortz and His Collections* (Moscow: Univ. of Idaho Press, 1996), 115–16.

3. This is often pronounced "Connard," from the German Conradt. The family patriarch on the South Branch, Jacob Conradt, was born in Bern, Switzerland.
4. Oleta Singleton, interview with author, Mar. 7, 2001.
5. Ibid.
6. Smith, Stewart, and Kyger, *Pennsylvania Germans*, 150.
7. Richard Chase, *The Jack Tales* (New York: Houghton Mifflin, 1943–71). Chase rewrote *The Jack Tales* from traditional sources, but I am sure the cats in his tales were part of the original narratives.
8. Cottrell interview.
9. See N. Betty Smith, *Jane Hicks Gentry: A Singer Among Singers* (Lexington: Univ. Press of Kentucky, 1998), 124–26, for a North Carolina example. Some argue for a German provenance for the Jack Tales, others for an Anglo/Celtic origin. See Smith, *Jane Hicks Gentry*, 56–57.
10. Marks interview. For other West Virginia/Appalachian tales with this motif, see Bayard, "Witchcraft Magic and Spirits," 51–52, and Porter, "Notes on the Folk-Lore," 115.
11. Russell, *History of Witchcraft*, 29.
12. Davies, *Witchcraft, Magic and Culture*, xii. In Newfoundland, the term *Old Hag* is used to describe this nightmare tradition. See David J. Hufford, "A New Approach to the 'Old Hag': The Nightmare Tradition Reexamined," in *American Folk Medicine*, ed. Hand, 74.
13. Porter, "Notes on the Folk-Lore," 107.
14. Dahmer interview, Pendleton County, Aug. 11, 1998.
15. See Bayard, "Witchcraft Magic and Spirits," 48.
16. Stith Thompson, *The Folktale* (New York: Holt, Rinehart and Winston, 1946), 250–51.
17. Another use of the term *witch riding* comes from the belief that if you awake with the feeling of a heavy weight upon your chest, a witch has gained power over you. See Davies, *Witchcraft, Magic and Culture*, xii.
18. Dahmer interview, Aug. 11, 1998.
19. Dahmer interview, Nov. 22, 1997.
20. See Herbert Halpert, "The Devil, the Fiddle and Dancing," in *Fields of Folklore: Essays in Honor of Kenneth S. Goldstein*, ed. Roger D. Abrahams (Bloomington, Ind.: Trickster Press, 1995), 44.
21. In all of the earliest accounts of fiddle playing in the Americas, it is African Americans who are playing. See Dena Epstein, *Sinful Tunes and Spirituals: Black Folk Music to the Civil War* (Urbana: Univ. of Illinois Press, 1977), 80.

Chapter 19

1. Francesco Maria Guazzo, *Compendium Maleficarum* (1608; reprint, New York: Dover, Montague Summers Edition, 1988), 93.
2. Guy Underwood, *The Pattern of the Past* (London: Sphere Books, 1972).
3. See Thompson, *Motif-Index of Folk Literature*, G249.3.

4. Ibid.
5. See ibid., G303.16.17.
6. Briggs, *Witches and Neighbors*, 207.
7. Opie and Tatem, *Dictionary of Superstitions*, 404.
8. Rexrode, "Take Moonshine According to Age," 42.
9. Drew Beisswenger, "Say Words and Take That Out: Alta Listenberger's Cures," unpublished MS, 1982.
10. Randolph, *Ozark Magic and Folklore*, 284.
11. Marks interview; Rose interview.
12. Marks interview.
13. Lilly interview.
14. Heatwole, *Shenandoah Voices*, 72.
15. Merrifield, *Archaeology of Ritual and Magic*, 155.
16. Funk, *Life of John Kline*, 213.
17. The "Old Christmas" date was used by Protestant Britain, which would not accept the Catholic Gregorian calendar. Christmas according to the Julian calendar was eleven days later than December 25.
18. Fleischhauer and Jabbour, *Hammons Family*, 6.
19. Beulah Blake interview, Braxton County, May 26, 1988.
20. Randolph, *Ozark Magic and Folklore*, 279.
21. Dieffenbach, "Powwowing among the Pennsylvania Germans," 34.
22. Bettina Bildhauer, "Blood," in *Medieval Folklore*, ed. Lindahl, McNamara, and Lindow, 47.

Chapter 20

1. Michael Bacci, "Votive Offerings," in *Medieval Folklore*, ed. Lindahl, McNamara, and Lindow, 425.
2. Russell, *Witchcraft in the Middle Ages*, 48.
3. Alderfer, *Ephrata Commune*, 170.
4. Grillot de Givry, *Witchcraft, Magic and Alchemy*, 100–102.
5. Lambert interview, Feb. 19, 1998; see Thompson, *Motif-Index of Folk Literature*, D2161.4.14.2 (bathing in consecrated water).
6. Porter, "Notes on the Folk-Lore," 107.
7. Smith, Stewart, and Kyger, *Pennsylvania Germans*, 152.
8. S. Liddell MacGregor Mathers, trans., *The Key of Solomon the King* (York Beach, Maine: Samuel Weiser, 1972), 86.
9. Behringer, "Witchcraft Studies in Austria, Germany and Switzerland," 78.
10. Wust, *Virginia Germans*, 66.
11. Summers, *History of Witchcraft and Demonology*, 84–85.
12. Dovie Lambert, interview with author, July 12, 1999.
13. Russell, *Witchcraft in the Middle Ages*, 249.
14. Summers, *History of Witchcraft and Demonology*, 85.
15. Thompson, *Motif-Index of Folk Literature*, M211.

16. *Doctor Faustus*, or just *Faustus*, embodies the motif/legend that is widespread in Western literature. Rewritten in 1587 (Anon.), 1604 (Marlow), 1789 (Lessing), 1804 (Chamisso), 1808–32 (Goethe), 1829 (Grabbe), 1846 (Berlioz), and 1836 (Lenau), it also shows up in numerous other pieces of literature and collections of folklore.

17. Grillot de Givry, *Witchcraft, Magic and Alchemy*, 116. Guazzo, *Compendium Maleficarum*, 13–19.

18. Russell, *History of Witchcraft*, 92.

19. Ruth Ann Musick, *Green Hills of Magic: West Virginia Folktales from Europe* (Lexington: Univ. Press of Kentucky, 1970), 23–25.

20. Russell, *Witchcraft in the Middle Ages*, 57.

Chapter 21

1. Dovie Lambert, interview with author, Jan. 28, 1998.

2. This form of pronouncing a word ending in *st* is found in old Appalachian speech in West Virginia. Similarly, some say a rope *twistes* or something *costes* too much.

3. Anthony Swiger, interview with author, June 29, 1995.

4. This rare belief shows up in a witch tale from the Valley that was collected in Indiana. See Ruth Ann Musick, "Indiana Witch Tales," *Journal of American Folklore* 63, no. 248 (Apr.–June 1950): 57.

5. Randolph, *Ozark Magic and Folklore*, 271.

6. Gary K. Waite, *Heresy, Magic, and Witchcraft in Early Modern Europe* (New York: Palgrave Macmillan, 2003), 165.

7. George Frederick Kunz, *The Curious Lore of Precious Stones* (Philadelphia: Lippincott, 1913; New York: Dover, 1971), 218.

8. Tom Ogden, *Wizards and Sorcerers: From Abracadabra to Zoroaster* (New York: Checkmark Books, 1997), 42.

9. Guiley, *Encyclopedia of Witchcraft*, 367.

10. Tyson Propst, interview with author, Dec. 3, 1998.

11. Cottrell interview.

12. Oscar Kuhns, *The German and Swiss Settlements of Colonial Pennsylvania: A Study of the So-Called Pennsylvania Dutch* (New York: Abingdon Press, 1914), 103.

13. Kunz, *Curious Lore of Precious Stones*, 185–86.

14. Thompson, *Hand of Destiny*, 134.

15. Robert Simmons, interview with author, May 18, 2000.

16. Blow flies lay their eggs on rotten meat, where their larva, maggots, will have food.

17. Dahmer and Mitchell interview.

18. Malcolm Jones, "Wild Man," in *Medieval Folklore*, ed. Lindahl, McNamara, and Lindow, 433.

19. Dahmer interview, Nov. 22, 1997.

20. Roberts, *Up Cutshin and Down Greasy*, 90–91.

21. Fleischhauer and Jabbour, *Hammons Family*, 23.

22. Suter, *Shenandoah Valley Folklife*, 108.

23. Collected by Dwight Diller; see Fleischhauer and Jabbour, *Hammons Family*, 8.

24. "A Cuar for gun that is Speld," reported in Butler, "Magic, Astrology," 521.

25. Collected by Dwight Diller in Fleischhauer and Jabbour, *Hammons Family*, 8–9.

26. Collected by Dwight Diller in ibid., 22–23.

Chapter 22

1. See Merrifield, *Archaeology of Ritual and Magic*.

2. Dahmer and Simmons interview.

3. Keplinger interview.

4. Porter, "Notes on the Folk-Lore," 113.

5. Randolph, *Seventh Day Baptists in Europe and America* 2:1084–85.

6. Winkler cites Julius Sachse, "Exorcism of Fire, Ephrata Cloister," *Proceedings of the Lancaster County Historical Society* 7:92.

7. Dahmer and Simmons interview.

8. See Walter O. Moeller, *The Mithraic Origin and Meanings of the Rotas-Sator Square* (Leiden: E. J. Brill, 1973).

9. Merrifield, *Archaeology of Ritual and Magic*, 142–43.

10. See David Ulansey, *The Origins of the Mithraic Mysteries: Cosmology and Salvation in the Ancient World* (New York: Oxford Univ. Press, 1989).

11. Thompson, *Hand of Destiny*, 237–38.

12. See Yoder and Graves, *Hex Signs*, for the most reasonable and scholarly discussion and analysis of this question.

Chapter 23

1. Hutton, *Triumph of the Moon*, and Norman Cohn, "The Non-Existent Society of Witches," in *Witches of the Atlantic World*, ed. Breslaw, 49–59.

2. Hutton, *Triumph of the Moon*.

3. John H. Wuorinen, *The Finns on the Delaware, 1638–1665: An Essay in American Colonial History* (New York: Columbia Univ. Press, 1938), 97–98.

4. Christian All Saints' Day, later All Souls' Day, redirected attention from the Celtic Samhain. The festivals are rooted in human consciousness. See Jack Santino, *All Around the Year: Holidays and Celebrations in American Life* (Urbana: Univ. of Illinois Press, 1994), 150–67.

5. Halpert, "Devil, the Fiddle and Dancing," uses the word mumming for the many different northern European traditions.

6. The Swedes came in 1638, English and Germans in the 1680s, Scots-Irish soon after. Each group brought versions of revelry to the New World. Charles E. Welch Jr., *OH! Dem Golden Slippers: The Story of the Philadelphia Mummers* (Philadelphia: Book Street Press, 1970), 13–19.

7. Guisers are beggars in disguise who, in nineteenth-century Staffordshire, performed a play in exchange for food. Welch, *OH! Dem Golden Slippers*, 13–15.

8. Henry Glassie, *All Silver and No Brass: An Irish Christmas Mumming* (Philadelphia: Univ. of Pennsylvania Press, 1985).

9. Ronald Hutton, *The Rise and Fall of Merry England: The Ritual Year, 1400–1700* (Oxford: Oxford Univ. Press, 1996), 8.

10. Glassie, *All Silver and No Brass*, 94–95.

11. This term is introduced by Alfred Shoemaker and used by Elmer L. Smith in *Shanghaiing or Fantasticals*, Valley Folklore 21 (Harrisonburg, Va.: Madison College, 1971).

12. E. T. Kirby, "The Origin of the Mummers Play," *Journal of American Folklore* 84, no. 333 (1971): 275–88.

13. The parade is based on marching string bands and fantastic costumes and head gear.

14. Don Yoder, afterword to *Christmas in Pennsylvania: A Folk-Cultural Study*, by Alfred L. Shoemaker (Kutztown: Pennsylvania Folklore Society, 1959; Mechanicsburg, Pa.: Stackpole Books, 1999), 133–42.

15. John Lindow, "Wild Hunt," in *Medieval Folklore*, ed. Lindahl, McNamara, and Lindow, 432.

16. Barrick, *German-American Folklore*, 146–47.

17. Simmons interview, July 8, 1998.

18. Smith, Stewart, and Kyger, *Pennsylvania Germans*, 119–20.

19. Ira Yoder and Susie Brenneman, "Negro Mountain Belsnickle," *The Castleman Chronicle* 67:1, 2, 13–14.

20. Suter, *Shenandoah Valley Folklife*, 36.

21. Frazer, *The Golden Bough*, 248.

22. Jocie Armentrout, interview with author, Dec. 30, 1991.

23. See Shoemaker, *Christmas in Pennsylvania*, 75; Barrick, *German-American Folklore*, 147, and Wentz, *Pennsylvania Dutch*, 136.

24. In a German-settled community in Newfoundland, similar belsnickling exists, and the ancestors of these Germans did not pass through Pennsylvania.

25. Pete Simmons, interview with author, Jan. 11, 2001.

26. Halpert, "Devil, the Fiddle and Dancing," 41.

27. Ruth L. Cline, "Belsnickles and Shanghais," *Journal of American Folklore* 71, no. 280 (1958): 165.

28. Yoder, afterword, 137.

29. Stephen Nissenbaum, *The Battle for Christmas: A Cultural History of America's Most Cherished Holiday* (New York: Vintage Books, 1997), 99.

30. Wentz, *Pennsylvania Dutch*, 131. Moore's authorship of "The Night Before Christmas" is questioned.

31. Wentz, *Pennsylvania Dutch*, 131.

32. Noted at Jordan Run, Hardy County, West Virginia.

33. Cline, "Belsnickles and Shanghais." Suter, *Shenandoah Valley Folklife*, 34–36.

34. Robert Simmons, interview with author, Mar. 17, 1992.

35. Suter, *Shenandoah Valley Folklife*, 34, and Cline, "Belsnickles and Shanghais."

36. Yoder, afterword to *Christmas in Pennsylvania*, 141.

37. Suter, *Shenandoah Valley Folklife*, 35.

38. Ibid., 36.

39. An eighteenth-century account of a band of Swedish youth who were dressed in masquerade, shouting and shooting guns. See Welch, *OH! Dem Golden Slippers*, 13.

40. See Walter L. Robbins, "Christmas Shooting Rounds in America and Their Background," *Journal of American Folklore* 86, no. 339 (Jan.–Mar. 1973): 48–52.

41. Smith, Stewart, and Kyger, *Pennsylvania Germans*, 106.

42. Most interviewees I asked said belsnickling stopped by New Year's Day.

43. Gerald Thomas, "Noel, La Chandler, Mardi Gras," in *Fields of Folklore*, ed. Abrahams, 300.

44. See *Helvetia*, prod. Milnes.

45. Ibid.

46. Frazer, *The Golden Bough*, 248. See Rammel, *Nowhere in America*, 63.

47. *Helvetia*, prod. Milnes.

48. Don Yoder, introduction to *Christmas in Pennsylvania*, xiii.

49. Herbert Halpert proposes this. Discussed in Yoder, afterword to *Christmas in Pennsylvania*, 140.

50. See Margaret Bennett, *The Last Stronghold: Scottish Gaelic Traditions in Newfoundland* (St. John's, Newfoundland: Breakwater Books, 1989), and Halpert, "Devil, the Fiddle and Dancing."

51. By J. Dahmer, May 29, 1903.

Afterword

1. Dahmer and Mitchell interview.

2. Reported from several sources by W. Hunter Lesser, *Rebels at the Gate: Lee and McClellan on the Front Line of a Nation Divided* (Naperville, Ill.: Sourcebooks, 2004), 140.

Bibliography

Books and Articles

Aarne, Antti, and Stith Thompson. *The Types of the Folktale: A Classification and Bibliography.* FF Communications no. 184. Helsinki: Suomalainen Tiedeakatemia, 1961.

Aberg, Alf. *The People of New Sweden: Our Colony on the Delaware River, 1638–1655.* Stockholm: Bokförlaget Natur och Kultur, 1988.

Abrahams, Roger D., ed. *Fields of Folklore: Essays in Honor of Kenneth S. Goldstein.* Bloomington, Ind.: Trickster Press, 1995.

Alderfer, E. G. *The Ephrata Commune: An Early American Counterculture.* Pittsburgh: Univ. of Pittsburgh Press, 1985.

Bacci, Michael. "Votive Offerings." In *Medieval Folklore*, ed. Lindahl, McNamara, and Lindow, 425–27.

Bach, Jeff. *Voices of the Turtledoves: The Sacred World of Ephrata.* University Park: Pennsylvania State Univ. Press, 2003.

Bailyn, Bernard, and Philip D. Morgan, eds. *Strangers within the Realm: Cultural Margins of the First British Empire.* Chapel Hill: Univ. of North Carolina Press, 1991.

Baker, Ronald L. *Hoosier Folk Legends.* Bloomington: Indiana Univ. Press, 1982.

Baroja, Julio Caro. "Magic and Religion in the Classical World." In *Witchcraft and Sorcery*, ed. Marwick, 67–75.

Barrick, Mac E. *German-American Folklore.* Little Rock, Ark.: August House, 1987.

Barry, Jonathan, Marianne Hester, and Gareth Roberts, eds. *Witchcraft in Early Modern Europe: Studies in Culture and Belief.* Cambridge: Cambridge Univ. Press, 1996.

Bayard, S. P. "Witchcraft Magic and Spirits on the Border of Pennsylvania and West Virginia." *Journal of American Folklore* 51, no. 199 (Jan.–Mar. 1938): 47–59.

Bealle, John. *Public Worship, Private Faith: Sacred Harp and American Folksong.* Athens: Univ. of Georgia Press, 1997.

Behringer, Wolfgang. "Witchcraft Studies in Austria, Germany, and Switzerland." In *Witchcraft in Early Modern Europe*, ed. Barry, Hester, and Roberts, 69–86.

Beisswenger, Drew. *Fiddling Way Out Yonder: The Life and Music of Melvin Wine.* Jackson: Univ. of Mississippi Press, 2002.

Bennett, Margaret. *The Last Stronghold: Scottish Gaelic Traditions in Newfoundland.* St. John's, Newfoundland: Breakwater Books, 1989.

Bergdall, Luther. "The Morgan Dasher Family: Ten Generations in America, 1737–1984." Moss Beach, Calif.: n.p., 1984.

Bildhauer, Bettina. "Blood." In *Medieval Folklore*, ed. Lindahl, McNamara, and Lindow, 45–47.

Bittinger, Emmert F. *Allegheny Passage: Churches and Families, West Marva District, Church of the Brethren, 1752–1990.* Camden, Maine: Penobscot Press, 1990.

Bohlman, Philip V., and Otto Holzapfel. *Land without Nightingales: Music in the Making of German America.* Madison: Max Kade Institute for German-American Studies, Univ. of Wisconsin, 2002.

Bosworth, A. S. *A History of Randolph County, West Virginia from Its Earliest Exploration and Settlement to the Present Time.* 1916. Reprint. Parsons, W.Va.: McClain, 1975.

Botkin, B. A. *A Treasury of New England Folklore.* New York: Bonanza Books, 1947.

Brandon, Elizabeth. "Folk Medicine in French Louisiana." In *American Folk Medicine,* ed. Hand, 215–34.

Brauner, Sigrid. *Fearless Wives and Frightened Shrews: The Construction of the Witch in Early Modern Germany.* Amherst: Univ. of Massachusetts Press, 1995.

Breslaw, Elaine G., ed. *Witches of the Atlantic World: A Historic Reader and Primary Source-book.* New York: New York Univ. Press, 2000.

Briggs, Robin. *Witches and Neighbors: The Social and Cultural Context of European Witchcraft.* New York: Penguin Books, 1996.

Brooke, John L. *The Refiner's Fire: The Making of Mormon Cosmology, 1644–1844.* Cambridge: Cambridge Univ. Press, 1996.

Butler, Jon. *Awash in a Sea of Faith: Christianizing the American People.* Cambridge: Harvard Univ. Press, 1990.

———. "Magic, Astrology, and the Early American Religious Heritage, 1600–1760." In *Witches of the Atlantic World,* ed. Breslaw, 516–24.

Campbell, John C. *The Southern Highlander and His Homeland.* 1921. Reprint. Lexington: Univ. Press of Kentucky, 1969.

Carmichael, Alexander. *Carmina Gadelica: Hymns and Incantations.* Hudson, N.Y.: Lindisfarne Press, 1994.

Cerniglia, Keith A. "The American Almanac and the Astrology Factor." http://www.earlyamerica.com/2003_spring/almanac.htm

Chán, Beatriz Barba de Piña. "Spells." In *Hidden Truths,* ed. Sullivan, 217–23.

Chase, Richard. *The Jack Tales.* New York: Houghton Mifflin, 1943–71.

Claussen, William E. *Pioneers Along the Manatawny.* Boyertown, Pa.: Gilbert,1968.

Cleek, George W. *Early Western Augusta Pioneers.* Staunton, Va.: Published by the author, 1957.

Cline, Ruth L. "Belsnickles and Shanghais." *Journal of American Folklore* 71, no. 280 (1958): 164–65.

Cohn, Norman. "The Non-Existent Society of Witches." In *Witches of the Atlantic World,* ed. Breslaw, 49–59.

Coffin, Tristram P., and Hennig Cohen, eds. *Folklore in America: Tales, Songs, Superstitions, Proverbs, Riddles, Games, Folk Drama and Folk Festival.* New York: Doubleday, 1966.

Comstock, H. E. *The Pottery of the Shenandoah Valley Region.* Winston-Salem, N.C.: Museum of Early Southern Decorative Arts, 1994.

Coudert, Allison P. "The Myth of the Improved Status of Protestant Women." In *Witches of the Atlantic World,* ed. Breslaw, 309–21.

Culianu, Ioan Petru. "Magic in Medieval and Renaissance Europe." In *Hidden Truths*, ed. Sullivan, 110–15.

Cunningham, Rodger. *Apples on the Flood: The Southern Mountain Experience*. Knoxville: Univ. of Tennessee Press, 1987.

Davidson, Hilda Ellis. "Supernatural Weapons." In *Medieval Folklore*, ed. Lindahl, McNamara, John Lindow, 395–97.

Davies, Owen. *Witchcraft, Magic and Culture, 1736–1951*. Manchester: Manchester Univ. Press, 1999.

Deskins, Charlotte H. "New Moon, True Moon: Love Lore from McDowell County." *Goldenseal Magazine* 12, no. 1 (1986): 62–64. Used with permission.

Dieffenbach, Victor C. "Powwowing among the Pennsylvania Germans." *Pennsylvania Folklife* 25, no. 2 (Winter 1975–76): 29–46.

Diffenderffer, Frank Ried. *The German Immigration into Pennsylvania through the Port of Philadelphia from 1700 to 1755*. Pt. 2. Lancaster: Pennsylvania German Society, 1900.

Dorson, Richard M. *Folklore and Folklife: An Introduction*. Chicago: Univ. of Chicago Press, 1972.

Dundes, Alan. *Interpreting Folklore*. Bloomington: Indiana Univ. Press, 1980.

———. *Life Is Like a Chicken Coop Ladder: A Study of German National Character through Folklore*. Detroit: Wayne State Univ. Press, 1989.

Eaton, Allen H. *Handicrafts of the Southern Highlands*. 1937. Reprint. New York: Dover Publications, 1973.

Epstein, Dena. *Sinful Tunes and Spirituals: Black Folk Music to the Civil War*. Urbana: Univ. of Illinois Press, 1977.

Eye, Walter L. "A Compilation of Simmons Descendants of Pendleton County, West Virginia." Unpublished MS, 1988.

———. "A Compilation of the Descendants of Abraham Pitsenbarger, Pendleton County, West Virginia." Unpublished MS, 1990.

———. "A History of the Descendants of John Michael Propst of Pendleton County, West Virginia." Unpublished MS, 1983.

Fischer, David Hackett. *Albion's Seed: Four British Folkways in America*. Oxford: Oxford Univ. Press, 1989.

Fleischhauer, Carl, and Alan Jabbour, eds. *The Hammons Family: A Study of a West Virginia Family's Traditions*. Washington, D.C.: Library of Congress, 1973.

Frazer, James George. *The Golden Bough*. 1922. Reprint. New York: Macmillan, 1950.

Fromm, Roger W. "The Migration and Settlement of Pennsylvania Germans in Maryland, Virginia and North Carolina and Their Effects on the Landscape." *Pennsylvania Folklife* 37, no. 1 (Autumn 1987): v.

Funk, Benjamin. *Life of John Kline: 1797–1864*. Broadway, Va.: Brethren Press, 1900.

Gager, John G. *Curse Tablets and Binding Spells from the Ancient World*. New York: Oxford Univ. Press, 1992.

Gaster, Theodor H. "Amulets and Talismans." In *Hidden Truths*, ed. Sullivan, 145–50.

Gebhard, Bruno. "The Interrelationship of Scientific and Folk Medicine in the United States of America since 1850." In *American Folk Medicine*, ed. Hand, 87–98.

Gevitz, Norman, ed. *Other Healers: Unorthodox Medicine in America*. Baltimore: John Hopkins Univ. Press, 1988.

Gibbons, Phebe Earle. *Pennsylvania Dutch and Other Essays*. 1872. Reprint. with an introduction by Don Yoder, Mechanicsburg, Pa: Stackpole Books, 2001.

Ginzburg, Carlo. *The Night Battles: Witchcraft and Agrarian Cults in the Sixteenth and Seventeenth Centuries*. Baltimore: John Hopkins Univ. Press, 1992.

Glassie, Henry. *All Silver and No Brass: An Irish Christmas Mumming*. Philadelphia: Univ. of Pennsylvania Press, 1983.

———. "Folk Art." In *Folklore and Folklife*, ed. Dorson, 253–80.

———. *Pattern in the Material Folk Culture of the Eastern United States*. Philadelphia: Univ. of Pennsylvania Press, 1968.

Grillot de Givry, Émile. *Witchcraft, Magic and Alchemy*. New York: Bonanza Books, n.d.

Guazzo, Francesco Maria. *Compendium Maleficarum*. 1608. Reprint. New York: Dover, Montague Summers Edition, 1988.

Guiley, Rosemary Ellen. *The Encyclopedia of Witches and Witchcraft*. New York: Facts on File Books, 1989.

Halpert, Herbert. "The Devil, the Fiddle and Dancing." In *Fields of Folklore*, ed. Abrahams, 44–54.

Hand, Wayland. "German American Folklore." *Journal of American Folklore* 60, no. 238 (1947): 366–72.

———, ed. *American Folk Medicine: A Symposium*. Berkeley: Univ. of California Press, 1976.

Heatwole, John L. *Shenandoah Voices: Folklore, Legends, and Traditions of the Valley*. Berryville, Va.: Rockbridge, 1995.

Hively, Rev. Earl. "Old Propst Church: First Lutheran Church in Pendleton County." N.p.: N.d.

Hohman, John George. *Pow-Wows; or Long Lost Friend: A Collection of Mysterious and Invaluable Arts and Remedies*. Various editions since 1820.

Hostetler, John A. "Folk Healing and Sympathy Healing among the Amish." In *American Folk Medicine*, ed. Hand, 249–58.

Hudler, George W. *Magical Mushrooms, Mischievous Molds*. Princeton, N.J.: Princeton Univ. Press, 1998.

Hufford, David J. "A New Approach to the 'Old Hag': The Nightmare Tradition Reexamined." In *American Folk Medicine*, ed. Hand, 73–85.

———."Contemporary Folk Medicine." In *Other Healers*, ed. Gevitz, 228–64.

Hutton, Ronald. *The Rise and Fall of Merry England: The Ritual Year, 1400–1700*. Oxford: Oxford Univ. Press, 1996.

———. *The Triumph of the Moon: A History of Modern Witchcraft*. Oxford: Oxford Univ. Press, 1999.

Imboden, William A., Jr. "Plant Hypnotics." In *American Folk Medicine*, ed. Hand, 159–67.

Jackson, Bruce. "The Other Kind of Doctor." In *American Folk Medicine*, ed. Hand, 259–72.

Jackson, George Pullen. *White Spirituals in the Southern Uplands.* Hatboro, Pa.: Folklore Associates, 1964.

Jones, Loyal. *Faith and Meaning in the Southern Uplands.* Urbana: Univ. of Illinois Press, 1999.

Jones, Malcolm. "Wild Man." In *Medieval Folklore,* ed. Lindahl, McNamara, and Lindow, 433–35.

Kauffman, Henry J. *Pennsylvania Dutch Folk Art.* 1946. Reprint. New York: Dover, 1964.

Kazal, Russell A. *Becoming Old Stock: The Paradox of German-American Identity.* Princeton, N.J.: Princeton Univ. Press, 2004.

Kercheval, Samuel. *A History of the Valley of Virginia.* 2d ed. 1833. Reprint. Woodstock, Va., 1850.

Kirby, E. T. "The Origin of the Mummers Play." *Journal of American Folklore* 84, no. 333 (1971): 275–88.

Kirkland, James, Holly F. Mathews, C. W. Sullivan III, and Karen Baldwin, eds. *Herbal and Magical Medicine: Traditional Healing Today.* Durham, N.C.: Duke Univ. Press, 1992.

Kors, Alan C., and Edward Peters. *Witchcraft in Europe, 1100–1700: A Documentary History.* Philadelphia: Univ. of Pennsylvania Press, 1972.

Korson, George. *Black Rock: Mining Folklore of the Pennsylvania Dutch.* Baltimore: John Hopkins Press, 1960.

Kramer, Heinrich, and James Sprenger. *Malleus Maleficarum.* 1486. Reprint. with a translation by Montague Summers. London: Pushkin Press, 1948.

Kraybill, Donald B., and Carl Desportes Bowman. *On the Backroad to Heaven: Old Order Hutterites, Mennonites, Amish, and Brethren.* Baltimore: Johns Hopkins Univ. Press, 2001.

Kuhns, Oscar. *The German and Swiss Settlements of Colonial Pennsylvania: A Study of the So-Called Pennsylvania Dutch.* New York: Abingdon Press, 1914.

Kunz, George Frederick. *The Curious Lore of Precious Stones.* Philadelphia: Lippincott, 1913; New York: Dover, 1971.

Law, Rachel Nash, and Cynthia W. Taylor. *Appalachian White Oak Basketmaking: Handing Down the Basket.* Knoxville: Univ. of Tennessee Press, 1991.

Lee, Dorothy D. "Greek Personal Anecdotes of the Supernatural." *Journal of American Folklore* 64, no. 253 (1951): 307–12.

Lehman, James H. *The Old Brethren.* Elgin, Ill.: Brethren Press, 1976.

Lesser, W. Hunter. *Rebels at the Gate: Lee and McClellan on the Front Line of a Nation Divided.* Naperville, Ill.: Sourcebooks, 2004.

Lewis, I. M. *Religion in Context: Cults and Charisma.* Cambridge: Cambridge Univ. Press, 1986.

Lindahl, Carl, John McNamara, and John Lindow, eds. *Medieval Folklore: A Guide to Myths, Legends, Tales, Beliefs, and Customs.* New York: Oxford Univ. Press, 2002.

Lindow, John. "Wild Hunt." In *Medieval Folklore,* ed. Lindahl, McNamara, and Lindow, 432–33.

Lindsay, William. "The Blacks of Pendleton County, West Virginia, 1850 to 1920." Unpublished genealogical work. N.d.

Little, Ruth. *Sticks and Stones: Three Centuries of North Carolina Grave Markers.* Chapel Hill: Univ. of North Carolina Press, 1998.

MacMaster, Richard K. *The History of Hardy County, 1786–1986.* Moorefield, W.Va.: Hardy County Public Library, 1986.

Martin, Charles E. *Hollybush: Folk Housing and Social Change in an Appalachian Community.* Knoxville: Univ. of Tennessee Press, 1984.

Marwick, Max, ed. *Witchcraft and Sorcery.* Middlesex, England: Penguin Books, 1970.

Mathers, S. Liddell MacGregor, trans. *The Key of Solomon the King.* York Beach, Maine: Samuel Weiser, 1972.

McWhiney, Grady. *Cracker Culture: Celtic Ways in the Old South.* Tuscaloosa: Univ. of Alabama Press, 1988.

McWhorter, Lucullus Virgil. *The Border Settlers of Northwestern Virginia from 1768 to 1795: Embracing the Life of Jesse Hughes and Other Noted Scouts of the Great Woods of the Trans-Allegheny.* Hamilton, Ohio: Republican Publishing, 1915.

Merrifield, Ralph. *The Archaeology of Ritual and Magic.* New York: New Amsterdam, 1988.

Milnes, Gerald. "Old Christmas and Belsnickles." *Goldenseal* 21, no. 4 (Winter 1995): 26–31.

———. *Play of a Fiddle: Traditional Music, Dance, and Folklore in West Virginia.* Lexington: Univ. Press of Kentucky, 1999.

Mitchell, Robert D., ed. *Appalachian Frontiers: Settlement, Society, and Development in the Preindustrial Era.* Lexington: Univ. Press of Kentucky, 1991.

Moeller, Walter O. *The Mithraic Origin and Meanings of the Rotas-Sator Square.* Leiden: E. J. Brill, 1973.

Monter, William E. *Witchcraft in France and Switzerland: The Borderlands during the Reformation.* Ithaca, N.Y.: Cornell Univ. Press, 1976.

Morgan, John. *The Log House in East Tennessee.* Knoxville: Univ. of Tennessee Press, 1990.

Morton, Oren F. *A History of Pendleton County, West Virginia.* 1910. Reprint. Harrisonburg, Va.: C. J. Carrier Company, 1995.

Musick, Ruth Ann. *Green Hills of Magic: West Virginia Folktales from Europe.* Lexington: Univ. Press of Kentucky, 1970.

———. "Indiana Witch Tales." *Journal of American Folklore* 63, no. 248 (Apr.–June 1950): 105–17.

Nassau, Mike. "Black Dutch." http://www.geocities.com/mikenassau/Black Dutch.htm

Nelson, Robert. *Finnish Magic: A Nation of Wizards, a World of Spirits.* St. Paul, Minn.: Llewellyn Publications, 1999.

Nikiforuk, Andrew. *The Fourth Horseman: A Short History of Epidemics, Plagues, Famines, and Other Scourges.* New York: M. Evans, 1991.

Nissenbaum, Stephen. *The Battle for Christmas: A Cultural History of America's Most Cherished Holiday.* New York: Vintage Books, 1997.

Notestein, Wallace. *A History of Witchcraft in England from 1558 to 1718.* New York: Thomas Y. Crowell, 1968.

Ogden, Tom. *Wizards and Sorcerers: From Abracadabra to Zoroaster.* New York: Checkmark Books, 1997.

Opie, Iona, and Moira Tatem, eds. *A Dictionary of Superstitions.* Oxford: Oxford Univ. Press, 1989.

Ozment, Steven. *Flesh and Spirit: Private Life in Early Modern Germany.* New York: Viking Press, 1999.

Payne, Dale. *Frontier Memories as Taken from the Shane Interviews of Rev. John Dabney Shane of the Draper Manuscripts.* N.p.: Published by the author, 2002. Taken from the Draper Manuscripts, State Historical Society of Wisconsin, Madison.

Pendleton County Commission. *Pendleton County West Virginia Past and Present.* Franklin, W.Va., 1991.

Porter, J. Hampden. "Notes on the Folk-Lore of the Mountain Whites of the Alleghenies." *Journal of American Folklore* 7, no. 25 (Apr.–Jun. 1894): 105–17.

Radbill, Samuel X. "The Role of Animals in Infant Feeding." In *American Folk Medicine,* ed. Hand, 21–30.

Raichelson, Richard. "The Social Context of Musical Instruments within the Pennsylvania German Culture." *Pennsylvania Folklife* 25, no. 1 (Autumn 1975): 35–44.

Rammel, Hal. *Nowhere in America: The Big Rock Candy Mountain and Other Comic Utopias.* Urbana: Univ. of Illinois Press, 1990.

Randolph, Corliss F., ed. *Seventh Day Baptists in Europe and America.* Vol. 2. Plainfield, N.J.: American Sabbath Tract Society, 1910.

Randolph, Vance. *Ozark Magic and Folklore.* 1947. Reprint. New York: Dover, 1964.

Ratterman, H. A. *Kentucky's German Pioneers.* Translated and edited by Don Heinrich Tolzmann. Bowie, Md.: Heritage Books, 2001.

Raudvere, Catharina. "Nightmare." In *Medieval Folklore,* ed. Lindahl, McNamara, and Lindow, 291–92.

Rehder, John B. *Appalachian Folkways.* Baltimore: Johns Hopkins Univ. Press, 2004.

Rexrode, Carmen R. "Take Moonshine According to Age: Healing in Pendleton County, West Virginia 1900–1940." Senior thesis, Harvard Univ., 1982.

Robacker, Earl F. *Arts of the Pennsylvania Dutch.* New York: Castle Books, 1965.

Robbins, Rossell Hope. *The Encyclopedia of Witchcraft and Demonology.* New York: Crown Publishers, Inc., 1959.

Robbins, Walter L. "Christmas Shooting Rounds in America and Their Background." *Journal of American Folklore* 86, no. 339 (Jan.–Mar. 1973): 48–52.

Roberts, Leonard W. *Up Cutshin and Down Greasy: Folkways of a Kentucky Mountain Family.* 1959. Reprint. Lexington: Univ. Press of Kentucky, 1988.

Roeber, A. G. "The Origin of Whatever Is Not English among Us: The Dutch-Speaking and German-Speaking Peoples of Colonial British America." In *Strangers within the Realm,* ed. Bailyn and Morgan, 220–83.

Russell, Jeffrey Burton. *A History of Witchcraft: Sorcerers, Heretics, and Pagans.* London: Thames and Hudson, 1980.

———. *Witchcraft in the Middle Ages.* Ithaca, N.Y.: Univ. of Cornell Press, 1972.

Santino, Jack. *All Around the Year: Holidays and Celebrations in American Life*. Urbana: Univ. of Illinois Press, 1994.

Sasche, Julius. *The German Pietists of Provincial Pennsylvania*. Philadelphia: P. C. Stockhousen, 1895.

———. "Exorcism of Fire, Ephrata Cloister." *Proceedings of the Lancaster County Histori cal Society* 7.

Schamschula, Eleonore. *A Pioneer of American Folklore: Karl Knortz and His Collections*. Moscow: Univ. of Idaho Press, 1996.

Schuricht, Herrmann. *History of the German Element in Virginia*. 2 vols. in 1. 1898–1900. Reprint. Baltimore: Genealogical Publishing, 1977.

Shapiro, Henry D. *"Appalachia on Our Mind." The Southern Mountains and Mountaineers in the American Consciousness, 1870–1920*. Chapel Hill: Univ. of North Carolina Press, 1978.

Shoemaker, Alfred L. *Christmas in Pennsylvania: A Folk-Cultural Study*. Kurtztown: Pennsylvania Folklore Society, 1959; Mechanicsburg, Pa.: Stackpole Books, 1999.

Slagle, A. Russell. "The Schlegel Family and the Rosicrucian Movement." *Pennsylvania Folklife* 25, no. 3 (Spring 1976): 32–38.

Smith, Elmer L. *Pottery: A Utilitarian Folk Craft*. Lebanon, Pa.: Applied Arts, 1972.

———. *Shanghaiing or Fantasticals*. Valley Folklore 21. Harrisonburg, Va.: Madison College, 1971.

Smith, Elmer L., John G. Stewart, and M. Ellsworth Kyger. *The Pennsylvania Germans of the Shenandoah Valley*. Pennsylvania German Folklore Society, vol. 26. Allentown, Pa.: Schlechter Printing, 1964.

Smith, L. Allen. *A Catalogue of Pre-revival Appalachian Dulcimers*. Columbia: Univ. of Missouri Press, 1983.

Smith, N. Betty. *Jane Hicks Gentry: A Singer Among Singers*. Lexington: Univ. Press of Kentucky, 1998.

Smith, Ralph Lee. *The Story of the Dulcimer*. Cosby, Tenn.: Crying Creek, 1986.

Sparks, Elder John. *The Roots of Appalachian Christianity: The Life and Legacy of Elder Shubal Stearns*. Lexington: Univ. Press of Kentucky, 2001.

Sullivan, Lawrence E., ed. *Hidden Truths: Magic, Alchemy, and the Occult*. New York: Macmillan, 1989.

Summers, Montague. *The History of Witchcraft and Demonology*. Seacaucus, N.J.: Castle Books, 1992.

Suter, Scott Hamilton. *Shenandoah Valley Folklife*. Jackson: Univ. Press of Mississippi, 1999.

Sutton, David H. *One's Own Hearth Is Like Gold: A History of Helvetia, West Virginia*. New York: Peter Lang, 1990.

Talbot, Charles H. "Folk Medicine and History." In *American Folk Medicine*, ed. Hand, 7–10.

Thomas, Gerald. "Noel, La Chandler, Mardi Gras." In *Fields of Folklore*, ed. Abrahams, 300–310.

Thomas, Keith. New York: Charles Scribner's Sons, 1971.

Thompson, C. J. S. *The Hand of Destiny: Folklore and Superstition for Everyday Life*. New York: Bell Publishing, 1989.

Thompson, Stith. *The Folktale*. New York: Holt, Rinehart and Winston, 1946.

———. *Motif-Index of Folk Literature: A Classification of Narrative Elements in Folktales, Ballads, Myths, Fables, Mediaeval Romances, Exempla, Fabliaux, Jest-Books, and Local Legends*. 6 vols. Bloomington: Indiana Univ. Press, 1955–58.

Torrey, E. Fuller. *The Mind Game: Witchdoctors and Psychiatrists*. New York: Emerson Hall, 1972.

Ulansey, David. *The Origins of the Mithraic Mysteries: Cosmology and Salvation in the Ancient World*. New York: Oxford Univ. Press, 1989.

Underwood, Guy. *The Pattern of the Past*. London: Sphere Books, 1972.

Vogt, Evon Z., and Peggy Golde. "Some Aspects of the Folklore of Water Witching in the United States." *Journal of American Folklore* 71, no. 282 (Oct.–Dec. 1958): 519–31.

Waite, Gary K. *Heresy, Magic, and Witchcraft in Early Modern Europe*. New York: Palgrave Macmillan, 2003.

Ward, Christopher. *The Dutch and Swedes on the Delaware, 1609–1664*. Philadelphia: Univ. of Pennsylvania Press, 1930.

Welch, Charles E., Jr. *OH! Dem Golden Slippers: The Story of the Philadelphia Mummers*. Philadelphia: Book Street Press, 1970.

Wentz, Richard E., ed. *Pennsylvania Dutch: Folk Spirituality*. New York: Paulist Press, 1993.

Weygandt, Cornelius. "The Red Hills." In *Pennsylvania Dutch*, ed. Wentz, 106–13.

Wilk, Gerald. *Americans from Germany*. New York: German Information Center, 1976.

Williams, Harrison. *Legends of Loudon*. Richmond: Garrett and Massie, 1938.

Williams, John Alexander. *Appalachia: A History*. Chapel Hill: Univ. of North Carolina Press, 2002.

Winkler, Louis D. "Pennsylvania German Astronomy and Astrology." *Pennsylvania Folklife*. Series of articles. Vols. 21–28 (Autumn 1972–Winter 1978–79).

Wuorinen, John H. *The Finns on the Delaware, 1638–1665: An Essay in American Colonial History*. New York: Columbia Univ. Press, 1938.

Wust, Klaus. *The Saint-Adventurers of the Virginia Frontier: Southern Outposts of Ephrata*. Edinburgh, Va.: Shenandoah History, 1977.

———. *The Virginia Germans*. Charlottesville: Univ. Press of Virginia, 1969.

Yamin, Rebecca, and Karen Bescherer Metheny, eds. *Landscape Archeology: Reading and Interpreting the American Historic Landscape*. Knoxville: Univ. of Tennessee Press, 1996.

Yoder, Don. "Folk Medicine." In *Folklore and Folklife*, ed. Dorson, 191–215.

———. *Groundhog Day*. Mechanicsburg, Pa.: Stackpole Books, 2003.

———. "Hohman and Romanus: Origins and Diffusion of the Pennsylvania German Powwow Manual." In *American Folk Medicine*, ed. Hand, 235–48.

Yoder, Don, and Thomas E. Graves. *Hex Signs: Pennsylvania Dutch Barn Symbols and Their Meaning*. Mechanicsburg, Pa.: Stackpole Books, 2000.

Yoder, Ira, and Susie Brenneman. "Negro Mountain Belsnickle." *The Castleman Chronicle* 67:1, 2, 13–14.

Young, Chester Raymond. "The Observance of Old Christmas in Southern Appalachia." *Appalachian Journal*, 1977.

Zika, Charles. "Images of Circe and Discourses of Witchcraft, 1480–1580." *Zeitenblicke*. Online journal, July 2002, http://www.zeitenblicke.de/2002/01/zika/zika.html.

Interviews

All interviews are by the author unless otherwise noted.4

Armentrout, Jocie. Randolph County, Dec. 30, 1991.

Blake, Beula. Braxton County, May 26, 1988.

Brown, Waneta, and Jack Mayse. Braxton County, May 4, 1988.

Case, Clyde. Braxton County, Mar. 21, 1995.

Cottrell, Mary. Randolph County, June 30, 2000.

Dahmer, Bill. Pendleton County, May 17, 2000.

Dahmer, Johnny Arvin. Pendleton County, Nov. 22, 1997; Jan. 8, Aug. 11, Aug. 12, 1998; Dec. 5, Dec. 11, 2001.

Dahmer, Johnny Arvin, and Dennis Mitchell. Pendleton County, Feb. 11, 2001.

———, and Eva Simmons. Pendleton County, Aug. 12, 1998.

Gray, Catfish. Mason County, Apr. 24, 1996.

Keplinger, Dana. Pendleton County, July 21, 2000.

Lambert, Dovie. Randolph County, Jan. 28, Feb. 19, 1998; July 12, 1999.

Lilly, Kent. Mercer County, Nov. 11, 1997.

Mann, Elouise. Randolph County, Dec. 1, 1995.

Marks, Phyllis. Gilmer County, Apr. 20, 1995.

May, William. Mingo County, May 24, 1995.

Nichols, Emogene. Braxton County, Sept. 21, 1990.

O'Brien, Sylvia. Clay County, Mar. 18, June 8, 2000.

Parsons, Phoeba. Calhoun County, Jan. 19, 1995.

Propst, Irvin. Pendleton County, July 21, 2000.

Propst, Tyson. Pendleton County, Dec. 3, 1998.

———, and Stanley Tyson, Pendleton County, Dec. 4, 1997.

Rose, Otis. Braxton County, July 21, 1995.

Saville, Hoy. Hardy County, June 29, 1995.

Simmons, Pete. Pendleton County, Jan. 11, 2001.

Simmons, Robert. Pendleton County, Mar. 17, 1992; Apr. 5, 1977; July 8, 1998; May 18, 2000.

Singleton, Oleta. Gilmer County, Mar. 7, 2001.

Smith, Glen. Wirt County, Feb. 15, 1995.

Smith, Thelma, and Sharon Walker. Interview by Kent Walker, Webster County, Apr. 11, 2005.

Stover, Hazel. Clay County, Oct. 2, 1995.

Swiger, Anthony. Randolph County, June 29, 1995.

Welch, Israel. Mineral County, June 30, 1995.

Documentary Films

Fiddles, Snakes and Dog Days: Old-Time Music and Lore in West Virginia. Produced by Gerald Milnes. VHS, color, 60 min. Augusta Heritage Center, Elkins, W.Va., 1997.

Helvetia: The Swiss of West Virginia. Produced by Gerald Milnes. VHS, color, 60 min. AHV-93. Augusta Heritage Center, Elkins, W.Va., 1993.

Signs, Cures and Witchery: Appalachian Cosmology and Belief. Produced by Gerald Milnes. VHS, color, 60 min. Augusta Heritage Center, Elkins, W.Va., 2001.

Twisted Laurel: Folk Art, Folklore and Music from the West Virginia Woods. Produced by Gerald Milnes. VHS, color, 30 min. AHV-99. Augusta Heritage Center, Elkins W.Va., 1999.

Index

Page numbers in **boldface** refer to illustrations.

African Americans, 16, 39, 52–53, 131–33, 153, 173, 220n21; Black Dutch, 131

Albertus, 105, 215n34

alchemy, xv, 3, 13, 15, 26–27, 91, 139

almanacs. *See* astrology

amulets, xv, 79, 83, 120, 163, 180–81. *See also* number squares; charms; tickets

Anabaptists, 2–3, 6, 24, 195

architecture, folk, xii, 15, **179**, 201, 212n5; *Laura*, tower for observing the heavens, 13–14; Pitsenbarger farm, 68–69, **70**, **71**, 212n4, 212n8

Armentrout, Jocie, 17, 159–60, 190

Arndt, Jacob, 43

art, folk, xii, xiv, 24, 26, 45–56; barns, 55, 56; basket making, 52, 53; clocks, 50; common motifs in, 49–50, 54–55, 72; coopering, 21, 53; fraktur design, 50; gravestones, xvi, 24, 29, 43, 49, 54, 55, 120; hex signs, 49, 52, 55, 180; interior decorative painting, 48, 49, 94, 173; iron forging, 50, 51; mountain rifles, 89; pottery, 50; powder horns, 3; trompe l'oeil, 49; weaving, 53; woodworking, 60. *See also* music, fiddle

ash wood, 156–57; baskets, 52

astrology, 3, 19, 26, 29–36, **93**; almanac man, **30**, 33–35; almanacs,

29–36, 39, 77, 81, 91–92, 158, 208n5, 208n7; and astronomy, 29–30, 32–33; dog days, 35; and farming practices 31–36, 133; and folk curing, 24, 30–31, 39, 80, 106, 115; and the moon, 30–32, 34–36, 50, 80–81, 115; and religion, 24, 30–31, 91, 169; zodiac, 30, 33–35, 50, 80

Augusta Heritage Center, 75, 203n14

belling. *See* serenading

belsnickling. *See* mumming

Benneville, George de, 21, 206n13

Bethabara. *See* Brethren

Black Bible, 161–62

Black Dutch. *See* ethnic groups in Appalachia; African Americans: Black Dutch

blood-stopping. *See* stopping blood

Boehme, Jacob, 19, 23, 43, 49, 175

Booger Hole, 138, 140–41, 219n14

Boone, Daniel, 11, 205n18

Brethren, 6–9, 15, 19–20, 22–24, 30–31, 46; and astrology, 19, 29–31, 91, 169; Bethabara, 8; clothing of, 8, 23; Dunker's Bottom, 8, 13–14, 22, 26; Ephrata Cloister, 7–8, 14–15, 20, 22, 26–27, 29, 45–46, 161, 178; and folk medicine, 13, 31, 91–92; and occult beliefs, 31, 37, 61, 150, 167–69; origins of, 19; other names for, 19; pacifism, xiii, 13, 27; saint-adventuring, 7–8, 19,

Index

Propst, Ailey, 129
Propst, Irvin, 38, 123, 203n9
Propst, John Michael, 17, 20, 46
Propst Louis, 171
Propst, Stanley, 46, 69, 80, **126**, 137
Propst, Tyson, 46, 53, **54**, 69, 127, 169

Quakers. *See* Friends

Rapp, George, 23
regional identity, xiii, 24, 42, 165, 204n16
Roberts, Leonard, 142, 171
Rose, Otis, 34, 36, 100–101
rotas-sator square, 61, 176–81, **178**. *See also* number squares
rye, x, 41–42

Sabbatarians. *See* Brethren
saint-adventuring. *See* Brethren
Sangmeister, Ezechiel, 22–23, 25
Sangmeister, Heinrich, 13, 15
Sauer, Christopher, 91–92
Schlaraffernland, 86
Schmidt, Johann Friederich, 29, 31
Schwenkfelders, 21
Scots-Irish/Anglo-Celts, ix–xiii, xv, 6, 9–10, 14–16, 23–24, 32, 42, 45, 110, 124, 131, 184–86, 191–93, 195–96
serenading, 63
shanghai. *See* mumming
Shafer, Lefty, 47
Sharp, Cecil, ix
Shoemaker, Alfred, xiii, 223n11
shivaree. *See* serenading
Simmons, Eva, 85–86, 90, 178
Simmons, Martin, 27

Simmons, Robert, 27, 63, 66, **148**; on belsnickling, 188, 190; on witchery, 89–90, 123, 126, 130, 147, 168
Simmons, Woody, 47, 151
Singleton, Oleta Poste, 142, 148–50
Siron, Simon, 50
Slaughter, Emogene Nichols, 94–96, 99, 102
Smith, Elmer, xi, xiii, 191
snakes: cures for snakebite, 100, 173; folklore surrounding, 35, 87, 101, 115, 125, 153, 157
Society of the Woman of the Wilderness, 21–22
solstice, 183–86, 191
spirituality, folk, xv, 17, 26, 29, 32, 35, 49, 90, 107, 124, 199–202
Sponaugle, Ray, 47
springs and springhouses, 68, 135, 159; and occult belief, 82, 89, 158, 161–62
Stewart, John G., xi
stopping blood, 16, 59–60, 75, 95, 102–3, 105
Swedenborg, Emanuel, 162
Swedes and Finns, 37–38, 184, 192, 209n2, 212n5, 223n6, 224n39

talismans, xv, 79, 163, 181. *See also* amulets; charms
Thomas, Jean, ix
Thompson, Burt, **134**
Thompson, Saul, 49
thresholds, 156
tickets: as amulets, 79–80, 83, 175; use in imitative magic, 78–79, 81–82, 89, 105, 145, 175
toads: and occult belief, 87, 109–10, 129, 159
tobacco, 58, 72

tokens. *See* death
transcendentalism, 26
trees: and astrology, 35–36; species and their medicinal uses, 94, 156–58
Trinity. *See* cures and curing

Valstead Act, 67
Vandalia, 11

Weather prediction, 31, 35, 76–77, 98–99
Wentz, Richard, xiii, 19, 45, 78, 190, 192
Wesley, John, 43
West Virginia: German settlement in, xi, xiii, 7, 8, 15–17. *See also* Grant County, W.Va.; Hampshire County, W.Va.; Hardy County, W.Va.; Pendleton County, W.Va.
Wetzel, Lewis, 9
William, Cratis, x
Wine, Melvin, 47
Winkler, Louis, xiii, 30–32
witch doctoring. *See* cures and curing; healers, curers, and witch doctors
"witch war," 72, 175–76
witches and witchery: becoming a witch, 162–64; bewitchment, 22, 78–80, 121–23, 137, 140–41, 147, 151, 158, 167–69, 173; and borrowing, 137, 141; and brooms, 37, 40, 119–20, 156, 176; involving dogs and guns, 171–74; involving milk, 86–87, 122, 135–39, **140**, 142–44, 148; the ergot fungus

theory, 41–42; familiars, 26, 87, 109–10, 150–51; and farming, 40, 81–82, 85–90, 121–22, 132–33, 136–37, 144–47, 158; and fertility/impotence 40, 109, 112, 117–18; fingernails, 119; four forms of witchcraft, 39–41; malevolent vs. benevolent, 25, 40–41, 111, 150, 163; midwives, 40, 100, 110, 112; night rides, 111; occult books and manuscripts, 161–62; origins of, 39–41, 109–12; persecution and torture of witches, 1–2, 37, 40, 42–43, 111, 116–18; and religious belief, 17, 38–39, 43, 61, 76, 78, 99–100, 107–8, 110, 124–25, 139, 169, 199–200; sexual aspects, 110–11, 116–19; shape shifting, 150–51, 168; social tension theory, 40, 62, 79, 124; in today's society, 110, 112, 151–52; witch balls (glass balls), 167–69; witch balls (hairballs), 119, 167–68; witch-riding, 122, 151–52, 220n17. *See also* amulets; cures and curing; curses and spells; divining; healers, curers, and witch doctors; magic; toads
Witt, Christopher, 29–30, 91
Wust, Klaus, xiii, 21, 46

Yoder, Don, xiii, 75, 186

Zinn, Gerhart and Margaretha, 8
Zinzendorf, Count, 20

Index

245

Signs, Cures, and Witchery was designed and typeset on a Macintosh OS 10.4 computer system using InDesign software. The body text is set in 10/13 Joanna and display type is set in Brothers Regular. This book was designed by Barbara Karwhite and typeset by Stephanie Thompson.